Backpacking
Pennsylvania

0 11557 03180 5

Backpacking Pennsylvania

37 Great Trails

Jeff Mitchell

STACKPOLE
BOOKS

Hiking and backpacking are inherently risky activities, with ever-changing conditions and numerous natural and man-made hazards. Please choose trails that are appropriate for your ability. Many trails in this guide have dangerous natural conditions demanding respect and experience. All persons using the trails in this guide do so at their own risk, and this guide is not a substitute for your own common sense, caution, and taking necessary safety precautions. The author and publisher disclaim any and all liability for conditions along the trails and routes of the hikes, occurrences along them, and the accuracy of the data, conditions, and information contained herein.

Library of Congress Cataloging-in-Publication Data

Mitchell, Jeff.
    Backpacking Pennsylvania : 37 great trails / Jeff Mitchell.
        p.   cm.
    ISBN 0-8117-3180-4 (pbk.)
        1. Backpacking–Pennsylvania–Guidebooks.   2. Hiking–
Pennsylvania–Guidebooks.   3. Trails–Pennsylvania–Guidebooks.
4. Pennsylvania–Guidebooks.   I. Title.
GV199.42.P4M578   2005
796.51′09748–dc22
                                                            2004008759

To Kaitlyn and Christian

Contents

Preface

Why do I enjoy backpacking? What's the point of hauling a big, heavy pack up and down mountains, across rocks and streams, while being dirty, sweaty, wet, and tired? The reasons are plenty.

There is something special about observing wildlife in the wilderness, climbing a mountain to behold a gorgeous view, or following a stream to a stunning waterfall. To view nature away from a car window is something to relish. To carry everything I need to survive on my back for a few days enforces my appreciation of the convenient life I live. I feel a sense of pride and accomplishment when I traverse the wilderness under my own power and determination. It's amazing what our bodies are capable of when given the opportunity to explore. The astonishing beauty of our world is best realized by simply walking through it. So many incredible places bear witness to the grandeur of our state, nation, and world. By respectfully visiting and experiencing these places, we can appreciate and protect them.

Mainstream America may view backpackers as antisocial oddities. After all, what kind of psychosis is required to hike through the woods only to sleep on the ground, in a tent, without a bed or bathroom? The reality is that the people you'll find along the trail are almost always the most selfless, gracious, interesting, and genuine people you'll ever meet. Backpacking reintroduces people not only to nature, but also to each other.

I hope this guide enables you to explore and enjoy the beautiful world with which you have been blessed.

Acknowledgments

Special thanks to all my friends and family. Very special thanks to Joe and Tessa Mitchell, Steve Davis, Ashley Leng, and my parents for all their invaluable help and hospitality, which helped make this book a reality. I also thank Bob Holliday, Jeff Sensenig, Bryan Mulvihill, Dan Wrona, Ed Shrimp, Matt LaRusso, Ian Strever, Wayne Gehris, and Carissa Longo.

This book would not be possible without the assistance and support of Kyle Weaver and Amy Cooper at Stackpole Books. Pennsylvania's backpacking trails would not exist without the assistance and cooperation provided by the Pennsylvania Department of Conservation and Natural Resources and the Pennsylvania Game Commission.

Finally, I express my appreciation to all the trail organizations and volunteers who have made these backpacking trails a reality through their hard work and determination.

Introduction

If you look for hiking guidebooks in the outdoors section of any bookstore, you will find that the vast majority are dedicated to dayhiking; few guidebooks even mention backpacking trails. This is odd, because backpackers are even more dedicated to hiking, and a guide covering trails of interest to them would be invaluable. I can't begin to count the number of times I've heard people ask where they can go backpacking, what to expect on the trail, or where to find a trailhead. This guidebook is designed to answer all of those questions.

Several backpacking trails in Pennsylvania have their own guides for sale; this guidebook is not intended to replace them. It does not offer a turn-by-turn or mile-by-mile description of the trails. Rather, it offers a descriptive overview of each trail, informing the backpacker of the terrain, features, highlights, difficulty, length, water availability, and directions to the trailheads. This guidebook is designed to be a single source of information for all of Pennsylvania's backpacking trails, to give you an idea of where you'd like to go and what to expect on your trip. For more in-depth information about a trail, it is advisable that you purchase a guide for that particular trail, if one is available.

Pennsylvania's Backpacking Trails

Pennsylvania is home to the most extensive system of backpacking trails east of the Rocky Mountains. Trails stitch the state, exploring the state's expansive isolated plateaus, eroded with countless glens, gorges, and canyons, as well as its spectacular ridges where the rocky terrain offers numerous vistas. The trails in this guide reveal vistas, rock formations, gorges, canyons, glens, waterfalls and cascades, wildlife, expansive isolation, and old-growth forests. With almost 5 million acres of public land, Pennsylvania offers backpackers plenty of room to explore. Considering its size and large population, the state has the most impressive amount of public land in the nation. With so many trails, so much beauty, and so much public land, Pennsylvania is a premier backpacking destination.

Although some backpackers dismiss Pennsylvania for its lack of high elevations such as those found in the Adirondack, White, or Great Smoky Mountains, what many fail to realize is that Pennsylvania has the second-highest mean elevation of any state in the East. (West Virginia has the highest.) Pennsylvania may not have mountains as high as those in other states, but it has many more of them. And the views are just as stunning.

Backpackers who overlook Pennsylvania are denying themselves incredible outdoor experiences. Here you will find the impressive Pine Creek Gorge along the West Rim Trail; the isolation, wildlife, and scenic streams of the Quehanna, Susquehannock, and Chuck Keiper Trails; and the views, history, and rock formations of the Link Trail. Pennsylvania's backpacking trails are varied, exploring different terrains, habitats, and natural features. They range from the very difficult Black Forest Trail to the easy Pinchot Trail. Some, like the Donut Hole Trail, offer a deep-woods experience; others, such as the Warrior Trail, pass through pastoral countryside. If you want to spend a night, hike the 7-mile Minister Creek Trail; if you have more time, the 260-mile-long Mid State Trail requires several weeks.

Pennsylvania's incredible selection of backpacking trails offers something for every backpacker.

Pennsylvania's Environmental Heritage

Pennsylvania's history and development are inextricably linked to its incredible natural resources. Beginning in the early to mid-1800s, the state was home to millions of acres of old-growth forests, the richest anthracite deposits in the country, expansive fields of bituminous coal, natural gas deposits, and some of the highest-quality oil fields in the world. These resources drove and developed the nation and brought great wealth to Pennsylvania, but they also were recklessly exploited, leading to environmental degradation.

Careless mining practices resulted in the pollution of hundreds of miles of streams and rivers with acid mine drainage, quite possibly Pennsylvania's most embarrassing environmental problem. This acidic pollutant renders waterways lifeless and gives the rocks and streambed an orange-red tint.

The incredible old-growth forests were ruthlessly clear-cut, resulting in rampant wildfires, massive soil erosion, and loss of habitat. To exploit the forests, logging companies constructed a system of logging roads, skid trails, and railroad grades throughout Pennsylvania's forests, remnants of which can still be found. By the early twentieth century, Pennsylvania's forests were devastated, and the logging industry had nearly extinguished itself. Today only a handful of old-growth forests remain in the state.

Ironically, it was the very destruction of Pennsylvania's old-growth forests that laid the foundation for the state's incredible amount of state forests and game lands. In the early 1900s, the state government became aware of the great damage done to watersheds and soil as a result of careless logging practices. Led by the renowned forester Joseph Rothrock, the state began to purchase large swaths of logged forests at greatly discounted prices, creating a state forest system that now exceeds 2 million acres. These forests were nurtured back to relative health, a system of wild and natural areas was established, and the state park system was greatly expanded. Instead of acquiring wealth from the exploitation of its forests, Pennsylvania now benefits from their preservation. Thanks to its state forests and game lands, the state has become a prime outdoor recreation destination.

What does all of this have to do with backpacking? As a result of Pennsylvania's expansive amount of public land, an impressive backpacking trail system was created for the enjoyment of all. The logging roads, skid trails, and railroad grades once built by logging companies to transport lumber now provide convenient and historic routes for trails. This unequaled trail system is a national model. By backpacking through Pennsylvania's forests and mountains, we can obtain a greater understanding of all that was lost and an appreciation of what will be regained. We must be mindful not to leave future generations the same sad legacy our forefathers left us.

Pennsylvania Trail Designations

There are two primary trail designations in Pennsylvania: National Scenic Trails and State Forest Trails.

National Scenic Trails: These trails are created by acts of Congress and are eligible for federal protection, funding, and support for route acquisition and corridor protection. Pennsylvania has three of these trails:

- Appalachian Trail
- North Country Trail
- Laurel Highlands Trail (as a segment of the Potomac Heritage Trail)

State Forest Trails: Sixteen backpacking trails have this designation. Many state forests provide free maps to several of these trails. Horseback riding, mountains bikes, and ATVs are prohibited. A person who hikes all of these trails will receive the State Forest Hiking Trail Award from the Pennsylvania Department of Conservation and Natural Resources.

- Black Forest Trail
- Bucktail Path
- Chuck Keiper Trail
- Donut Hole Trail
- Elk Trail
- John P. Saylor Trail
- Lost Turkey Trail
- Loyalsock Trail
- Mid State Trail
- Old Loggers Path
- Pinchot Trail
- Quehanna Trail
- Susquehannock Trail System
- Thunder Swamp Trail
- Tuscarora Trail
- West Rim Trail

Camping Regulations

It is important to be mindful of the different camping regulations of the various agencies that have jurisdiction over the land through which the trails run.

State Parks: Backcountry camping is not permitted in state parks, except for those with designated backcountry sites. The only option is to camp at designated campsites, if they are available, and pay the fees. If you want to use a shower at a state park, you must pay a fee and/or make arrangements with that park.

State Game Lands: The Pennsylvania Game Commission (PGC) forbids camping on state game lands, with the exception of the Appalachian Trail. This prohibition makes it very difficult, if not impossible, to backpack a few trails in this guide in their entirety. The only option is to ask for and obtain written permission from the PGC to camp on state game lands.

State Forests: State forests have the most liberal camping policies, with the following guidelines:

- Backpackers spending no more than one night at a campsite do not need a permit.
- Groups of ten or more need letters of authorization from the district forester.
- Camp at least 100 feet from water and 25 feet from the trail.
- Small campfires are permissible except when the fire danger is high, very high, or extreme, and from March 1 to May 25 and October 1 to December 1.
- Camping in designated natural areas may be restricted.
- Follow "leave no trace" ethics, and leave a campsite cleaner than when you found it.

Allegheny National Forest: Backcountry camping is liberally permitted along trails within the forest, except within 1,500 feet of the tree line along the Allegheny Reservoir.

Backpacking during Hunting Season

Every trail passes through public land open to hunting. During hunting season, wearing fluorescent orange while backpacking is required by the Pennsylvania Game Commission. Try not to disturb a hunt or wildlife, and be considerate of hunters. It's important for backpackers to be respectful of other outdoor users. For more information about hunting seasons, visit www.pgc.state.pa.us. Hunting is not permitted on Sundays.

Trailhead Parking

Many trailheads are located in isolated areas, and vandalism of vehicles does occasionally occur. To protect your vehicle, make sure it is locked, all windows are closed, and anything of value is placed out of sight. Taking commonsense precautions will help keep your vehicle safe.

To park overnight at a state park, you are often required to register your vehicle for free at the park office; it's always a good idea to call the park and advise them you'll be parking overnight. To park overnight in a state forest, call ahead and let officials know where you'll be parking so they can keep an eye out for your vehicle. If you keep the park, forest, or other agency informed of your vehicle and whereabouts, they'll be in a better position to help you should the need arise.

Maps

It is very important to have a map and a guide, if one is available, of any trail you plan to backpack. Pennsylvania's state forests provide free, quality maps for several trails. Maps to most Allegheny National Forest trails are also free. Maps and guides are available for several other trails in this guide as well. Maps for all of Pennsylvania's state game lands can be purchased for a few dollars or downloaded for free from www.pgc.state.pa.us.

Backpacking Safety

It never ceases to amaze me how many people backpack without taking even minimal precautions to ensure their safety. Important precautions include the following:

- Tell someone where you will be backpacking, and if you can, hike with a friend.
- Wear proper footwear, and dress appropriately for the weather and elevation. Synthetic materials and wool are recommended. Avoid cotton, which loses its insulating capacity when wet and dries very slowly, putting you at risk of hypothermia. Never backpack in cold temperatures unless you have the proper equipment and experience.
- Water is absolutely critical, regardless of how easy or short the trail. Always carry a water filter or other chemical treatment; all wilderness water sources must be treated.
- Take along sufficient food.
- Obtain a map, learn how to read it, and acquire as much information as possible about the trail you plan to backpack.
- Carry a flashlight and a small medical pack.
- Check the weather report before leaving.
- Choose trails that are appropriate for your ability and experience.
- Be careful when hiking along or crossing streams or creeks with high water. Always unbuckle your hip belt when crossing deep streams.

Sign Trail Registers

Most trails in this guide have occasional trail registers. It's important to sign them for several reasons:

- Safety. If something were to happen to you on the trail, it would be easier to determine your location and direction if you had signed the register.
- Government assistance. It's easier for parks or agencies to acquire grants and funding to preserve and maintain trails that are being used. The most accurate way to determine use is by the number of names in a register.

- Trail conditions and warnings. Previous backpackers often write about trail conditions, give warnings, and note experiences on the trail, which are often helpful to subsequent backpackers.
- Camaraderie. Registers create a sense of kinship and camaraderie on the trail.

Backpacking Etiquette

Always show respect toward nature. Please observe the following:

- Pack out everything that you carried in; if you can, also pack out litter left by others.
- Do not pick vegetation or disturb, harm, or feed wildlife.
- Do not take shortcuts, particularly through switchbacks, which causes erosion.
- Do not deface, remove, carve into, or damage anything.
- Follow all rules and regulations established by the park, forest, game land, or other agency.
- When camping, follow "leave no trace" ethics.

Respect Private and Public Property

Many trails in this guide cross private property at some point. To maintain good relations with the owners, backpackers must treat private property with the highest respect. When crossing private property, do not litter, camp without permission, build fires, loiter, or damage property. Pass through as quickly and quietly as possible. If camping is permitted, do not become a nuisance; keep the noise level down, and change your clothes and relieve yourself discreetly. Shelters along the Warrior and Baker Trails are located on private property. At some of these shelters, you must ask the landowner for permission before staying for the night.

Anyone involved with trail organizations knows that working with private property owners to permit a trail crossing is a constant source of concern. To ensure the survival of many of Pennsylvania's backpacking trails, the cooperation and trust of these owners is absolutely critical. After all, would you want a stranger causing problems on your property?

Public land also must be respected. Too many people feel they have the right to use, pollute, and exploit public land any way they see fit. Always follow regulations of public agencies regarding the use of their lands, and help pack out litter or clear dump sites. We all need to be more appreciative of the public land that has been provided for our benefit.

Bears

The black bear calls Pennsylvania home, with the greatest concentrations in the Poconos and in the north-central region of the state. Black bears can be found along most of the state's backpacking trails. For the experienced backpacker, seeing a bear is a highlight of a trip, because these shy, retiring creatures avoid human interaction. For the beginning backpacker, no other animal causes more stress or worry.

Black bears do not need to be feared; they need to be treated with intelligence and respect. In all my years of backpacking, I have only seen a bear twice: a cub climbing a tree along the Link Trail and an adult along the Mid State Trail. Always avoid cubs and keep your distance from them, because their mother will be overprotective and more likely to be aggressive. Make noise when hiking through thick brush; surprising a bear can result in an attack. Clapping or talking is generally sufficient. Always rig your food in a tree, along with soap, toothpaste, and utensils, and avoid cooking meat when camping. Never keep food in your tent, as a hungry bear will slice through the tent easily.

If you do find yourself faced with an aggressive bear, back away slowly, avoid eye contact, and wave and clap your hands to make yourself appear larger. If a bear does charge you, it typically will be a bluff. If a black bear does attack you, however, you must fight back. The strategy of playing dead applies to brown or grizzly bears, which do not live in Pennsylvania. For this reason, I carry a trusty hiking stick. Hiking with a partner would further discourage a bear attack.

There is no need to be alarmed. In almost every case, a bear will leave the area where you are hiking without your ever knowing it was there. It has been several decades since a human was attacked by a bear in Pennsylvania. Because bears are heavily hunted, and not commonly fed, in the state, they do not pose the same problem or nuisance as those found in the Adirondacks or Shenandoah and Great Smoky Mountains National Parks. You must be prepared, however, in the unlikely situation that you are confronted with an aggressive bear.

Snakes

Pennsylvania is home to three species of venomous snakes: the timber rattlesnake, eastern copperhead, and massasauga.

The timber rattlesnake grows to 35 to 74 inches, is most active between April and October, and occurs in two phases: the common black-brown phase and the rare yellow phase. This snake often enjoys sunning on rocks. The habitat for the timber rattlesnake is throughout much of the state, but you are more likely to see it along trails in the north-central part of the state, and along dry, rocky, ridgetop trails. The eastern copperhead grows to 22 to 53 inches and also enjoys sunning on rocks. It also lives throughout much of the state but tends to be more common along trails in the north-central part of the state.

The massasauga is another kind of rattlesnake that is rarely found in Pennsylvania. It is highly unlikely that you will ever see one. It grows to 18 to 39 inches and generally lives in swamp, bogs, wetlands, or rivers. This snake lives only in the far western part of the state.

Like bears, snakes tend to be shy creatures that are afraid of humans. Snakebites are rare and typically occur when people try to harass or handle a snake. When you approach a snake, always give it a wide berth and observe it from a safe distance. Do not harm snakes, as they are becoming increasingly rare and may be protected by law. Most of my snake encounters have been along rocks exposed to the sun, so be mindful when hiking this type of terrain. Thankfully, rattlesnakes almost always let you know if you are getting too close with a shrill rattle. If you hear the rattle, freeze and locate the snake with your eyes before proceeding.

If a snake does bite you, seek medical attention immediately. Stay calm and hydrated. The venom of these snakes is generally not fatal to an adult but can kill a small child. Keep the wound below the level of the heart, clean, and immobilized as best you can.

In all of my backpacking trips, I've seen poisonous snakes only about four times. Most of these encounters have been along trails in the north-central part of the state. These sightings are a highlight of any trip. Because snakes are so crucial to our ecosystems, please respect them.

Stinging Nettle

Various species of nettles grow throughout the United States. In Pennsylvania, stinging nettles tend to grow in large groups or patches in shaded, wet areas, including streams and glens. They are often found along the trails of north-central Pennsylvania. The plants have heart-shaped leaves and are generally 1 to 3 feet in height but can grow as high as 5 feet. The stems have fine needles that pierce the skin and deliver formic acid, causing a red, itchy, burning rash that may have welts and blisters. This condition is temporary and can be alleviated by water, saliva, baking powder, or other alkaline substance.

Stinging nettles are most prevalent in summer months and can be extremely irritating while you're hiking. The best defense is simply to wear long pants while hiking through areas with nettles.

Lyme Disease

Lyme disease is a bacterial infection transmitted by the bites of infected deer ticks. In Pennsylvania, very few tick bites actually lead to the disease. When a person is bitten by an infected deer tick, symptoms develop in a few days to weeks. A circular rash envelops the bite and flulike symptoms result. If caught early enough, the disease can be successfully treated with antibiotics.

The risk of infection increases when the tick is attached for thirty-six to forty-eight hours. Most people will find a full-grown tick within that time, so the greatest risk of infection comes from tiny ticks in the nymph stage, which are about the size of the period at the end of this sentence.

Deer ticks are common in the woods, but they tend to prefer grassy and brushy areas. Some insect repellents are effective against ticks. The best defense is to wear long pants and sleeves and to inspect your body for ticks at the end of the day.

Giardiasis

All water sources, even pristine springs, must be treated before drinking. There is no reason why any backpacker should become infected with giardiasis or any other water-borne bacterial or microbial infection. With today's lightweight and effective water filters and various chemical purifiers, any backpacker can obtain safe water easily and conveniently.

Giardiasis wreaks havoc with the digestive and intestinal tracts. It can be successfully treated with appropriate medical attention.

Backpacking through Pennsylvania's Seasons

Winter: Winter is a surprisingly popular time to backpack. There are no bugs, stifling heat, or crowds. Water sources tend to be more prevalent along drier trails, and the lack of leaves affords more views, allowing you to peer deep into the forest and observe features that are concealed by foliage at other times of year. Snow cover presents a profusion of animal tracks that add interest to a hike. Do not attempt winter backpacking, however, unless you are experienced and have the proper equipment, including snowshoes or crampons.

The Quehanna, Susquehannock, Allegheny Front, Old Loggers Path, and Loyalsock Trails incorporate extensive cross-country skiing trails and are ideal for snowshoeing. The John P. Saylor, Lost Turkey, Pinchot, and Laurel Highlands Trails as well as most trails in the Allegheny National Forest, are also excellent for snowshoeing. North-central Pennsylvania, the Allegheny National Forest, and the Laurel Highlands tend to receive the heaviest snowfalls in the state.

Spring: With plentiful water, budding trees, and profusion of wild-flowers and wildlife, spring is an excellent time to backpack in Pennsylvania. Waterfalls and streams often are filled with water and at their most impressive; however, fording swollen streams can be difficult and dangerous, and trails can be wet and boggy. Spring in Pennsylvania tends to be temperate and wet. Snow sometimes lingers into mid-April in higher elevations. Lengthening days enable you to cover more miles and longer trails.

Summer: For many people, summer is the least favorite season to backpack in Pennsylvania. It's often hot and humid, and bugs are a nuisance. Water sources diminish greatly along many of the dry ridgetop trails. The good news is that most trails pass through mountain laurel and rhododendron, whose incredible blooms are a highlight of any hike. Mountain laurel blooms in late June and early July, and rhododendron in mid-July. Blueberries also can be found along most trails; the berries ripen in July.

Autumn: Autumn is probably the favorite season for backpackers. The weather is cool and crisp, and water sources are more available. The highlight is the incredible changing foliage colors that sweep through the expansive hardwood forests. In Pennsylvania, this foliage lasts from late September to late October, depending on the region. Elk are growing in numbers in the state, and if you are hiking the Elk or Quehanna Trail, you may hear these magnificent animals bugling during the rut in late September through October. When hiking in autumn, be aware of hunting seasons, and make sure to wear fluorescent orange.

Backpacking for Beginners

Many dayhikers are interested in backpacking. Making the transition is surprisingly easy. Follow these simple tips for your first trip:

- Choose a relatively short, easy trail offering a one-night trip.
- Acquire a map, and learn everything about the trail you plan to backpack.

- Purchase or rent the proper equipment. You'll need a pack that's at least 3,500 cubic inches in volume; a sleeping bag (rated to at least 20 degrees F for three-season backpacking) or liner (if backpacking in summer); a sleeping pad, especially if backpacking in cold temperatures; a tent; a water filter or chemical treatment; and hiking boots. This may sound like a lot of equipment, but it will last you a lifetime if you take care of it.
- Don't pack too heavy; an unbearably heavy pack will ruin any trip. Concentrate on packing light and taking only what you'll need. Pack dehydrated foods.
- Take along a friend familiar with backpacking.
- Learn about "leave no trace" ethics, outdoor survival skills, and how to rig your food properly.

There's a wealth of how-to guides available for beginning backpackers. Also check: www.backpacker.com and www.thebackpacker.com for informative forums.

These trails are ideal for your first few trips:

- Section hike of the Appalachian Trail
- Pinchot Trail
- Minister Creek Trail
- Morrison Trail
- Twin Lakes Trail
- Section hike of the North Country Trail
- Hickory Creek Trail
- Tracy Ridge Hiking Trail System
- Piper Loop
- John P. Saylor Trail
- Gerard Hiking Trail
- Quebec Run Wild Area
- Bear Run Nature Reserve
- Thunder Swamp Trail
- Section hike of the Laurel Highlands Trail
- Raccoon Creek State Park
- Allegheny Front Trail
- Section hike of the Conestoga Trail
- Section hike of the Mason-Dixon Trail

Keystone Trails Association

The Keystone Trails Association (KTA) was formed in 1956. It is Pennsylvania's premier trail organization and also serves as an umbrella over the state's various trail clubs. The KTA promotes the protection, maintenance, and preservation of hiking trails. It holds several weekend trips to maintain trails across the state, as well as weeklong excursions in summer. With Pennsylvania's trails facing increasing challenges, the KTA has put growing emphasis on governmental cooperation and the promotion of hiking and backpacking. Please consider joining and supporting the KTA. Keystone Trails Association, P.O. Box 129, Confluence, PA 15424-0129; phone: 814-395-9696; e-mail: info@kta-hike.org; website: www.kta-hike.org.

Trail Maintenance

Almost every Pennsylvania backpacking trail is primarily maintained by volunteers, who expend tens of thousands of hours every year. Trails should be sustained by the people who use them; it is unrealistic to expect state agencies to maintain these trails for us. Many beautiful backpacking trails throughout the state are in danger of disappearing. State and national parks and forests are always looking for volunteers, and numerous trail organizations, such as the Keystone Trails Association, do an extensive amount of trail work. Most trails have their own clubs that maintain the trails; these clubs are always looking for volunteers. Many people find they enjoy the camaraderie of trail work more than backpacking. It is imperative that every backpacker help maintain the trails they use. Even volunteering a few hours every year would make an incredible difference.

Endangered Hiking Trails

In 2003, the Keystone Trails Association established the Endangered Hiking Trails designation to provide awareness and support for threatened trails. The initial list included seven trails: Conestoga, Mason-Dixon, Horse-Shoe, Baker, Mid State, Warrior, and Link Trails. Although Pennsylvania is blessed with many trails, some of them face significant problems, as follows:

Landowner permission: Several trails face the threat of having their routes severed if a landowner withdraws permission for a trail crossing. This is a significant concern that can easily terminate a trail's existence. Trail organizations are moving toward written easement agreements, instead of verbal assurances, to help protect trail routes. Many trails are increasingly being forced onto roads because private landowners retract permission or new owners do not want a trail crossing their property. Because obtaining easements is costly and time-consuming, assistance from state and local governments is crucial. You can help by joining and supporting trail organizations.

Under use: In a way, simply hiking a trail helps maintain it. A government agency or local organization will not move forward to protect and maintain trails if they are not being used. One of the purposes of this guidebook is to provide information about lesser-known trails so they will be used and survive. Many backpackers are looking to escape crowded trails to find isolation, wildlife, and peaceful camping along relatively unknown or overlooked trails. Pennsylvania has a greater selection of these trails than any other state. Consider backpacking lesser-known trails to ensure their survival.

Camping restrictions: The Pennsylvania Game Commission (PGC) forbids camping on game lands, except along the Appalachian Trail, but it has been gracious enough to permit several backpacking trails to cross game lands. It makes no sense to permit backpacking trails to cross game lands yet forbid backcountry camping, which is the reason for establishing a backpacking trail in the first place. A reasonable alternative would be to allow camping at designated sites along approved backpacking trails. State game lands are primarily funded by hunters' licenses; if necessary, the PGC should institute a fee or permit program so that other outdoor enthusiasts can help finance game lands. The PGC's camping policy makes it impossible, or very difficult, to backpack several trails in their entirety, including the Mid State, Link, Tuscarora, North Country, Horse-Shoe, Mason-Dixon, and Lost Turkey Trails. As a result, the viability of these trails is threatened.

Development affecting trail corridor: Rampant development has forced portions of several trails, including the Horse-Shoe, Mason-Dixon, Conestoga, Baker, and Warrior Trails, onto roads. The Appalachian Trail's segment through the Cumberland Valley also faces increasing development. Walking on the road has little appeal for backpackers, and increased development affects the availability of campsites, making these trails more difficult to backpack. Without state or federal protection, there is little a trail organization can do to protect its corridor when it is located primarily on private land that is succumbing to intense development.

Lack of established trailheads and road signs: No backpacker wants to drive several hours only to get lost trying to find the trailhead, or to discover that there is no trailhead. The future of Pennsylvania's trails requires established trailheads, with sufficient parking and information signs, as well as road signs indicating where the trailheads can be found.

Lesser-Known and Isolated Trails

Are you searching for isolated, lonely trails that offer opportunities to view wildlife, camp at peaceful locations, or simply provide some solace? Are you tired of the crowds that descend upon the better-known trails? Are you frustrated by the stringent camping regulations in those places? Well, you're in luck. No other state can match Pennsylvania's varied selection of isolated, lesser-known backpacking trails that are just begging to be explored. Try a trail you haven't backpacked before; you won't regret it. These trails tend to be the most isolated:

- Link Trail
- Susquehannock Trail System
- Mid State Trail
- Bucktail Path
- Chuck Keiper Trail
- Donut Hole Trail
- Quehanna Trail
- Allegheny Front Trail
- Tuscarora Trail
- Elk Trail
- Lost Turkey Trail
- Terrace Mountain Trail

Better-Known Trails

These trails are more popular but are rarely overcrowded and typically offer plenty of isolation. You may have these trails to yourself, but expect company on holiday and summer weekends, when you can also expect to share popular campsites. Some sections of these trails are popular with dayhikers.

- Old Loggers Path
- Black Forest Trail
- Loyalsock Trail
- West Rim Trail
- Thunder Swamp Trail
- Pinchot Trail
- John P. Saylor Trail
- North Country Trail
- Morrison Trail
- Hickory Creek Trail
- Laurel Highlands Trail

Popular Hiking Trails

These trails tend to be the most popular, and sections of the trails may appear overcrowded during summer and holiday weekends, when you can also anticipate sharing popular campsites. Consider hiking less popular trails to enjoy some isolation and to help ensure their survival.

- Appalachian Trail
- Minister Creek Trail

Trail Conditions

Trail conditions are constantly changing. Trails are often rerouted, blazes are repainted or changed, and side trails may be built, expanded, or abandoned. A trail that is in excellent condition one day may be covered with blowdowns after a storm. Trails are often severed by private property owners and have to be rerouted. It is impossible for this guidebook to identify all the changes that may have occurred along Pennsylvania's numerous backpacking trails, and conditions may have changed since the time of this writing. Major trail problems are often listed on the Keystone Trails Association's website, www.kta-hike.org, or on websites for individual trails.

Northeastern Pennsylvania: Pocono and Endless Mountains

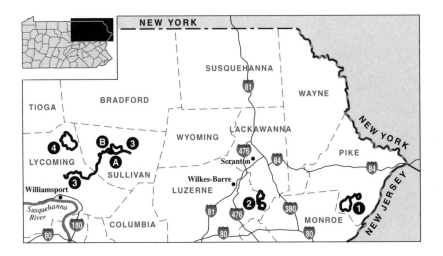

The Pocono Mountains is technically a plateau harboring unique habitats and ecosystems. Rain falls and collects on the top of the plateau, forming a complex and extensive system of swamps, wetlands, bogs, fens, lakes, ponds, springs, and streams. Streams drain the top of the plateau and descend over its edge, creating some of the most impressive waterfalls in the Mid-Atlantic, including Raymondskill, Pinchot, and Dingmans Falls. Two backpacking trails can be found on the Pocono Plateau: Thunder Swamp Trail and Pinchot Trail. Both trails are very similar in that they are mostly level with mild changes in elevation; there are numerous swamps and wetlands; the forests are dominated by hardwoods, with hemlocks and pines found near streams; and both are rocky. Neither features the sizable waterfalls that make the Poconos famous.

The Endless Mountains are a part of the Allegheny Plateau and feature four beautiful trails: the famed Loyalsock Trail, the Loyalsock–Link Loop, the Worlds End Loop, and the Old Loggers Path. These trails feature greater variations of elevation, numerous vistas, waterfalls, gorges, glens, and scenic streams. The incredible beauty and hiking opportunities of the Endless Mountains are just beginning to be realized.

1. Thunder Swamp Trail

Length: 28.2 miles consisting of a loop, a connector trail, and a small loop around Big Bear Swamp in the Stillwater Natural Area; 16.7 miles of side trails, which usually reconnect to the main trail.

Duration: 2 to 3 days.

Difficulty: Easy to moderate.

Terrain: Generally level with mild changes in elevation; greatest change is about 250 feet. Terrain often rocky, with numerous streams and wetlands.

Trail conditions: Trail is established and generally blazed well; side trails may be unestablished. Most major stream crossings have bridges, but most smaller streams do not have bridges. Sections of trail often wet, muddy, and boggy; trail is often rocky.

Blazes: Orange; side trails red.

Water: Generally plentiful.

Vegetation: Hardwoods dominate, with occasional hemlocks and pines; understory primarily mountain laurel, rhododendron, ferns, and saplings.

Highlights: Scenic streams, wetlands, Saw Creek, cascades, Bushkill Creek, beaver dam, Stillwater Natural Area, and Big Bear Swamp.

Maintained by: Delaware State Forest, volunteers.

Contact info: Delaware State Forest, Rte. 611, HC1 Box 95A, Swiftwater, PA 18370-9723; phone 570-895-4000; e-mail: fd19@state.pa.us; websites: www.dcnr.state.pa.us/forestry/hiking/stateforests/forests/delaware/delaware. htm, www.dcnr.state.pa.us/forestry/hiking/thunder.htm, ww.kta-hike.org.

Maps and guides: Detailed map available for free from the Delaware State Forest; no guide available.

Trailhead directions: From the north, get off at Exit 30 of I-84, and proceed 10.5 miles south on PA 402 to the Burnt Mills trailhead on your left (at the corner of PA 402 and Bushkill Road). The main trailhead is 16.4 miles south on PA 402 from I-84. From I-80, exit onto PA 209 north to Marshalls Creek; bear left and follow PA 402 north for 8.5 miles to the main trailhead, which will be on your right.

The Thunder Swamp Trail (TST) is a great place for beginning backpackers because it is accessible and mostly level, though rocky, with moderate changes in elevation. The trail system also offers numerous red-blazed side trails that can be used to extend your hike or for dayhikes. These side trails have scenery similar to that along the TST.

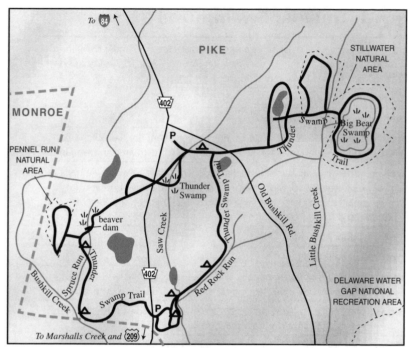

Hike 1: Thunder Swamp Trail

Hiking the trail counterclockwise from the main trailhead parking area along PA 402, proceed north from the trailhead and gradually descend for 1.3 miles to Saw Creek, passing two connector trails to the right along the way. At the juncture with the second red side trail at Saw Creek, there is a nice campsite capable of accommodating several tents in a glade. This particular side trail is very scenic as it follows Saw Creek downstream for .8 mile, with cascades and hemlocks. About .4 mile down this trail is an excellent campsite underneath hemlocks along the creek.

Cross Saw Creek over a bridge and proceed upstream along Red Rock Run. Both are scenic streams with cascades. Follow Red Rock Run for 1.4 miles, passing a few small potential campsites. Red Rock Run has one cascade that drops 30 feet down a sloping rock face. Bear left onto Luke Road, an old forest road. Follow this road across level terrain for 1.3 miles, then bear left on Red Rock Run Road, which you follow for .2 mile. The TST reenters the forest, and over the next 2 miles the trail makes a gradual ascent, levels off and passes through wetlands, and makes a gradual descent before crossing Whittaker Road, a gated forest road. The trail continues for 1.4 miles before reaching a forest road and an important juncture.

To the left, the TST continues onto the main loop and will return you to the main trailhead. To the right, the TST is a 4.7-mile-long connector trail that links with a 3.6-mile-loop around Big Bear Swamp in the Stillwater Natural Area. This description will begin with the connector trail and loop around Big Bear Swamp, and then return to this juncture to describe the remainder of the main loop.

Bear right off the forest road, and follow the trail for .4 mile to Old Bushkill Road; a parking area is off to the left. Cross the road and continue for 1.5 miles to an old forest road and a side trail to the left. Follow the road for .3 mile before bearing left and cross Painter Swamp Creek. Follow the trail for .8 mile until you reach another side trail to your left; this trail leads to a loop around a wetland that is the headwaters of Painter Swamp Creek. The TST begins a mild ascent for .5 mile to gated Coon Swamp Road. Cross the road, which is another side trail that forms a half loop through the northern section of the Stillwater Natural Area. Enter the natural area which features mixed hardwoods and spruce-fir wetlands. After .4 mile, a side trail connects from the left; this is the same half loop just described. Cross scenic Little Bushkill Creek, and in .5 mile you reach the juncture with the beginning of the 3.6-mile-loop around Big Bear Swamp, a very large, scenic, and diverse wetland. Views of this swamp are limited due to thick vegetation. This isolated, foreboding area provided a sanctuary for men evading conscription during the Civil War. Retrace your steps to the main loop.

On the main loop, follow the orange-and-red blazed forest road for .7 mile before reaching Saw Creek. The TST turns left, and the side trail continues straight along the road for 1 mile, where it ends at a parking area at the juncture of PA 402 and Old Bushkill Road. Over the next 1.4 miles, the TST heads downstream along Saw Creek, crossing it once; passes a side trail to the left, and bears away from Saw Creek. Then the TST meets PA 402 and the side trail rejoins from the left. Cross PA 402. For the next 2.8 miles, the trail is level but is often very rocky. The TST gradually descends to Spruce Run and bears left around a scenic wetland. Cross a side stream and Spruce Run at the foot of a large beaver dam. Potential campsites are downstream. The trail climbs above Spruce Run and meets a side trail to the right. This .5-mile trail connects to a 3-mile loop in Pennel Run Natural Area, which features wetlands, a small mountain stream, and a diverse forest of aspen, birch, and oak.

The TST gradually descends and crosses Spruce Run, follows the run downstream for .3 mile before bearing left, and climbs to Snow Hill Road, with a parking area to the left. Cross the road and begin a gradual but rocky 160-foot descent over 1.9 miles to beautiful Bushkill Creek. This large creek features some of the nicest campsites along the entire trail. Upstream, the creek widens into a large pool. The TST bears left away from the creek and ascends gradually a total of 240 feet over almost a mile. The trail levels off and follows the edge of the plateau before turning right and descending to a small stream. Over the next 1.5 miles, you pass near wetlands and through pockets of hemlock and pine before reaching PA 402 and the main trailhead.

🥾🥾 2. Pinchot Trail

Length: 24-mile loop.

Duration: 1.5 to 2 days.

Difficulty: Easy.

Terrain: Typically level with gentle ascents and descents. Occasionally rocky.

Trail conditions: Trail is established and blazed well. Several sections very brushy. Many small stream crossings without bridges. Trail often wet, boggy, and muddy in sections that skirt wetlands and swamps.

Blazes: Orange (formerly blue); side trails red.

Water: Generally plentiful.

Vegetation: Sections near wetlands feature diverse vegetation, with thick stands of rhododendron, mountain laurel, spruce, white birch, hemlock, beech, and oak; drier sections of the trail are open hardwoods dominated by oaks.

Highlights: Big Pine Hill Vista, diverse forests, wetlands, scenic streams, Choke and Painter Creeks, rhododendron and mountain laurel, Spruce Swamp Natural Area.

Maintained by: Lackawanna State Forest, Keystone Trails Association, volunteers.

Contact info: Lackawanna State Forest, 401 Samters Bldg., 101 Penn Ave., Scranton, PA 18503; phone: 570-963-3048; e-mail: fd11@state.pa.us; websites: www.dcnr.state.pa.us/forestry/stateforests/forests/lackawanna/lackawanna.htm, www.dcnr.state.pa.us/forestry/hiking/pinchot.htm, www.kta-hike-org.

Maps and guides: Free maps available from the Lackawanna State Forest; no guide available.

Trailhead directions: From I-81, take Exit 175 onto PA 315 and proceed north about 1 mile into Dupont. Turn right at a light onto Suscon Road (SR 2035), also known as Bear Creek Road, and follow it for 11.7 miles. The trailhead will be on your left and can be easy to miss if driving fast. From the Pennsylvania Turnpike, exit at White Haven and follow PA 940 east for almost 6 miles to Blakeslee. In Blakeslee, turn left onto PA 115 toward Wilkes-Barre. Follow PA 115 for 3.7 miles and cross the Leigh River; continue for an additional 1.3 miles, and turn right onto SR 2040. Follow this road for 5 miles to Thornhurst. In Thornhurst, turn left onto SR 2016 and follow 4.2 miles to the trailhead on your right.

The relatively easy Pinchot Trail (PT) is a great weekend hike, featuring diverse forest types, scenic streams, wetlands, and an excellent vista from Big Pine Hill. Although a loop, the PT nearly bisects itself, making it convenient to hike only the northern or southern section of the trail. The trail is rocky in sections and passes through thick stands of mountain laurel and rhododendron, making it a prime destination in late June and July, when these plants bloom. The PT is an ideal trail for the beginning backpacker. The trail was named after Gifford Pinchot, the father of American forestry, who lived in Milford, Pennsylvania. The trailhead is located in a scenic pine grove with ample parking.

To hike the trail counterclockwise, proceed north from the trailhead, passing the large trail sign. The PT is unique in that segments of this backpacking trail have their own names, this one being the Powder Magazine Trail. You'll find various trail signs while hiking the loop. Begin a gradual ascent, pass a register, and turn right where the red-blazed Pine Hill Trail joins from the left. This trail intersects with the Frank Gantz Trail, named after the trail's founder, and climbs to Big Pine Hill before rejoining with the PT on the other side of the loop.

A gradual descent follows and you'll reach Pittston Road, a dirt forestry road. Turn left and follow the road for a short distance, then turn right, leaving the road. Cross small Spring Run as it gurgles underneath rocks, pass a campsite, and begin a gradual ascent along the Sassafras Hill Trail. Upon reaching the top, the trail turns left, and level hiking follows for 1.3 miles as the trail crosses the top of the plateau; along the way, you pass a forest road, a few open meadows, a forest of

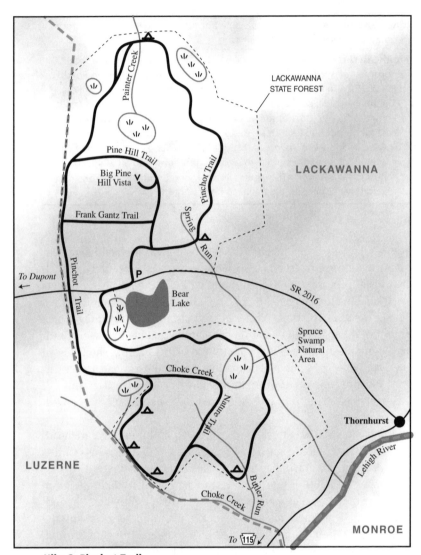

Hike 2: Pinchot Trail

white birch, and small wetlands. Bear left and begin a gradual descent, skirting Hayes Run Swamp. The PT turns left and descends to a small seasonal stream with possible camping. A steep, rocky descent follows to scenic Painter Creek, with beautiful camping underneath hemlocks and spruce. Cross the creek and pass a red-blazed side trail, which provides a scenic shortcut, and begin a short but steep ascent. Turn left at the crest of the plateau. The side trail rejoins and the PT passes near Painter Creek Swamp, with spruce trees. Cross Pittston Road again and begin a mild ascent along the Scrub Oak Trail for almost a mile, until you reach the Pine Hill Trail to your left at a grassy forest road.

Leave the PT and follow this trail for a side trip to Big Pine Hill. Pine Hill Trail is level and wraps around the northern flank of Big Pine Hill, passing boulders and rock outcrops. Bear right onto a forest road and climb to the top of Big Pine Hill, where you will find stunted scrub oak and spruce, and an observation platform offering an exceptional 360-degree view. To the north, you can see the Moosic Mountains, Bald Mountain, Miller Mountain, North Mountain, and the Allegheny Front. To the south is the Pocono Plateau, with isolated knobs similar to Big Pine Hill. Because Big Pine Hill rises about 200 feet above the surrounding plateau, it is subject to high winds and colder temperatures, resulting in a scrub oak ecosystem with stunted vegetation, a rarity in Pennsylvania. Retrace your steps to the PT.

For the next 2 miles, the trail proceeds south and closely follows the state forest boundary. The terrain is level with a gradual descent; this section of trail is especially brushy. Along the way, you pass the Frank Gantz Trail to your left and begin a gradual descent to the road, passing a small stream.

You now begin to hike the southern loop. This section of the PT is more brushy as it tunnels through thickets of mountain laurel and rhododendron. Expect trail conditions to be wetter as the trail passes around more wetlands. After crossing the road, the trail continues to follow the boundary and passes near a small stream. Bear right onto Tannery Road, which the PT follows a short distance before turning right. The PT rejoins the road and reaches a parking area with a sign for the Choke Creek Nature Trail. This red-blazed trail follows Tannery Road. Turn right and follow the PT through thickets of rhododendron, mountain laurel, spruce, and oak. The forest here is particularly diverse, and at times the trail is brushy. Cross several small streams and seep springs. Camping is possible in the open hardwood forest along a small stream. Begin a gradual descent to Choke Creek. This scenic stream features about three different campsites. The PT follows the stream closely for about a mile; at high water, Choke Creek floods the trail. You'll come upon one of the trail's most scenic campsites where the creek makes a sharp right along ledges and boulders. Above this bend is a great place to camp beneath spruce and hemlocks.

Soon thereafter, the PT turns left along a private-property line which it follows for about .75 mile. Cross a small stream and reach the Choke Creek Nature Trail to your left and a sign for the Butler Run Trail. Follow the PT through level terrain and open hardwoods as the trail passes near a wetland and descends to Butler Run. After crossing the run, you'll find another nice campsite in an open glade. Cross Sand Spring Road and hike over .75 mile to Phelps Road; turn left and follow the road for a short distance before reentering the forest. For the next .75 mile, the trail ascends gradually, passing small streams before reaching Tannery Road. Cross the road and more small streams as the trail skirts the edge of the Spruce Swamp Natural Area. Cross an old forest road and begin a rocky 200-foot climb over .75 mile along the Stone Lookout Trail (there is not a view, as the name might seem to imply), and follow the trail as it descends to Balsam Swamp and skirts its edge.

You will again meet Tannery Road. Follow it to your right and hike SR 2016. Turn right and walk along the road to the trailhead parking area, .75 mile away.

🥾 3. Loyalsock Trail

Length: 59.28-mile linear trail.

Duration: 4 to 7 days.

Difficulty: Moderate to difficult.

Terrain: Eroded plateau with many streams, gorges, and glens. Numerous ascents and descents, ranging from 200 to 1,100 feet. Steep and rocky in sections.

Trail conditions: Trail is established and blazed well; side trails not as well established, and blazes may be faded or harder to locate. Some sections are wet and boggy. Several stream crossings, most without bridges; some can be difficult in high water. Briers, stinging nettle, and brush can be a problem along certain sections.

Blazes: Red/yellow; connector trails have red Xs and spur trails have either white or blue.

Water: Generally plentiful.

Vegetation: Forests dominated by hardwoods, with occasional understory of mountain laurel and ferns; hemlocks and pines frequently found along streams and gorges.

Highlights: Vistas, waterfalls and cascades, rock formations and outcrops, scenic mountain streams, Kettle Creek Gorge, Worlds End State Park, Canyon Vista, Loyalsock Gorge, Angel Falls, Ketchum Creek waterfalls, the Haystacks, Smiths Knob, High Knob Overlook.

Maintained by: Alpine Club of Williamsport, Keystone Trails Association, volunteers.

Contact info:

Alpine Club of Williamsport, P.O. Box 501, Williamsport, PA 17703; e-mail: alpineclublt@suscom.net; website: www.lycoming.org/alpine/.

Wyoming State Forest, 274 Arbutus Park Road, Bloomsburg, PA 17815; phone: 570-387-4255; e-mail: fd20@state.pa.us; websites: www.dcnr.state.pa.us/forestry/stateforests/forests/wyoming/wyoming.htm, www.dcnr.state.pa.us/forestry/hiking/loysock.htm, www.kta-hike.org.

Tiadaghton State Forest, 423 E. Central Ave., S. Williamsport, PA 17702; phone: 570-327-3450; e-mail: fd12@state.pa.us; website: www.dcnr.state.pa.us/forestry/stateforests/forests/tiadaghton/tiadaghton.htm.

Worlds End State Park, P.O. Box 62, Forksville, PA 18616-0062; phone: 570-942-3287; e-mail: worldsendsp@state.pa.us; website: ww.dcnr.state.pa.us/stateparks/parks/worldsend.asp.

Maps and guides: Both can be purchased from the Alpine Club of Williamsport; trail also shown on free map from Wyoming State Forest.

Trailhead directions:

Eastern trailhead: From Dushore, head south on US 220 and cross the Loyalsock Creek; proceed .8 mile farther and turn right onto Mead Road (there is a sign for the Loyalsock Trail). Follow Mead Road for .2 mile to large parking area and restrooms. From Laporte, proceed north about 3 miles on US 220 to Mead Road, which will be on your left.

Worlds End State Park: From the Williamsport area, proceed north on PA 87 to Forksville and turn right onto PA 154; the park is 2 miles farther. Upon entering the park, cross the bridge and turn left into the parking area, then drive up to the park office. From US 220 near Laporte, turn onto PA 154; the park is 7 miles farther.

Brunnerdale Road: Proceeding north on US 220 from Hughesville, turn left onto PA 42 at Muncy Valley. Follow PA 42 for about 3 miles, going uphill, and turn left onto Brunnerdale Road, a dirt road; you will also see a sign for Hunters Lake. Follow Brunnerdale Road for about 4 miles. A parking area is on the right before reaching the juncture with Ogdonia Road. From the Montoursville exit of I-180, proceed north on PA 87 for 20.9 miles and turn right onto Ogdonia Road, a dirt road, and follow it for 3.5 miles. Bear left onto Brunnerdale Road; the parking area will be to your left. Ogdonia Road is about 2.2 miles south of Hillsgrove along PA 87. This trailhead may be difficult to reach in winter.

Western trailhead: This trailhead is right along PA 87, with limited parking, and it is easy to miss. From the Montoursville area exit along I-180, head north on PA 87 for about 8.5 miles; the trailhead will be on your right.

The Loyalsock Trail (LT) is one of Pennsylvania's venerable trails. Few other Pennsylvania trails can compare in beauty, notoriety, and difficulty. The LT was first established in the early 1950s, making it among the oldest backpacking trails in the nation. The trail was first laid out by an Explorer Scout post from Williamsport, Pennsylvania. In 1953, the Alpine Club of Williamsport was created to maintain the trail, and the LT was extended from its original 30.7 miles to its present length between 1960 and 1962. Several relocations have taken place since then.

The LT is named after the beautiful Loyalsock Creek, a sizable stream known for its scenery and whitewater rapids. Loyalsock is a derivative of the Indian phrase *Lawi-saquick,* meaning "middle creek," because the Loyalsock is in between the Lycoming and Muncy Creeks.

The LT often follows old logging and railroad grades and old forest roads. Other sections of the trail, however, are narrow, rocky, and steep. Besides the main trail, there are three other types of trails: The red X trails are connector trails, beginning and ending along the LT; the white trails are unmaintained spur trails; and the blue trails connect parking areas to other trails in the LT system. This description below includes the main trail and most of the red X trails.

If you are planning to hike the entire trail, I suggest you hike from west to east, because the parking area at the western trailhead along PA 87 is very limited and right along the highway. Park your car at the large parking area along Mead Road, at the eastern trailhead, and hire a shuttle to the western trailhead. This is unnecessary if you're hiking

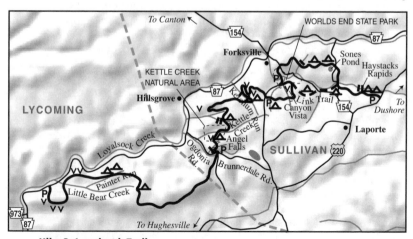

Hike 3: Loyalsock Trail

with others and are using two cars to shuttle. If you are hiking just a portion of the LT, Worlds End State Park is another excellent trailhead; just let the park office know you'll be leaving your car overnight. There is also a small parking area along Brunnerdale Road near Angel Falls. The hike is described here in sections from west to east (PA 87 near Loyalsockville to US 220 near Ringdale).

Section One: PA 87 to Brunnerdale Road

From the western trailhead, the LT makes a short, steep ascent and then turns right on an old forest road, which it follows for a short distance. The trail then turns left and begins your initiation rite, a steep, rocky, eroded 800-vertical-foot ascent to Laurel Flat. The LT passes between ledges and boulders, and it has a few switchbacks across the rocky terrain. At one point you are treated to a nice vista of the Loyalsock Creek and its steep-walled valley. You will pass Sock Rock, a flat, oval boulder. As the trail nears the top of the plateau, the terrain becomes very rocky, with large boulders and ledges.

When you reach Laurel Flat, the rocks virtually disappear and are replaced with a thick understory of mountain laurel. The trail is mostly flat as it wanders through a diverse forest dominated by hardwoods along with some hemlocks and pine trees. RX-1 joins sharply from the left, and the LT soon meets a grassy forest road. Bear left, passing seep springs and a small stream, which may not be running during dry periods. The trail follows the grassy forest road and begins a mild ascent. The LT turns left and reenters the forest, continuing its gradual ascent to the Allegheny Ridge. You will follow the crest of this ridge for almost a mile along exposed ledges; two main vistas and several partial vistas look over the hilly farmlands to the south. The LT descends from the crest of the ridge, and RX-1 rejoins from the left on another grassy old forest road. Bear right here, following this grassy road. Soon the trail turns left and reenters the forest to begin its descent of Pete's Hollow. The LT often follows the bed of this ephemeral stream, passing through a scenic forest of many sizable hemlocks. The descent is rocky and increasingly steepens. You will pass to the left of an extensive blow-down, exposing a sizable ledge off to your right. The trail soon reaches the forest ranger headquarters and crosses scenic Little Bear Run. This is the last water source before you begin the ascent to Smith's Knob and descend to Painter Run.

Now begins the LT's biggest climb, a 1,100-foot ascent to Smith's Knob. At first the terrain is steep, but it slowly becomes more gradual.

Hardwoods dominate, with a thick understory of striped maple and ferns. The LT reaches Laurel Ridge, becomes more level, and passes a white trail to the left. This trail may be hard to notice. You are then offered views of the Loyalsock and its deep valley. The LT bears right on another old woods road, and a blue trail joins from the left. This blue trail descends all the way to PA 87.

Ahead is RX-2, a connector trail that avoids the climb to Smith's Knob. The LT turns left from the old forest road and begins a final steep ascent over loose rock. The trail ascends the western flank of the knob and passes a vista; the hardwood forest is very open with little undergrowth. You then reach Smith's Knob at a dry campsite. From a cliff, there is an extensive view of the Loyalsock and the mountains to the east. The distinctive peak of Smith's Knob is a geologic anamoly in a region dominated by plateaus. From here, you begin a very steep, eroded descent from the knob, passing ciffs and exposed ledges to your left. The trail levels off and passes another vista, and RX-2 rejoins from the right. After a gradual descent, you reach beautiful Painter Run, a small mountain stream harboring brook trout. Painter Run bounces along a rocky streambed carpeted with moss as it disappears down its glen. You will find water and campsites here.

The LT follows Painter Run upstream, and a white trail, W-2, leaves from the left and goes to a vista of Smith's Knob; RX-3 leaves from the right. The white trail is a 1.4-mile-long semiloop and rejoins the LT .2 mile farther. The trail crosses Painter Run again, where there are more campsites. Then it follows the run almost to its source, passes the other end of RX-3, crosses over Red Ridge, and descends into the headwaters of Snake Run. A half mile farther, there are more campsites along the small Snake Run.

The trail bears right on an old woods road through a hardwood forest. It soon begins another gradual ascent over a ridge and then a descent to Shingle Run; RX-4 joins from the right. From Shingle Run, the LT begins another gradual ascent, turns right, and continues its ascent until it descends to Big Grand Dad Run, which is about 1.25 miles from Shingle Run. Following the run upstream, you'll pass a register. The trail climbs Long Ridge, and RX-4 rejoins from the right; you can follow RX-4 for .3 mile to a forest road accessible to cars. The LT descends from Long Ridge, following an old forest road. At mile 14.82, the trail leaves the Tiadaghton State Forest and crosses private land until mile 21.14, where the LT enters the Wyoming State Forest. No camping is permitted along the portion of trail over private land.

From mile 14.82, the trail descends from the Allegheny Front and crosses Laurel Run. The LT descends again and bears left onto a dirt road, which it follows for more than 2 miles and climbs the Allegheny Front. The trail passes near Highland Lake, and almost .75 mile farther is the historic Wind Whistle Inn. More road walking follows, as the trail passes a road to the right that goes to Camp Genesee and a road to the left that goes to Crystal Lake Camps. The LT finally leaves the road, gradually ascends along an old forest road, crosses the Lycoming–Sullivan County line, and continues to climb to the highest point along the trail at 2,140 feet. This point is anticlimactic, as there is no view. You will notice many No Trespassing signs along the trail, thanks to neighboring hunting clubs. The trail begins a long, gradual descent along this gentle old forest road for about 1.25 miles, until the LT enters the Wyoming State Forest. The forest is dominated by hardwoods, with an occasional understory of mountain laurel; off to your left, you may notice small boulders and exposed ledges. Continue the gradual descent for more than .5 mile until you reach the intersection of Ogdonia and Brunnerdale Roads, both well-maintained forest roads. The trail turns right onto Brunnerdale Road and begins a slight descent to a parking area to the left.

Section Two: Brunnerdale Road to Worlds End State Park

This section of the LT is one of the most scenic in the Mid-Atlantic region. The trail winds through gorges and glens, offering a showcase of views, waterfalls, and streams. Such scenery does come at a price, with numerous, and steep, climbs and descents, typically ranging from 200 to 500 vertical feet.

From the parking area, the trail follows Ogdonia Run downstream and fords Brunnerdale Run, where the two streams meet. The LT continues to follow Ogdonia Run downstream underneath scenic hemlocks for about .4 mile. Make a sharp right onto an old forest road. The unblazed trail to the left was the LT's former approach to Angel Falls; it was rerouted to curb erosion and habitat damage around the falls. The LT bears left and climbs about 300 feet along an old forest road. At the top, you'll pass a dry campsite and reach Falls Run. A blue-blazed spur trail to your left goes to Angel Falls.

Angel Falls is a beautiful 80-foot waterfall. The spur trail goes to the top of the falls, where there is a nice view of Ogdonia Run's gorge, and switchbacks to the bottom. Rhododendron, mountain laurel, and hemlocks surround the crest of the falls. Although it is very tempting to camp at this beautiful location, overuse has begun to take its toll on the falls.

Back on the LT, you'll follow Falls Run upstream, almost to its source, passing small campsites along the way. You will make a short ascent and cut through brush and saplings before making a steep descent into Kettle Creek Gorge, another exceptional highlight. Cross a small stream and seep springs, and turn left onto the short, blue-blazed spur trail to Kettle Creek Vista. Here you will also find a beautiful, large campsite; you couldn't dream of a nicer location. The vista offers a wonderful view of the graceful gorge from exposed ledges. Kettle Creek can be heard down below. Because the vista is down within the gorge, you are surrounded by its 800-foot slopes.

The LT descends into the gorge and fords scenic Kettle Creek, which can be difficult in high water. The trail turns right upstream, following an old railroad grade. You'll find another campsite near a cascade and deep pool. For .5 mile, the trail follows the creek before turning left and making a steep ascent. More campsites are along Kettle Creek. The trail makes a 400-foot climb, levels off, and passes through an area of blowdowns and thick briers. Then it crosses McCarty Road (an old forest road) and passes through open, sizable hardwoods before reaching a campsite at Dutters Run. Dutters Run is about 1.3 miles from Kettle Creek.

The trail descends along Dutters Run, crossing it seven times amid small waterfalls and cascades. You'll bear right and climb out of the glen to Mary's View, from which you'll see the distinctive V of Dry Run Gorge, High Knob, and Smith's Knob. Sign the register. The trail crosses Dry Run Road at a small parking lot and turns left toward High Knob. The LT is mostly level as it traverses a hardwood forest for more than a mile before it turns right and climbs switchbacks to High Knob. When you reach High Knob Road, there is a view; impressive High Knob Overlook is less than .25 mile to your left along the road. It is a worthwhile side trip, offering a view over seven counties of Pennsylvania's high plateau.

Cross over High Knob and the other access road. The surrounding forest is sparse as a result of windstorms and insect infestation. Briers can be a problem. Descend and cross the west and east branches of Cape Run, a small stream, and make an ascent to a logging road. Here the trail turns left and passes through Split Rock, a collection of boulders and rock outcrops. Follow another old forest road from Split Rock, where briers can be a problem. The trail turns left and enters a mature hardwood forest, and the briers diminish. Mostly level hiking follows until you reach Ketchum Run, about 1.5 miles from Split Rock.

Cross Ketchum Run and turn left, heading downstream amid scenic hemlocks and passing a campsite. Follow the run downstream for .3 mile, until you reach a register and a very scenic campsite in a glade. As you are about to see, Ketchum Run Gorge is a highlight with its waterfalls, cascades, flumes, and rugged scenery. Follow the trail from the register as it traverses the edge of the gorge over eroded, steep, and rocky terrain. The gorge narrows, with rock outcrops and impressive flumes. The LT makes a sharp right and ascends the gorge above 15-foot Lee's Falls. RX-6 follows the run, crossing it twice, amid cascades; do not follow this short, rocky trail in high water. Climb 200 feet up the side of the gorge to a narrow view of Lee's Falls at the top of a landslide. The trail descends back to Ketchum Run; RX-6 joins from the left. The LT bears right and continues to follow this beautiful run downstream. Along the way, you'll pass a powerful cascade and deep pool; more cascades and flumes follow. The trail reaches 16-foot Rode's Falls and its small pool; descend the ladder next to the falls. RX-7 is a short, steep trail bypassing the ladder. A beautiful, small campsite lies at the bottom of the falls.

The LT leaves Ketchum Run and climbs the side of the gorge to Lower Alpine View. This is a cliff-top vista overlooking the Loyalsock Creek valley. Level hiking for a few hundred yard follows along an old forest road until the trail begins a steep climb to Alpine View underneath hemlocks. Before reaching the view, you'll pass a section with thick briers and brush. Alpine View offers a beautiful view of the Loyalsock Creek and Ketchum Run Gorge; you'll also find a grassy glade and dry campsite here. After .25 mile, the trail crosses Coal Mine Road, a dirt forest road with parking off to your right. Level hiking follows for the next 2.75 miles, as the LT crosses the top of the plateau and passes the Worlds End Trail and cross-country skiing trails before descending to Double Run Road.

Cross the road and continue to descend to Double Run, which you must ford. Turn right on an old railroad grade underneath hemlocks and pass some campsites. The trail makes a gradual ascent before the short climb to Winners Knob, followed by a short, steep descent. The LT continues a gradual descent through a hardwood forest and passes rock ledges before entering the shallow glen of the East Branch Double Run, a scenic stream with many cascades, and Mineral Spring, a sulfer spring. There are some small campsites, but Mineral Spring Road is nearby.

Climb up the bank, cross the road, and enter the rocky glen of Mineral Spring Falls, a sloping 20-foot falls. Climb out of the glen and bear left, traversing the top of the plateau for 1.3 miles until you reach famous Canyon Vista, which overlooks the Loyalsock Gorge and beautiful Worlds End State Park. The view is exceptional. The Rock Garden is on the other side of Cold Run Road, featuring rock outcrops, passageways, and boulders. Here the LT also meets the Link Trail (RX-8). The Link can be used with a part of the LT to backpack an excellent loop trail.

The LT crosses Cold Run Road behind the vista and bears left, separating from the Link, recrosses Cold Run Road, and makes a steep, rocky 200-foot descent. Bear left, and the trail levels off before descending over very rocky terrain underneath hemlocks. Cross Mineral Springs Road and descend to Double Run, where the Loyalsock again meets the Link Trail. Cross both branches of Double Run and proceed on the bank going upstream along West Branch Double Run, a scenic stream with cascades, deep pools, and Cottonwood Falls, which is a short distance from the LT. The LT climbs gradually, crosses Double Run Road, and makes a sharp right onto Pioneer Road, the original road through Worlds End, abandoned in 1895. Notice the large boulders off to your right. For the next .5 mile, the trail is level until it reaches scenic Worlds End Vista. Then it sharply descends over 300 feet to PA 87 and the new park office. Here you also will find a concession stand that sells food, snacks, and some supplies between Memorial Day and Labor Day.

Section Three: Worlds End State Park to Mead Road and US 220

To park at Worlds End overnight, you need to register your vehicle with the park office. Start this hike by crossing the Loyalsock Creek, and turn left to begin the climb to High Rock Vista. Cross High Rock Run, above High Rock Falls, and start a very steep, rocky ascent to the vista. Large boulders and hemlocks cover the terrain. High Rock Vista offers a scenic view of Worlds End. The LT continues a moderate climb up High Rock Run's glen, passing small cascades. The trail crosses Loyalsock Road and traverses the top of the plateau; sections of the trail follow old forest roads that are often wet. Cross Loyalsock Road again and descend to Big Run, where you'll find a beaver dam underneath pine trees. Cross the run and follow an old forest road as it traverses the side of the glen to Ken's Window, a narrow view of Big Run's glen. Begin a steep descent to Tom's Run, with campsites, and scenic Alpine Falls encased in a rocky glen. Another waterfall is downstream, off the trail. For the next 3 miles, the trail is generally level. You'll cross small streams, then the Loyalsock Road again, and pass Porky's Den, a ledge where porcupines live, evidenced by large piles of droppings, before you finally reach Sones Pond, with scenic campsites underneath hemlocks.

From Sones Pond, the LT makes a gradual descent through exposed rock ledges and cliffs before making a steep descent to the Loyalsock Creek. Cross the historic Horseheads Bridge (also known as Jakersville Bridge); more scenic campsites are along the Link Trail, just downstream. The trail begins a mild ascent before leveling off, following old forest roads and a railroad grade for about 2.7 miles, until the trail makes a sharp left and steeply descends to the famous Haystacks Rapids. At the turn of the century, loggers tried to blast the Haystacks because they hindered logging runs. The Haystacks are boulders of Burgoon sandstone and create Class IV rapids in high water. This is a great place to swim, explore, or relax. Beautiful campsites are located around the rapids. Please treat this special place with respect. For the next mile, the LT follows the scenic Loyalsock Creek upstream, occasionally passing great campsites. The trail ascends away from the creek and reaches a railroad grade, which it follows for about .3 mile. Before turning right to make the climb to the parking area, it is worthwhile to visit Dutchman Falls, along RX-11. The end of the trail is at the large parking area along Mead Road.

3a. Loyalsock–Link Loop

Length: The loop is 17 miles; the spur along the Loyalsock Trail between the loop and parking area along Mead Rd., near US 220, is 4 miles one-way; Link Trail is 7 miles long.

Duration: 1.5 to 2.5 days.

Difficulty: Moderate.

Terrain: Ascents and descents are often steep and rocky and range from 400 to 800 feet, separated by periods of level hiking across the plateau. Trail occasionally follows old logging roads and grades.

Trail conditions: The Link Trail is well blazed, but is not as well established as the Loyalsock Trail. Small stream crossings without bridges. Can be brushy in sections; briers also an occasional problem.

Blazes: Loyalsock Trail portion is red and yellow; Link Trail is a red X on yellow.

Water: Generally plentiful; trail passes many streams and a few springs.

Vegetation: Forests dominated by hardwoods, hemlocks, and pines, some open areas from logging.

Highlights: Similar to the Loyalsock Trail: Haystacks Rapids, Dutchman Falls, Flat Rock, Canyon Vista, waterfalls and cascades, Worlds End State Park, Alpine Falls, High Rock Falls and Vista, Sones Pond.

Maintained by: Alpine Club of Williamsport, Keystone Trails Association.

Contact info:
Alpine Club of Williamsport, P.O. Box 501, Williamsport, PA 17703; e-mail: alpineclublt@suscom.net; website: www.lycoming.org/apline/.
Wyoming State Forest, 274 Arbutur Park Rd., Bloomsburg, PA 17815; phone: 570-387-4255; e-mail: fd20@state.pa.us; websites: www.dcnr.state.pa.us/forestry/hiking/loyalsock.htm, www.dcnr.state.pa.us/forestry/stateforests/forests/wyoming/wyoming.htm, www.kta-hike.org.
Worlds End State Park, P.O. Box 62, Forksville, PA 18616-0062; phone: 570-924-3287; e-mail: worldsendsp@state.pa.us; website: www.dcnr.state.pa.us/stateparks/parks/worldsend.asp.

Maps and guides: Can be purchased from the Alpine Club of Williamsport; link trail also shown on free map from Wyoming State Forest.

Trailhead directions:
Eastern trailhead: From Dushore, head south on US 220 and cross the Loyalsock Creek; proceed .8 mile farther and turn right onto Mead Road (there is a sign for the Loyalsock Trail). Follow Mead Road for .2 mile to a large parking area and restrooms. From Laporte, proceed north about 3 miles to Mead Road, which will be on your left.
Worlds End State Park: From the Williamsport area, proceed north on PA 87 to Forksville, and turn right onto PA 154. The park is 2 miles farther. Upon entering the park, cross the bridge, turn left into the parking area, and drive up to the park office. From US 220 near Laporte, turn onto PA 154; the park is 7 miles farther.

This is an excellent weekend backpacking trip, offering great scenery and campsites. If you have only one night to spare, hike the loop, beginning and ending at Worlds End. If you have two or more nights, begin at the Loyalsock Trail trailhead along Mead Road. If you're arriving later in the afternoon or evening, I suggest spending your first night at the spectacular Haystacks Rapids, only about 2 miles from the trailhead.

To hike the Loyalsock Trail west to the beginning of the loop at the Horseheads Iron Bridge, following the Link Trail to the Loyalsock Trail at Worlds End, and then back to the bridge, begin at the Mead Road parking area.

From the trailhead, follow the LT as it descends steeply to the railroad grade; nearby is scenic Dutchman Falls. Follow the LT along the railroad grade for .3 mile, until it suddenly turns right and descends to the Loyalsock Creek. You can also follow the grade to the Haystacks. The trail follows its namesake creek, passing nice campsites before reaching the Haystacks. The LT then ascends steeply back to the railroad grade and continues west for almost 2 miles to the Horseheads Iron Bridge and the beginning of the Link Trail. The LT crosses the bridge to the right; you'll return to this spot after completing the loop.

The Link follows the scenic Loyalsock downstream through a scenic pine and hemlock grove. You'll find great campsites along this section; it's an ideal locale to camp if you're hiking just the loop. Continue to follow the creek until you must make a steep 150-foot climb up to PA 154 because the trail was washed out downstream. Follow PA 154 for a short distance before making a steep descent back to the creek. Con-

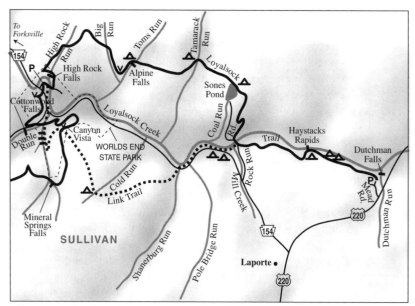

Hike 3a: Loyalsock–Link Loop

tinue to follow the Loyalsock downstream under hemlocks and pines. You will cross Pole Bridge Run as it cascades into the Loyalsock and reach Flat Rock, a large sandstone ledge bordering a deep pool along the Loyalsock. This is an ideal place to rest, swim, or fish. The scenery is beautiful. If the water is high, you will have to hike along PA 154.

The Link Trail crosses PA 154 and Shanerburg Run, then begins ascending, the side of the glen for a total of 450 vertical feet. The forest changes from hemlocks to hardwoods. For the next mile, the terrain is mostly level as the trail follows old forest roads and grades through hardwoods, hemlocks, and glades. Cross Cold Run Road and enter Cold Run's shallow glen with deep hemlocks. Cross small Cold Run; campsites can be found here. The trail bears right and climbs past ledges to a large, open area of logging activity. Expect to see deer through here. Reenter the diverse forest and fairly level terrain. After almost another mile, you will pass over large sandstone ledges with deep fractures. You soon join the LT and reach Canyon Vista and the Rock Garden.

The trail leaves the scenic vista to the left and makes a rapid descent to Mineral Springs Road and beautiful Double Run. Follow the trail downstream, passing waterfalls, flumes, boulders, and cascades. The terrain is very rocky but also very scenic. You will reach the juncture of both branches of Double Run; the trail crosses both branches, heads downstream along the left bank, and crosses PA 154. You will once again join the Loyalsock as you traverse ledges right along the creek. Here you will find a deep pool, carvings dating back to 1906, and numerous wildflowers. The surrounding gorge and the large Loyalsock Creek make for excellent scenery. Canyon Vista can be seen high above to your right. In high water, hiking this section of the trail would be impossible and dangerous. The Link crosses the rocky floodplain and ends at the LT along the park road as it crosses the Loyalsock Creek. To the left along the road are the park office, concession stand, and parking area. For those of you just hiking the loop, you'll begin your hike from here.

You will now follow the LT to your right, back to the Horseheads Iron Bridge, which is a little over 9 miles away. Cross the Loyalsock Creek and turn left to begin the climb to High Rock Vista. Cross High Rock Run, above High Rock Falls, and start a very steep, rocky ascent to the vista. Large boulders and hemlocks cover the terrain. High Rock Vista offers a scenic view of Worlds End. The LT continues a moderate climb up High Rock Run's glen, passing small cascades. The trail crosses Loyalsock Road and traverses the top of the plateau; sections of the trail follow old forest roads that are often wet. Cross Loyalsock Road again and descend to Big Run, where you'll find a beaver dam underneath pine trees. Cross the run and follow an old forest road as it traverses the side of the glen to Ken's Window, a narrow view of Big Run's glen. Begin a steep descent to Tom's Run, with campsites and scenic Alpine Falls encases in a rocky glen. Another waterfall is downstream, off the trail. For the next 3 miles, the train is generally level. You'll cross small streams, then the Loyalsock Road again, and pass Porky's Den, a ledge where porcupines live, evidenced by large piles of droppings before you finally reach Sones Pond, with scenic campsites underneath hemlocks.

From Sones Ponds, the LT makes a gradual descent through exposed rock ledges and cliffs before making a steep descent to the Loyalsock Creek. Cross the historic Horseheads Bridge. Retrace your steps to Mead Road, or if you are just hiking the loop, continue on the Link Trail to Worlds End State Park.

3b. *Worlds End Loop*

Length: 12-mile loop.

Duration: 1 to 2 days.

Difficulty: Moderate.

Terrain: Trail often rocky, rugged, and wet, with several stream crossings. Ascents and descents range from 100 to 700 feet and can be steep.

Trail conditions: Worlds End Trail is not well established between Worlds End State Park and the top of the plateau. Trail is brushy and briers are sometimes a problem. Faded, inconsistent blazes may be hard to follow to the top of the plateau. Otherwise, the trail often follows wide, grassy old forest roads.

Blazes: Worlds End Trail, red blazes; Loyalsock Trail, red and yellow blazes; Link Trail, yellow with red X.

Water: Generally plentiful.

Vegetation: Northern hardwoods predominate, with hemlocks, pines, and pine plantations; understory of mountain laurel.

Highlights: Worlds End State Park, Worlds End Vista, Loyalsock Canyon, Mineral Springs Falls, Canyon Vista, Double Run, Loyalsock Creek, Cottonwood Falls, access to Ketchum Run Gorge.

Maintained by: Alpine Club of Williamsport, volunteers.

Contact info:

Alpine Club of Williamsport, P.O. Box 501, Williamsport, PA 17703; e-mail: alpineclublt@suscom.net; website: www.lycoming.org/alpine/.

Wyoming State Forest, 274 Arbutus Park Rd., Bloomsburg, PA 17815; phone: 570-387-4255; e-mail: fd20@state.pa.us; websites: www.dcnr.state.pa.us/forestry/hiking/loyalsock.htm, www.dcnr.state.pa.us/forestry/stateforests/forests/wyoming/wyoming.htm, www.kta-hike.org.

Worlds End State Park, P.O. Box 62, Forksville, PA 18616-0062; phone: 570-924-3287; e-mail: worldsendsp@state.pa.us; website: www.dcnr.state.pa.us/stateparks/parks/worldsend.asp.

Maps and guides: Maps and guides of the Loyalsock Trail available from Alpine Club of Williamsport for purchase; free map of Loyalsock Trail also shown on the Wyoming State Forest map; Worlds End Trail shown on Wyoming State Forest and Worlds End State Park maps.

Trailhead directions:

Worlds End State Park: From the Williamsport area, proceed north on PA 87 to Forksville, and turn right onto PA 154; the park is 2 miles farther. Upon entering the park, cross the bridge, turn left into the parking area, and drive up to the park office. From US 220 near Laporte, turn onto PA 154; the park is 7 miles farther.

With its 800-foot-deep gorge, waterfalls, vistas, whitewater, and spectacular scenery, Worlds End State Park is a premier hiking and backpacking destination. The park serves as a primary trailhead for the Loyalsock Trail (LT) and the Loyalsock–Link Loop. The LT has long been popular with backpackers, and the Loyalsock–Link Loop is attracting more and more attention. There is yet another loop that is worth backpacking: the Worlds End Loop, formed by the 3.25-mile-long Worlds End Trail and the LT. This 12-mile loop is ideal for a weekend and can also be used to incorporate a side trip into the spectacular Ketchum Creek Gorge.

To hike the trail counterclockwise from Worlds End State Park, begin at the park office. Follow the red-blazed Worlds End Trail and the LT across PA 154, through a picnic area, and up the side of the gorge. The 350-vertical-foot ascent steepens under hemlocks until you reach Pioneer Road and the Worlds End Vista. The vista offers a narrow, scenic view of the Loyalsock Creek and swimming area. The terrain below the vista is incredibly steep. The Pioneer Road was the original road that traversed the gorge and connected Eagles Mere to Forksville; it was abandoned in 1895.

The LT makes a sharp left and follows Pioneer Road; the Worlds End Trail continues straight. Make a short ascent until the trail levels off along a bench, or flat area, along the gorge. Sections of this trail are unestablished and brushy, and blazes may be inconsistent. Stinging nettles are a problem along this section of trail in summer. Begin another ascent, following switchbacks of an old forest road. This steep ascent climbs an additional 400 feet to the top of the plateau underneath rock ledges and outcrops. You will enter an open area, appearing to be a salvage cut, where the trail may be difficult to follow. Bear right and follow the remnants of an old logging road as it gradually climbs uphill underneath blowdowns. Here the trail is also blazed with orange lids, several rusted. Fortunately, the trail quickly joins a wide, grassy, cross-country ski trail and gated forest road at a trail sign. Bear right and follow the trail along the edge of the plateau. The Loyalsock Creek can be heard far below. For about the next 2.5 miles, the Worlds End Trail is level or rolling as it follows the wide, grassy trail through open glades, which

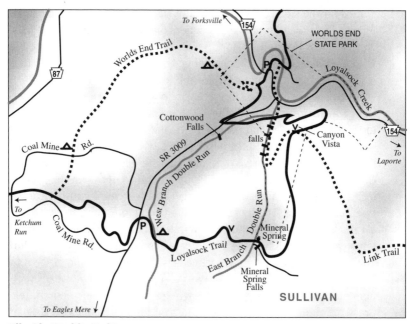

Hike 3b: World's End Loop

would make nice, dry campsites (the first glade is near a small seasonal stream), and scenic hemlock groves. Blazes are spaced far apart, and birch saplings and brush encroach on the trail in several sections, but the trail is easy to follow. The trail merges with Randall Road, a grassy, gated forest road, and crosses the headwaters of Scar Run. Before the gate, bear right, crossing small streams and passing through a scenic pine plantation with seep springs, old foundations, and a campsite that is nice even though it is close to Coal Mine Road. Cross the road and hike across the top of the plateau for .6 mile along a wide, grassy trail until you reach the LT. The juncture is easy to miss; you went too far if you reach a powerline swath.

If you'd like to extend your hike and camp in a beautiful location, turn right onto the LT and hike for about 2.5 miles into Ketchum Run Gorge. The LT passes a powerline, crosses Coal Mine Road, and follows the edge of Ketchum Run Gorge. After enjoying Alpine View (a possible dry campsite), the trail descends to a bench along the gorge and reaches Lower Alpine View. Another descent brings you to Ketchum Run and the scenic Rode's Falls. Here you will find a small campsite and a ladder alongside the falls. Above are more scenic cascades. Proceed upstream along this gorgeous stream. The LT then climbs up the side of the gorge, but a rugged side trail, RX-6, can be followed upstream to Lee's Falls, where the LT rejoins. Above the falls, you will pass through an impressive chasm and reach a grassy glade with a register and beautiful camping. You'll have to retrace your steps in the morning, but the beauty of this gorge is worth the extra effort.

If you choose to forego the side trip to Ketchum Run, turn left onto the LT at its juncture with the Worlds End Trail. The LT is level for more than 1.5 miles and passes areas that were once mined. Make a moderate 180-vertical-foot descent to Double Run Road. Cross the road near a parking area and continue the descent to Double Run. Cross the run and proceed up a side stream underneath deep hemlocks and along a railroad grade. A few small, scenic campsites can be found in this area. The trail enters a hardwood forest and crosses a forest road. Begin a short climb up Winner Knob, only to make a short but steep descent. Continue a moderate descent and cross Double Run Trail. The LT passes between rock ledges and makes a mild descent to East Branch of Double Run. This is a pretty cascading stream with hemlocks and Mineral Spring; downstream are flumes and chutes. Cross the run and Mineral Springs Road. The trail enters a rocky glen with Mineral Springs Falls. Proceed upstream and begin to bear left, leaving the stream and crossing another small stream. For the next mile or so, the terrain is rolling or level as the trail enters Worlds End State Park and reaches the beautiful Canyon Vista overlooking the gorges and glens of the Loyalsock Creek and Double Run.

From the vista, you can take either the LT or the Link Trail. The Link Trail is a more scenic descent and is not as rocky. Both trails have steep descents, but the Link also proceeds along Double Run, with its waterfalls, cascades, and boulders. At the confluence of the branches of Double Run, the LT rejoins; cross the run. You can follow the green-and-white blazed Double Run Nature Trail to the left and proceed upstream to Cottonwood Falls. Otherwise, follow the Link Trail to the right, cross PA 154, and hike along the ledges of the Loyalsock, bordered by a deep pool. Reach the park road and turn left to the park office.

4. Old Loggers Path

Length: 27-mile loop trail.

Duration: 1 ½ to 3 days.

Difficulty: Moderate.

Terrain: Eroded plateau with numerous streams. Trail often follows old forest roads and grades. Ascents and descents tend to be gradual with some steep sections; they range between 200 and 800 feet. Sometimes rocky, particularly between Sprout Point and Masten. Numerous stream crossings.

Trail conditions: Trail blazed well and established. Few stream crossings have bridges; crossing Pleasant Stream during high water is very difficult. Briers an occasional problem.

Blazes: Orange; spur and connector trails blue.

Water: Plentiful; trails crosses and passes many streams and springs.

Vegetation: Forests dominated by hardwoods, with occasional understory of mountain laurel and ferns; hemlocks and pines occasionally found along streams.

Highlights: Waterfalls and cascades, rock formations and outcrops, scenic mountain streams, history, Rock Run, Sharp Top Vista, Sullivan Mountain vistas, wildlife, large railroad grade.

Maintained by: Individual volunteers, Keystone Trails Association, Tiadaghton State Forest, volunteers.

Contact info:
Tiadaghton State Forest, 423 E. Central Ave., S. Williamsport, PA 17702;
phone: 570-327-3450; e-mail: fd12@state.pa.us; websites:
www.dcnr.state.pa.us/forestry/stateforests/forests/tiadaghton/tiadaghton.htm,
www.dcnr.state.pa.us/forestry/hiking/logger.htm, www.kta-hike.org.

Maps and guides: Free map available from Tiadaghton State Forest;
no guides available.

Trailhead directions: Traditional trailhead located at Masten. From
Forksville, proceed on PA 154 north to Shunk, where PA 154 makes a sharp
right. Go straight on another paved road, and follow it 3.7 miles to Ellenton. At Ellenton, turn left on a dirt road, SR 1013, and follow 1.1 miles to
a Y. Bear left on another dirt road, SR 1015, and follow it 1.5 miles to Masten. From PA 14 and Marsh Hill, follow Pleasant Stream Road for 9.4 miles
to Masten; the road becomes dirt after 2 miles. Parking is somewhat limited. Trailheads may be difficult to reach if there is snow.

The Old Loggers Path (OLP) is one of Pennsylvania's premier loop
trails. The OLP showcases some of the state's most scenic areas,
with sweeping vistas, cascading streams, rock outcrops, and Rock Run,
a stream of exceptional beauty. Because the OLP offers so much scenery
along an ideal weekend loop, it is becoming increasingly popular.

The main trailhead is located at Masten, an abandoned logging
town. Pennsylvania is dotted with abandoned lumber and mining
towns. At one time, Masten was a thriving lumber community with
churches, bars, and numerous homes. Once all the lumber was
exploited, Masten began to decline. The Depression reinvigorated
Masten with a Civilian Conservation Corps camp. Once World War II
began, the town disappeared for good. Today there are a few hunting
camps, sunken foundations, and a towering chimney located in a
spruce grove at the trailhead.

If you're beginning your hike on a Friday afternoon, hike the loop
counterclockwise so that you will be able to camp along beautiful
Rock Run, about 6 miles from Masten. If you are more determined,
you may be able to make camp at Doe Run, which is about 10 miles
from Masten. If you plan to take two and a half days for your hike,
with your first day being a whole day, hiking the loop clockwise from
Masten may be your best bet, camping at Pleasant Stream the first
night and Rock Run the second.

To hike the loop counterclockwise from Masten, begin by hiking down (west) on Pleasant Stream Road. Below is a grove of spruce trees with a towering chimney. This is a popular place to camp, although it is right along the road. The OLP soon makes a right and leaves the road, ascending the side of the plateau via an old logging grade. This trail often follows old forest roads, grades, and railroad grades. The forest you see around you is typical of the OLP: mature hardwood forest with an understory of ferns, saplings, brush, and some mountain laurel. There are few areas with hemlock or pine. You will enter the gentle glen carved by Hoghouse Run, a small stream. The trail crosses the stream, ascends the other side, and passes a campsite. Hiking for the next .6 mile is level as the OLP passes through meadows and makes a left to begin a steeper ascent up the plateau. Once again the trail follows an old forest road.

When I hiked along this section one late-spring morning, a fawn came bounding down the trail by itself. It was about 10 feet away from

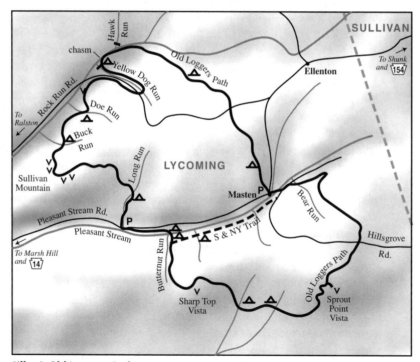

Hike 4: Old Loggers Path

me when it finally stopped. I stood perfectly still as the fawn sniffed the area and tried to figure out what I was; it finally bounded away. Wildlife experiences like this make backpacking all the more worthwhile. The OLP offers a chance to view much wildlife, especially deer, wild turkeys, pheasant, grouse, vultures, and the occasional bear.

The OLP finally reaches the top of the plateau, a climb of almost 500 vertical feet from Masten, and turns right on a forest road. The blue blazes you see are for the Cherry Ridge Trail, a 6-mile loop. Ahead are Ellenton Ridge Road and a small parking area. The trail follows the road for a short distance before it turns right into the forest and joins a wide, grassy old logging road. The OLP makes a sharp left turn and begins a gradual descent into the Rock Run watershed. The trail levels off, crosses a small stream after about a mile, and bears right to begin a long, gradual descent along the side of the gorge carved by beautiful Rock Run. The OLP continues its descent for about 1.5 miles, passing under a few hemlocks. Rock Run can be heard and occasionally seen. The descent accelerates until the trail finally joins Rock Run; there is a campsite below to the right.

Rock Run is considered to be one of Pennsylvania's most scenic streams, and it's easy to see why. There are overhanging ledges, boulders, cascades, and deep pools. Hawk Run tumbles into Rock Run over a small waterfall. The OLP only comes within about 200 feet of Rock Run, but it's easy to do some off-trail exploring. Follow the run downstream to where Yellow Dog Run descends from the left and cascades over a rock face directly into Rock Run. Here Rock Run has carved a tight chasm into solid rock, creating deep, oblong pools and cascades. The scenery is exceptional. This is a great place to take a break and refresh yourself. If you camp here, please treat this special place with the highest level of respect. A larger campsite can be found on the other side of Yellow Dog Run.

Unfortunately, the OLP's rendezvous with Rock Run is brief. Follow the trail as it turns left and ascends the plateau again. The OLP follows another old forest road above the glen carved by Yellow Dog Run, ascending 600 feet over more than a mile. At times the trail is eroded and there are some seep springs. Deep in the glen of Yellow Dog Run is a 20-foot waterfall, which is hidden from the trail when there are leaves on the trees. Upon reaching the top of the plateau, the trail curves right and crosses Yellow Dog Run. Bear right on Yellow Dog Road and follow it for a short distance, passing a small parking area. Bear left where the trail reenters the forest, passing a register. For about the next 4 miles, the trail is mostly level as it follows the edge of the plateau above Rock Run's gorge. You cross a pipeline swath and soon reach a short, blue-blazed spur trail to the right, which takes you to a vista of Rock Run's beautiful gorge, reaching a depth of 1,000 feet. There is also a register here.

The OLP continues along the plateau, passing a pretty meadow to the left. It eventually bears left and crosses Doe Run, where there are more scenic campsites near the cascading stream. The trail returns to the edge of the plateau above Rock Run until turning left toward Buck Run. There are many large boulders along this stretch of the trail, the largest being the size of small houses near where the trail crosses small Buck Run. You'll find a few small campsites here underneath hemlocks. The OLP makes a sharp right onto Ellenton Ridge Road, another abandoned road. To the left, you pass a juncture with Crandalltown Trail, a shortcut to avoid Sullivan Mountain. The OLP follows Ellenton Ridge Road for about .5 mile, until the trail makes a sharp left to ascend Sullivan Mountain. This turn is very easy to miss, so pay attention to the blazes; it's easy to just follow grassy Ellenton Ridge Road, which continues straight.

Begin a steep, short, rocky ascent to the summit of Sullivan Mountain, with its many vistas. Upon reaching the top, the trail bears right through laurel and passes boulders. You soon reach the first two excellent vistas, which overlook the high plateau to the west from exposed ledges and rock faces. You can clearly see the gorges and glens carved by Rock Run, Miners Run, and other tributaries. Sunsets are memorable from these vantage points. Large boulders and ledges dot the forest behind you. From here the OLP makes a mild ascent and turns left through an open meadow of ferns. The trail makes another mild ascent to the rim of a series of exposed, crumbling ledges, with a vista to the south over Pleasant Stream's gorge. Continuing along the trail, a boulder is perched upright within a crevasse along one of the ledges. The OLP reenters the forest, slightly descends, and comes to Sullivan Mountain's last vista, a large, exposed ledge overlooking Sixth Bottom Hollow and Pleasant Stream's gorge. The setting is almost completely undisturbed.

The trail soon begins a steep descent past boulders and through ledges, then makes a sharp right at a large hemlock and campsite; here is yet another old forest road, Crandalltown Road. Mostly level hiking follows, and you pass through the same pipeline swath that you crossed previously near Yellow Dog Road. More level hiking follows, until the trail bears right and makes an increasingly steep descent into Long Run's glen. Long Run is another scenic little mountain stream, with small cascades, pools, and even native brook trout. The trail passes a few small campsites, crosses the run, and uses a logging grade. Follow the grade downstream, above the run, and keep an eye on the blazes where the trail descends to and crosses the run. Continue downstream until you reach Pleasant Stream Road at a small parking area. The OLP crosses the road and turns left onto a railroad grade, which the trail follows for almost a mile. Pleasant Stream can be heard off to your right, and at times you are treated to a glimpse of the stream where it flows up along the grade.

The trail turns right, descends from the grade, and passes an unsigned juncture with Butternut Trail. Ahead is a nice campsite. There is no bridge, so you must ford the stream. This is an easy task when the water is at low or normal levels; at higher levels, caution is required. After crossing the stream, you encounter more nice campsites. The trail bears left as it ascends Butternut Run's gentle glen along an old logging grade. Pass the juncture with the blue-blazed S & NY Trail to your left, an ideal 3.34-mile connector trail that divides the OLP into two loops. This easy, rolling trail follows Pleasant Stream high on a bank, passes a vista created where a landslide eroded the embankment, and crosses Rock Spring Run, with potential campsites. The trail joins its namesake, the S & NY Railroad grade, for level, easy hiking to Hillsgrove Road. Parts of the large grade have been eroded by small streams. When you reach the road, turn left and follow it for .25 mile to Pleasant Stream Road and the OLP.

Back on the OLP along Butternut Run, continue a gradual climb that ascends 500 feet over a mile. As you near the top of the plateau, briers can become a problem, as the forest canopy here has been ravaged by blowdowns and insect infestation. There are many scags and areas dominated by ferns.

The OLP reaches a dirt road, crosses it, and bears left, traversing the edge of Burnett's Ridge. You pass eroding ledges and broken views to the south. After a slight ascent, you reach spectacular Sharp Top Vista. From here you are treated to an expansive, wooded view of the valley below. The view is relatively undisturbed, as there are no towns and few farms. To the south rise Jacoby, Cove, and Camp Mountains, and you can see the water gap carved by Plunketts Creek between Cove and Camp Mountains. To the east are Goosebury Mountain and High Knob Overlook, another famous vista.

The trail now leaves the edge of the plateau and makes a gradual descent. You then turn right and make a steep, eroded descent for about 300 feet. The descent becomes more gradual as the trail enters a forest of stately hardwoods. The OLP crosses a small stream with a few campsites and stays generally rolling as it crosses a few more small streams before reaching Cascade Road at a small parking lot. The trail crosses the road and begins a gradual ascent, skirting the side of an overgrown meadow. The climb becomes steeper as the OLP once again ascends the plateau. You soon reach a side trail to your right, heading to Sprout Point Vista. There are many briers along this short trail. Sprout Point is mostly overgrown and offers only a narrow window of the valley below for a view. There is a dry campsite here.

From the vista, the OLP continues its ascent and then levels off until the trail makes a short climb up to a logging road and passes to the left of a clear-cut. You then make a gradual descent to Hillsgrove Road and a small stream. There is no parking along this road. The OLP reenters the forest, makes a slight ascent, and bears right. The terrain becomes increasingly rocky, with seep springs; off to your left are Bear Run and small wetlands. The trail joins a rocky grade and begins to descend along the side of Bear Run's scenic glen. Hemlocks and laurel are common along this section of the trail. The trail follows the large grade as it turns right and continues to descend. You soon reach a large, impressive railroad grade, on which the OLP makes a sharp left. Below to your right are Pleasant Stream and a mature hardwood forest. This area is very scenic, and the effort it took to build this massive grade is incredible, especially where it crosses Bear Run. The OLP then turns right and descends from the grade through a grove of spruce. You pass a register and soon reach Pleasant Stream Road. Turn left on the road and follow it for .5 mile back to your car. Along the way, you pass hunting cabins, one with a piped spring, and foundations, which are all that remains of Masten. Your car is just ahead.

Southeastern Pennsylvania

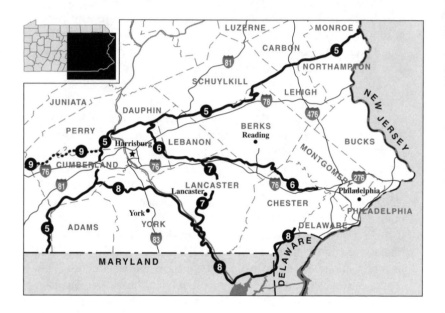

This area is the most heavily populated in the entire state. Rapid urban sprawl has begun to affect this region's agricultural heritage, environment, and backpacking trails. Development has forced much of the Horse-Shoe, Mason-Dixon, and Conestoga Trails onto roads. The Appalachian Trail corridor near Carlisle is being encroached on by housing developments. Fortunately, these trails have diligent volunteers working on their behalf; the simple fact that these trails exist is a testament to the dedication of the volunteers.

Southeastern Pennsylvania has fine backpacking opportunities. The Appalachian Trail is the world's most famous trail and is synonymous with backpacking. The trail traverses South Mountain, with views, rock outcrops and formations, and scenic streams. Thereafter, the trail crosses the Cumberland Valley and follows the crests of ridges with numerous water gaps and vistas, including the impressive Pinnacle and Delaware Water Gap.

My favorite natural feature in this part of the state is the Susquehanna River Gorge. The Susquehanna River, nearly 2 miles in width in places, has carved a gorge almost 400 feet deep into the Piedmont. You'll find excellent vistas, rock outcrops, boulders, cliffs of schist, and countless islands with rocky spires thrusting out of the river. Numerous streams have carved side gorges and glens with cascades, rapids, waterfalls, boulders, hemlock groves, and rhododendron thickets. Muddy, Tucquan, Otter, Pequea, and Codorus Creeks and Kelly Run are some of the most scenic streams in the state. Another amazing feature lies underneath the Susquehanna: The river has carved incredible tubs and potholes into the bedrock. And finally, the gorge is home to an incredible diversity of plants and wildlife, and includes the world's first refuge for bald eagles, Johnson Island. The Susquehanna River Gorge is a truly special place that is in need of greater protection. Two trails, the Mason-Dixon and Conestoga, explore parts of the gorge and feature the finest scenery.

Backpacking trails can exist on private property and populated areas, but they are in need of special support. The benefits they offer the communities through which they pass more than justify their existence.

 5. Appalachian Trail

Length: 232-mile linear trail (Pennsylvania's section).

Duration: 2 to 3 weeks.

Difficulty: Easy to difficult.

Terrain: Over South Mountain, elevation changes range from 200 to 800 feet; moderately rocky terrain with stream crossings. Flat and easy across the Cumberland Valley. Across the Susquehanna River, dry, rolling ridgelines, very rocky in sections; elevation changes range from 400 to 1,100 feet where passing through water gaps and valleys. Trail often follows old grades and forest roads.

Trail conditions: Trail is established and blazed well.

Blazes: White; side trails blue. The trail often crosses through game lands with survey boundaries marked with irregular, large white paint marks on trees; do not confuse these with blazes for the trail, which are smaller, uniform rectangles.

Water: Between Maryland and the Susquehanna River, there are usually sufficient sources of water during periods of normal precipitation. Between the Susquehanna River and the Delaware Water Gap, the dry ridgetops have few streams or springs; side trails often lead to springs off the ridge. Carry extra containers for water.

Vegetation: Hardwoods predominate, with occasional hemlocks and pines; understory of mountain laurel and brush.

Highlights: Excellent vistas, Chimney Rocks, Susquehanna River, Caledonia State Park, Pine Grove Furnace State Park, St. Anthony's Wilderness, Swatara State Park, the Pinnacle, Knife Edge, Bear Rocks, Bake Oven Knob, Lehigh Gap, Wolf Rocks, Delaware Water Gap.

Maintained by: Various volunteer groups.

Contact info:

Michaux State Forest, 10099 Lincoln Way East, Fayetteville, PA 17222; phone: 717-352-2211; e-mail: fd01@state.pa.us; websites: www.dcnr.state.pa.us/forestry/stateforests/forests/michaux/michaux.htm, www.dcnr.state.pa.us/forestry/hiking/at.htm.

Weiser State Forest, Box 99, Cressona, PA 17929; phone: 570-385-7800; e-mail: fd18@state.pa.us; website: www.dcnr.state.pa.us/forestry/stateforests/forests/weiser/weiser.htm.

Appalachian Trail Conference, 799 Washington St., P.O. Box 807, Harpers Ferry, WV 25425-0807; phone: 304-535-6331; websites: www.appalachiantrail.org, www.nps.gov/appa.

Delaware Water Gap National Recreation Area, HQ—River Rd., Rt. 309,
Bushkill, PA 18324-9999; e-mail: DEWA_Interpretation@nps.gov;
website: www.nps.gov/dewa.

Caledonia State Park, 40 Rocky Mountain Rd., Fayetteville, PA 17222-9610;
phone: 717-352-2161; e-mail: caledoniasp@state.pa.us; website:
www.dcnr.state.pa.us/stateparks/parks/caledonia.asp.

Pine Grove Furnace State Park, 1100 Pine Grove Rd., Gardners, PA 17324;
phone: 717-486-7174; e-mail: pinegrovesp@state.pa.us; website:
www.dcnr.state.pa.us/stateparks/parks/pinegrovefurnace.asp.

Swatara State Park, c/o Memorial Lake, Grantville, PA 17028-9682;
phone: 717-865-6470; e-mail: memorialsp@state.pa.us;
website: www.dcnr.state.pa.us/stateparks/parks/swatara.asp.

Maps and guides: Both available for sale.

Trailhead directions:

Caledonia State Park: The park is located at the intersection of US 30 and PA
233. Along US 30, the park is 10 miles east of Chambersburg and 13 miles
west of Gettysburg.

Pine Grove Furnace State Park: From I-81, take Exit 37 and proceed on PA 233
south for 8 miles to the state park.

PA 850: The trail crosses PA 850 near Keystone, about 9 miles west of
Marysville. There is a parking lot on the left side of the road.

Duncannon (US 22/322 and PA 147): From I-81, take Exit 67B onto US
22/322 west for 11.5 miles. Before the highway crosses the Susquehanna
River, exit onto PA 147 north. Parking areas will be on the left, and a trail
sign on the right.

Swatara State Park: From I-81, take Exit 90 and proceed to Lickdale. Turn left
onto PA 72, follow to its juncture with PA 443, and turn left. A parking
area is on the left.

Port Clinton/PA 61: From I-78, take Exit 29B to Pottsville. Follow PA 61 north
for 1.5 miles, and turn right onto Blue Mountain Road. Parking is available
along the road at the trail crossing. Heading south on PA 61, 17 miles
south of Pottsville and .4 mile south of Port Clinton, turn left onto Blue
Mountain Road.

PA 309: The trailhead along PA 309 is located at the crest of Blue Mountain,
accessed by a game commission road on the east side of PA 309. The trailhead is 11.4 miles south of Tamaqua and 3 miles south of the PA 895 juncture at Snyders with PA 309. From the north, pass Blue Mountain Summit
restaurant to the right, and make the next left, which is easy to miss, onto
a game commission road with a parking area for fifteen to twenty cars.
From the Allentown area, proceed north on PA 309 from the US 22 juncture for 20 miles before you reach Blue Mountain Summit restaurant, and
turn right onto the game commission road.

Lehigh Gap: To reach the gap, drive east on PA 248 from Palmerton for 2
miles, or west on PA 248 for 12.5 miles from the juncture with PA 512 at
Bath. Cross the PA 873 bridge across the Lehigh River. There is very limited
parking on the right at a trail sign. To reach a much larger parking area,
from the juncture of PA 873 and PA 248, follow PA 248 east through a light
and pass the juncture with PA 145. About .1 mile past the light is an incon-
spicuous dirt road on the left, which goes to a large parking area offering
a view of the gap.

Wind Gap: From the town of Wind Gap, at the juncture of SR 1007 and PA
512, proceed north on SR 1007, also known as Broadway, and ascend up
Blue Mountain for .8 mile. There is a small gravel parking area on the right,
across from a trailer park.

Delaware Water Gap: From I-80, take Exit 310 and continue straight. Turn left
onto PA 611 (Main Street). Continue for a few blocks and turn right onto
Mountain Road, where there is a sign for the trail. Turn left on the next
paved road, which leads to a trail sign and gravel parking area.

The Appalachian Trail (AT) is the most famous and popular trail in
the world; it is synonymous with backpacking. Not surprisingly, it
is the most heavily hiked trail in Pennsylvania.

Although the AT often represents the limit of many backpackers
experiences in Pennsylvania, it is not among the state's most scenic
trails. While it has plenty of rock outcrops, vistas, and tradition, the
trail offers little wilderness or isolation. Numerous roads and highways
bisect the trail; development, farms, and towns are often encountered
along the corridor. The AT passes through a few small towns, which
are often hiker-friendly and add to the trail's uniqueness. Everyone
should backpack the venerable AT, but realize that it does not represent
the apex of Pennsylvania's trails. Because the AT has been described in
depth by countless other guides, this description of the hike, heading
south to north, is abbreviated.

Section One: Pen Mar to Susquehanna River

For the first 40 miles, the AT traverses the rolling mountainous terrain
of South Mountain and Michaux State Forest. Many backpackers consider this section of Pennsylvania's AT to be the most scenic and enjoyable, and it is very popular. Here you'll find several streams, sufficient
water, scenic vistas, and terrain that is not overwhelmingly rocky.

After passing through Pen Mar Park and crossing the Maryland-
Pennsylvania border, the AT descends and crosses Falls Creek. A 500-

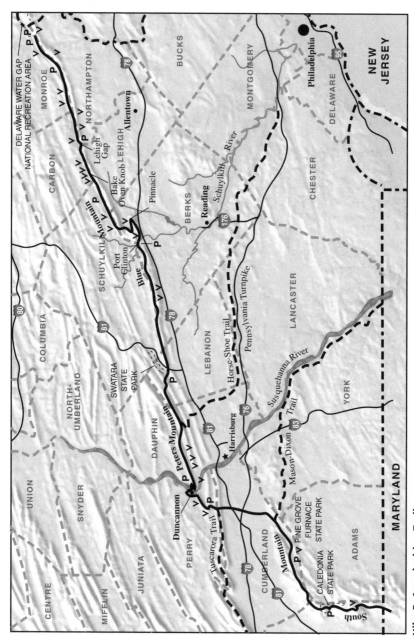

Hike 5: Appalachian Trail

foot ascent over .7 mile follows as the trail climbs Mount Dunlop, crossing Buena Vista Road and a spring along the way. Descend mildly to Old Route 16. Continue the descent into Michaux State Forest and cross PA 16. Begin a mild ascent along Mackey Run and cross Rattlesnake Run Road. Bailey Spring is .3 mile farther, and rolling terrain ensues for a mile, until the trail reaches Deerlick Run shelters and a spring. Begin a gradual 2-mile descent, which can be steep at times, and reach Antietam Shelter and Creek. Drinking from Antietam Creek is not advised. Cross Rattlesnake Run and Old Forge Roads; a small parking area is at the latter. Proceed upstream along scenic Tumbling Run, which features a spring, campsites, and Tumbling Run Shelter. Side trails lead to the run, spring, and the PATC-owned Hermitage Cabin; interesting cliffs and rock outcrops are in this vicinity. The AT begins a 500-foot climb over a mile to Buzzard Peak; a side trail leads to spectacular Chimney Rocks, offering an impressive vista to the east and Waynesboro Reservoir.

For the next 2 miles, the AT follows the crest of Snowy Mountain, before passing a side trail to Snowy Mountain Tower. At more than 2,000 feet in elevation, this is the highest point along the AT in Pennsylvania. Descend 300 feet over .5 mile to Snowy Mountain Road, and continue 1 mile to PA 233. Ascend the crest of Rocky Mountain; you reach Rocky Mountain Shelters about 2 miles from PA 233. Over the next 3 miles, the AT descends gradually to US 30 and Caledonia State Park. The park offers water, restrooms, parking, telephones, and camping and showers for a fee. From the state park, begin a steep 500-foot climb over .7 mile up Chinquapin Hill. The AT levels off, and the blue-blazed Locust Gap Trail joins from the left. Pass a spring and begin a 300-foot climb over .5 mile into a glen before reaching the Quarry Gap Shelters. Continue a 300-foot climb out of the glen, and follow the crest of the mountain to Sandy Sod. For the next 3.5 miles, the trail traverses the rolling summit of Big Piney Flat Ridge and crosses several dirt forest roads. Then it makes a 250-foot descent over .4 mile into a glen with a small stream and the Milesburn Cabin, owned by the Potomac Appalachian Trail Club. A side trail to the left proceeds downstream to a spring.

Climb out of the glen and reach the top of Big Flat Ridge; level hiking ensues for 2 miles before the trail drops into a shallow glen with a spring and the new Birch Run Shelter. The AT climbs gradually up the headwaters of the glen, then follows level and rolling terrain for 4 miles across the top of South Mountain and Big Flat, crossing dirt forest roads and passing near the Big Flat fire tower. Now you descend

600 feet over 2 miles and reach a juncture with the blue-blazed Sunset Rocks Trail and Tom's Run Shelters, with a spring. The trail resumes its rolling and level nature for 2 miles, crosses a stream with nice campsites, and reaches the juncture with the other end of Sunset Rocks Trail. This scenic, rugged side trail winds through impressive rock outcrops, boulders, and vistas along Sunset Rocks. The AT follows an old forest road for 1.7 miles to PA 233 and Pine Grove Furnace State Park. This scenic, historic park features the Ironmaster Mansion Hostel, a preserved iron furnace stack, water, restrooms, a seasonal concession stand, and campsites for a fee.

After passing through the park, begin your ascent up Piney Mountain, a 400-foot climb over a mile. Near the top, a side trail to the left leads to the impressive Pole Steeple, an imposing rock outcrop with views. Continue a moderate climb to the crest of Piney Mountain, followed by a 3.7-mile descent along the northwestern flank of the mountain, until you reach blue-blazed side trails to springs and Tagg Run Shelters. Over the next 3 miles, you descend and cross Hunters Run Road and PA 34, climb 600 feet over 1.2 miles, and descend more than 300 vertical feet to PA 94. Rolling and rocky terrain ensues for more than a mile, until the AT begins a 500-foot climb over .5 mile to the crest of Rocky Ridge. The climb becomes increasingly steeper, with switchbacks. At the top are a nice vista to the south and a maze of boulders and rock outcrops. Descend more gradually off the ridge to Whiskey Spring and the western terminus of the Mason-Dixon Trail to the right. Climb over another ridge, descend to a saddle, and surmount another hill. The following descent leads to Little Dogwood Run. Rolling and rocky terrain follows for the next mile, and the trail passes the White Rocks Trail to the right, which leads to outcrops of quartzite. Shortly thereafter is Center Point Knob, the traditional center point of the AT. Descend 800 feet over a mile to the Cumberland Valley, and proceed north to Boiling Springs, a quaint town with restaurants, hotels, amenities, the Appalachian Trail Conference Field Office, Children's Lake, and Yellow Breeches Creek, a famous limestone trout stream.

For about the next 13 miles, the trail crosses the Cumberland Valley before ascending Blue Mountain. This segment of trail is very flat and traverses farmlands with several road crossings and two interstate highways. The charming agricultural heritage of the valley and trail corridor is giving way to increased development. This part of the trail provides little shade and lots of sun exposure, so carry extra water and protect yourself from the sun.

After crossing large Conodoguinet Creek via a bridge, the trail passes through rolling and hilly terrain until it begins its ascent up Blue Mountain. Here the AT enters the ridge and valley geological province, which will define the remainder of the trail in Pennsylvania, as it crosses valleys and water gaps and follows ridgetops. The AT has a special relationship with Blue Mountain, returning to the crest of this mountain and following it for a substantial distance between Swatara and the Delaware Water Gap.

Begin the 800-foot climb over .7 mile to the crest of Blue Mountain. The climb becomes increasingly steeper, with switchbacks. At the top is an important four-way juncture with two other trails: the Tuscarora Trail to the left and the Darlington Trail to the right. The Tuscarora is a side trail to the AT and returns to it in Shenandoah National Park, Virginia. Just ahead, a side trail to the right leads to Darlington Shelter and a spring. Descend 600 feet over a mile into the wooded valley between Blue and Little Mountains. Climb around the flank of Little Mountain, and descend gradually to open fields and a parking area along PA 850. After crossing the road, the trail reenters the woods and follows old forest roads for the next mile before ascending Cove Mountain, a 600-foot climb over .6 mile. Cove Mountain offers the first ridgetop hiking of the AT in Pennsylvania and a taste of the state's famous rocks. Follow the ridgeline to a vista at a pipeline swath; continue to follow the ridge for 4 miles before reaching scenic Hawks Rock Vista overlooking farms, Shermans Creek, and the confluence of Juniata and Susquehanna Rivers. Begin an 800-foot descent over a mile to the Susquehanna River. This descent is initially steep, with switchbacks, but becomes more gradual as the trail drops along the side of Cove Mountain. You reach a road along the Susquehanna River, where there is a bar to the right. Follow the road to the left, cross a bridge over Shermans Creek, and enter Duncannon, where there are several businesses and amenities. Pass through the town, and cross over the Juniata River and the Susquehanna River via the Clarks Ferry Bridge along busy US 22/322. The Susquehanna is the largest river along the entire AT.

Section Two: Susquehanna River to Port Clinton

For its remainder in Pennsylvania, the AT is a ridgetop trail. Along the ridges, the terrain is rolling but very rocky in sections. Numerous vistas are a highlight of this section; however, water is scarce and you must carry extra containers. The greatest elevation changes are found where the trail drops off the ridge to cross a valley or water gap. How did these ridges become so rocky? You can blame the ice age; although glaciers never reached this far south, the constant freezing and thawing broke up the rocks that form the crests of these ridges. Pennsylvania's other ridgetop trails offer similar terrain, but the Link, Tuscarora, and Mid State Trails are even more rocky and rugged, with greater isolation and wilderness. Most of the vistas along this section are early in the hike from the top of Peters Mountain.

After crossing the river, the trail ascends and levels as it follows the side of Peters Mountain. The ascent becomes steeper and rockier as you climb the western edge of the mountain, within the gap carved by the river. Here you find numerous rock outcrops and several fine vistas. Several climbs are steep and rocky; at the crest of Peters Mountain, the trail follows the ridgetop. Pass blue-blazed side trails to a camping area, and a spring. To this point from the river, the AT climbed 900 feet over 3 miles. Follow the ridge for the next 4 miles across rocky terrain, with views and rock outcrops. The trail reaches PA 225, with a nearby parking area; cross over the highway via a new pedestrian bridge.

The next 3 miles to Peters Mountain Shelter features similar terrain, and Table Rock offers nice views to the south. A blue-blazed side trail leads to the shelter; a spring is farther down the mountain but is hard to reach. The AT follows the rocky, rolling ridge of Peters Mountain for 6 more miles, with occasional views. Along the way, you pass Shikellimy Rocks, which offer a nice view to the south. Now you begin a 700-foot descent over a mile to PA 325. During the descent, a blue-blazed trail to the right leads to a spring. Cross PA 325, with a large parking area. The trail crosses Clark Creek and begins a long climb of 1,100 feet over 3 miles up Stony Mountain. At the crest of the mountain, the Horse-Shoe Trail joins from the right and extends all the way to Valley Forge. The trail crosses small Rattling Run and follows the crest of Sharp Mountain across rolling terrain for more than 7 miles through St. Anthony's Wilderness, the second-longest roadless area in the state. This wilderness contains numerous side trails offering great dayhiking opportunities and the remnants of abandoned logging and mining towns, old grades, forest roads, and inclined planes. The AT descends gradually into Rausch Gap, and a blue-blazed side trail to the right leads to Rausch Gap Shelter and a spring. Continue your descent to a road and cross Rausch Run. The AT crosses another small stream and begins a gradual ascent through a gap in Second Mountain, descending 500 feet over a mile off Second Mountain, and then following roads to PA 443. Level hiking follows as the trail enters Swatara State Park and crosses Swatara Creek over the historic Waterville Bridge, which once spanned famous Pine Creek in north-central Pennsylvania. Traffic from I-81 can be heard and seen above; pass under the interstate's bridges.

Now begin a climb back up to the ridgetop of Blue Mountain, a 500-foot climb over a mile. Upon reaching the ridgetop, the AT continues a gradual ascent for a mile. Hike over rolling, rocky terrain, following the ridge for almost 6 more miles, until you reach blue-blazed trails. The one to the left leads to a spring, the one to the right the William Penn Shelter. Two more miles of similar terrain follow, until the trail crosses PA 645. Continue along the ridge of Blue Mountain for an additional 2 miles before reaching Kimmel Lookout, which offers a great view to the south over farmlands and small towns. Shortly thereafter, you come to PA 501, with a parking area. Cross the highway, and a side trail leads to an enclosed shelter; .4 mile farther, another side trail leads to Pilger Run Spring, a historic water source. The AT gradually ascends through rocky terrain before reaching Round Head and a vista. A side trail to the right leads to Shower Steps, rock-hewn steps that descend to PA 501 and a spring. Follow the edge and side of the mountain to a glen with camping and a spring. Climb gradually out of the glen to the crest of Blue Mountain, and in about 3 miles the trail crosses PA 183, with parking.

Rolling hiking ensues, and in 1.3 miles a side trail to the right leads to Black Swatara Spring. Similar terrain follows for 4 miles, when the AT reaches the Sand Spring Trail to the right; a spring can be found a short distance down this trail. The Sand Spring Trail is about 2 miles long and descends to Northkill Creek and a parking area. In another mile, the AT passes a side trail to the left leading to Eagles Nest Shelter and a nearby spring. Over the next 6 miles, the terrain continues to be rolling and rocky in sections. The trail passes through woodlands, near open meadows, and along a few forest roads. As always, the AT continues to follow the ridgetop of Blue Mountain. Auburn Lookout offers a nice view to the south; soon thereafter, you begin a descent to Port Clinton, into a water gap carved by the Schuylkill River. This is a 900-foot descent over 1.3 miles, which steepens near the bottom.

Cross over the Schuylkill River and enter Port Clinton, a hiker-friendly town with water, the Port Clinton Hotel, Appalachian Outfitters, and other services.

Section Three: Port Clinton to Delaware Water Gap

This section is even more rocky and rugged than the previous, which sometimes had monotonous woodland hiking. You'll also find a much greater selection of impressive vistas from the numerous rock outcrops and talus slopes, including the famous Pinnacle. The trail continues to follow the ridge of Blue Mountain. Water is particularly scarce along this section, but the combination of rugged terrain and sweeping vistas makes this section of the AT both challenging and enjoyable.

From Port Clinton, proceed downstream along the Schuylkill River and cross beneath PA 61. Begin a steep climb via numerous switchbacks to the ridgetop of Blue Mountain. The initial ascent is 600 feet over .7 mile to the crest of the ridge; there are some nice views and a precipitous drop to the Schuylkill River. Continue a gradual 300-foot climb over a mile to the crest of Blue Mountain. The trail drops to the side of the mountain and passes a side trail to the right leading to Pocahontas Spring. Descend along the flank of Blue Mountain into the Hamburg Borough Watershed lands. You reach Furnace Creek, where a road to the right leads to a parking area.

The next segment of trail to the Pinnacle is very popular with dayhikers. Cross the creek and pass a side trail to Windsor Furnace Shelter and a spring. Begin a gradual 600-foot climb over 2 miles to Pulpit Rock, offering an excellent view from a rock outcrop. An astronomical park is nearby. The trail follows rolling, rocky terrain for the next 2 miles before reaching the spectacular Pinnacle, a massive outcrop offering the finest vista between Virginia and Massachusetts along the AT. An excellent panorama reveals farmlands, towns, Hawk Mountain, and the long ridge of Blue Mountain. A small cave system can be explored beneath the outcrop.

Return to the AT, and in another 2 miles you pass a short side trail to the left leading to Gold Spring. Rolling hiking follows for a mile before the AT begins its descent from Blue Mountain to the valley below. This is a long, gradual descent of 800 feet over 3 miles to SR 2018. A side trail to the right leads to Eckville Shelter. Cross the road and then a small stream and wet areas. Follow old logging roads as the trail climbs back up Blue Mountain; this is an 800-foot ascent over about a mile. The climb steepens near the top, where a side trail to the left leads to the world-famous Hawk Mountain Sanctuary, known for its views and raptor migrations. The AT bears rights and follows the crest of Blue Mountain. Pass Dan's Pulpit, a rock outcrop offering a narrow view to the south. Over the next 3 miles, the trail navigates rolling, rocky terrain and passes a few vistas before reaching Tri-County Corner, where Berks, Lehigh, and Schuylkill Counties meet, with another fine vista. In another 1.3 miles, you reach a side trail to the right leading to Allentown Shelter, from which another trail descends farther to a spring. Continue to follow the rocky ridgetop for about 4 miles, until you reach PA 309, with a restaurant and parking area.

The segment between PA 309 and the Lehigh Gap is rocky and rugged, with rock outcrops and several fine vistas. The trail bears right along PA 309, crosses it, and continues along the ridgetop of Blue Mountain. After almost 2 miles, you pass a powerline swath with views; a side trail to the left leads to the New Tripoli Campsite and spring. A mile farther, the trail crosses the Knife Edge (not to be confused with the more famous Knife Edge along the AT on Mount Katahdin, Maine), a series of cliffs and outcrops with views. Rough, rugged terrain persists for another mile, then the trail passes near Bear Rocks, an impressive rock outcrop with expansive views from the top. Proceed along old forest roads, then cross a game commission road and large parking area. The AT begins a very rocky ascent to Bake Oven Knob, a popular raptor flyover. The knob is ringed with talus slopes and offers a nice vista to the north and an exceptional vista to the south from a cliff. Descend from the vista across extremely rocky terrain. Bake Oven Knob Shelter and a seasonal spring are .5 mile farther, accessed by a side trail to the right. In typical fashion, the trail follows the ridgetop for about 7 miles, passing more vistas, talus slopes, rock outcrops, and the Pennsylvania Turnpike tunnel. Begin a 1,000-foot descent over 2 miles into Lehigh Gap, passing the Outerbridge Shelter, with a spring. A side trail leads to Devil's Pulpit, a rock outcrop offering a great view within the Lehigh Gap. Here the north face of Blue Mountain is denuded of all vegetation due to decades of zinc smelting.

Bear left onto SR 4024 and cross over the Lehigh River. Nearby is Palmerton, a trail town famous for its hospitality; through-hikers are allowed to stay at the borough hall. Cross PA 248 before beginning a

1.5-mile-long, 900-foot ascent back to the ridgetop of Blue Mountain. The ascent is steep and rocky in places, with more vistas. Springs along this section are spaced far apart and tend to be seasonal; it is imperative to carry sufficient water and containers. For the next 3 miles, follow the rolling terrain of the ridge, passing several vistas, before making a mild descent into Little Gap. Cross SR 4001, ascend the ridge, and pass a view to the north. Approximately 4.5 miles farther is Delps Trail, descending to the right for .3 mile to a spring. Rolling and level hiking continues for 6 miles, until the trail reaches blue-blazed Katellen Trail to the right, a side trail leading to a shelter and springs. Hahn's Lookout is 3.5 miles farther and offers a nice vista to the south. Shortly thereafter is another nice vista looking to the north. The AT begins its 400-foot descent via switchbacks over .7 mile into Wind Gap. Pass under PA 33 and cross a road with parking.

In typical fashion, the trail climbs out of Wind Gap to the crest of Blue Mountain; this 400-foot ascent over .6 mile has steep sections. Follow the wide ridgetop of Blue Mountain across rolling and level terrain for about 4 miles. The trail then inconspicuously leaves Blue Mountain and follows Kittatinny Mountain, which the trail follows for its remainder in Pennsylvania. Two miles farther, pass a series of rugged rock outcrops known as Wolf Rocks, with nice views. Descend gradually and cross PA 191, with parking. Ascend gradually, and in .7 mile you reach a side trail to popular Kirkridge Shelter, where a side trail leads to the Kirkridge Retreat, with a tap for water. This shelter is popular because it is close to PA 191; the remainder of the trail to the Delaware Water Gap is popular with both dayhikers and weekend backpackers. The AT passes vistas looking to the south and the terrain is rolling and rocky as the trail traverses the ridgetop. After 3 miles, you reach Mount Minsi and begin the long descent into the famous Delaware Water Gap, an impressive geologic feature. The descent is rocky and rugged as it passes near cliffs, ledges, and excellent vistas. The AT drops 1,000 feet over 2 miles, and several sections are steep. Along the way, you pass small streams, small Lake Lenape, and a parking area. Enter the town of Delaware Water Gap, cross PA 611, and reach the I-80 bridge, which the trail crosses over the Delaware River into New Jersey.

6. Horse-Shoe Trail

Length: 140-mile linear trail.

Duration: 9 to 14 days.

Difficulty: Easy to moderate.

Terrain: Rolling, pastoral countryside with rolling terrain. A few short, steep ascents and descents. The most difficult part of the trail is at its western juncture, with rocky terrain and ascents and descents ranging from 200 to 1,000 feet.

Trail conditions: Trail is established and generally blazed well, but some sections may be brushy. Trail often rerouted. Extensive road walking, sometimes through small towns and villages.

Blazes: Yellow.

Water: Generally plentiful; trail crosses several streams. Many of these streams may be polluted, however, from development and agricultural runoff. Because there is so much road walking through developed and agricultural areas, expect a lot of sun exposure; carry extra water and containers.

Vegetation: Extensive farmlands and pastoral countryside; hardwoods predominate along trail; trail corridor mostly developed.

Highlights: Valley Forge National Historical Park, Great Valley Nature Center, Brandywine Trail, Welkinweir Nature Preserve, Warwick County Park, Falls of French Creek, Hopewell Furnace National Historic Site, French Creek State Park, Middle Creek Wildlife Management Area, Conestoga Trail, Hershey, Swatara Creek, Stony Creek, Appalachian Trail, Amish culture, covered bridges, iron furnaces, historic features, and pastoral views.

Maintained by: Horse-Shoe Trail Club, volunteers.

Contact info:

Horse-Shoe Trail Club, P.O. Box 182, Birchrunville, PA 19421-0182; websites: www.n99.com/hst/, www.kta-hike.org.

French Creek State Park, 843 Park Rd., Elverson, PA 19520-9523; phone: 610-582-9680; e-mail: frenchcreeksp@state.pa.us; website: www.dcnr.state.pa.us/stateparks/parks/frenchcreek.asp.

Valley Forge National Historical Park, P.O. Box 953, Valley Forge, PA 19482-0953; phone: 610-783-1077; e-mail: VAFO_Superintendent@nps.gov; website: www.nps.gov/vafo.

Warwick County Park, 382 County Park Rd., Pottstown, PA 19465; phone: 610-469-1916; website: www.chesco.org/ccparks/index.html.

Hopewell Furnace National Historic Site, 2 Marle Blvd. Lane, Elverson, PA 19520; phone: 610-582-8773; e-mail: HOFU_Superintendent@nps.gov; website: www.nps.gov/hofu.

Middle Creek Wildlife Management Area, P.O. Box 110, Kleinfeltersville, PA 17039; phone: 717-733-1512.

Maps and guides: Both available for sale from Horse-Shoe Trail Club.

Trailhead directions:

Valley Forge National Historical Park: From Philadelphia, proceed on I-76 west and take Exit 327, the last one before the tollbooth. Make a right at first light; at the next light, make another right onto N. Gulph Road. Follow for about 1.5 miles, until the road becomes two-lane; turn left at light into the park. From Reading, proceed on US 422 east. Take the Valley Forge exit. Turn right off the exit ramp and merge into the center lane. The park entrance is straight ahead. The trailhead is located on the western side of the park. From the Welcome Center, follow PA 23 west for 2.5 miles; pass the juncture with PA 252 and cross Valley Creek. The trail begins along a gravel road to the left. The closest parking is at Washington's Headquarters.

Warwick County Park: From Pottstown, take PA 100 south to PA 23 west. Follow PA 23 west for 4 miles to Knauertown. Turn left onto County Park Road, before Village Market; the park entrance is on the left. From the Downington exit of the PA Turnpike, take PA 100 north to PA 23 west. Follow PA 23 west for 4 miles to Knauertown. Turn left onto County Park Road, before Village Market; the park entrance is on the left.

French Creek State Park: The trail crosses many roads through the park. From Birdsboro, take PA 345 south for 4.4 miles into the park. Turn right into the East Entrance, and follow Park Road for 1.8 miles to the park office. From Warwick and PA 23, follow PA 345 north for 2.5 miles, and turn left at the South Entrance. Follow the road to Park Road, and turn right; the park office will be on the right. The trail crosses Park Road in between the park office and Scotts Run Road.

Middle Creek Wildlife Management Area: From PA 897 at Kleinfeltersville, follow Hopeland Road south for 3 miles to where the trail crosses below the dam. Parking is available .3 mile farther down the road, where you can follow Middle Creek Trail to the right to the Horse-Shoe Trail. The trail is located about 2.7 miles north of Hopeland, along Kleinfeltersville Road.

US 322: From the juncture with PA 501 at Brickerville, follow US 322 west for 2.1 miles. A parking area and trail sign will be on the right.

The Horse-Shoe Trail (HST) is one of Pennsylvania's most historic, and unfortunately, threatened trails. As the name implies, the trail is intended not only for hikers and backpackers, but also horseback riders. The Horse-Shoe Trail Club was formed in 1935 with the hope of creating a trail connecting Philadelphia to the Appalachian Trail, a truly ambitious endeavor. The HST was first established in 1947, traversing the extensive farmlands that existed at the time in southeastern Pennsylvania.

Not surprisingly, as urban sprawl and housing developments began to overtake farmlands, the HST has been increasingly forced onto roads. Because the HST is under constant threat of having its route severed by a private property owner, it is designated as an Endangered Hiking Trail. The simple fact that a trail of this length and scenic value is able to exist in the most developed area of Pennsylvania is astounding and a tribute to the countless volunteers who have worked to make the HST a continuing reality. The trail explores some of the most scenic regions in this part of the state and provides excellent outdoor recreational opportunities. It is a great asset to this region and must be preserved.

The HST is a very historic trail, passings near many forges, mills, homes, furnaces, monuments, and even a ditch dug by Hessian prisoners of war during the Revolution. This trail offers a walking history tour of one of the most historic regions in the United States.

The HST forms the backbone of a surprising web of trails in southeastern Pennsylvania. The Brandywine Trail joins the HST near Welkinweir, proceeding 27 miles south and joining with the Mason-Dixon Trail. The Conestoga Trail meets the HST near Brickerville, heading 60 miles south to meet the Mason-Dixon Trail. The HST ends at its juncture with the Appalachian Trail.

Primitive backcountry camping along the HST is virtually nonexistent. Extensive stretches over road, private property, state game lands, and state and county parks offer no primitive camping. The only options are to camp at state parks or private campgrounds for a fee, or to stay at hostels. Refer to the HST club's trail guide for potential places to camp. Because of the lack of backcountry campsites and the extensive road walking through developed areas, towns, and farmlands, the HST is typically dayhiked, and therefore the description that follows is abbreviated.

To hike the trail from east to west, from Valley Forge National Historical Park, begin a 400-foot ascent over .7 mile to the top of the ridge. This ascent is steep in parts. For the next 2 miles, follow this ridge over Mount Misery, Mount Joy, and Diamond Rock Hill. The HST now follows roads for more than 2 miles to PA 29, then traverses rolling countryside for more than 3 miles before following roads another 9 miles or so. Road walking ends as the trail traverses hilly, wooded terrain for 2 miles and reaches the Welkinweir Preserve. Rolling, bucolic terrain continues for 2.5 miles as the HST reaches sce-

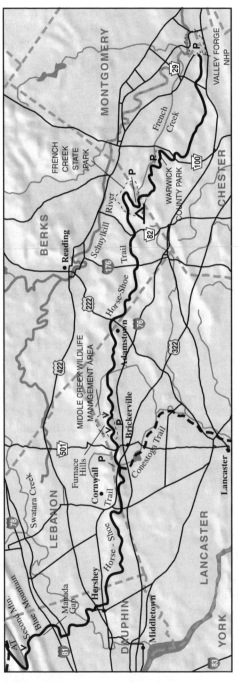

Hike 6: Horse-Shoe Trail

nic French Creek and Warwick County Park. Here you pass the Falls of French Creek, where the creek cascades over and around diabase boulders. Leaving the park, the trail follows a road to Knauertown, then begins a mile-long gradual ascent. Gradually descending from the hill, the HST turns left onto a railroad grade. After 1.5 miles, you leave the grade and hike through rolling countryside to Hopewell Village National Historic Site and French Creek State Park.

Follow the trail around Hopewell Lake and pass near the campground in French Creek State Park. Begin a 3.5-mile partial loop around a hill, and reach Scotts Run Lake. Continue to hike through hilly countryside for more than 8 miles, until you reach Buck Hollow Road. Turn left on the road, and follow it for 2.5 miles to Plowville. Cross over I-176 along a road, and continue to follow the trail. For the next 12 miles, the HST continues to explore the scenic, hilly countryside of southwestern Berks County. This is an enjoyable section of trail with relatively little road walking. After entering Lancaster County along the crest of Adamstown Ridge, you descend gradually and cross PA 897. Gradually climb another ridge and descend again before following roads to the north of Denver, where you climb yet another ridge and descend to a valley. For the next 4 miles, the trail follows this low ridgeline, with increasing altitude and through somewhat isolated surroundings.

The next 12 miles of the HST are among the most scenic along the entire trail. The trail explores the Furnace Hills and Black Oak Ridge, with fine views, relative isolation, woodland scenery, and scenic streams. Fortunately, much of this area is protected as state game lands. Descend to Girl Scout Road, and then gradually climb along Furnace Hill Road. Pass a vista and Millstone Road, then descend to Hopeland Road and the outlet for Middle Creek Lake. Climb more steeply, 400 feet over a mile, to the rolling crest of Black Oak Ridge, with nice vistas. Descend to Segloch Run and Road. Climb over Cannon Hill and descend steeply to Furnace Run and PA 501. Once again, climb up the ridge, and then descend to US 322 and Pumping Station Road. The trail crosses scenic Hammer Creek; nearby is the Upper Hopewell Forge Monument, which is also the northern terminus of the Conestoga Trail.

Climb the ridge once again. Reach the site of the Cornwall Fire Tower, the highest point of the trail thus far, and descend steeply to Penryn Park. Follow a powerline swath and descend to a creek. Proceed north for 2 miles along roads, then begin a 300-foot climb over a mile up Governor Dick Hill, with a view. To the west is Mount Gretna Heights. Descend to Pinch Road and enter State Game Lands 145 via old roads and grades across easy terrain. After 3 miles, cross a road south of Colebrook and continue along an easy, old road. Cross Conewago Creek over a bridge and cross PA 241. For the next 4 miles, the trail navigates rolling countryside and woodlands, with little road walking. After you pass Mountain View Height, you hike along roads for more than 3 miles to the Dauphin County line.

For the next 9 miles to Swatara Creek, the trail follows several roads and cuts across farmlands south of Hershey. Pass through the heavily developed area around Hershey, and continue to primarily follow roads before crossing Swatara Creek. For the subsequent 11 miles, the trail follows roads past houses and farms and across rolling terrain to Manada Gap and PA 443. Follow PA 443 for .5 mile, and turn right onto Dunlop Road. Leave the road to the left and enter the Fort Indiantown Gap Military Reservation.

The final 16 miles of the HST begins to resemble a typical backpacking trail, with far more rugged terrain and plenty of isolation. For 4 miles, the trail gradually climbs to the southern flank of Second Mountain, follows the flank across level terrain, and drops slightly to a pipeline swath. Bear right and follow the swath to the crest of Second Mountain, with an excellent view. This is a 600-foot climb over a mile that becomes increasingly steep and rocky at the top. The HST descends from the ridge along the swath; the descent is initially steep and rocky but becomes more moderate. This is a 900-foot descent over 1.7 miles. Cross beautiful Stony Creek and a railroad grade. Follow a game commission road to the top of Sharp Mountain, climbing 1,100 feet over 3 miles. Hike across the flat, level crest of Sharp Mountain for 3 miles, and then descend gradually along scenic Devils Race Course, with cascades. Cross the stream and climb 600 feet over 1.2 miles to the juncture with the Appalachian Trail, where the HST ends.

7. Conestoga Trail

Length: 63-mile linear trail.

Duration: 4 to 6 days.

Difficulty: Easy to moderate.

Terrain: Trail often follows roads through farmlands, villages, small towns, and developed areas. The northern half of the trail traverses rolling farmlands; the southern half is more difficult, traversing the Susquehanna River Gorge and its side glens, with some ascents being steep and rocky and ranging from 100 to 300 vertical feet.

Trail conditions: Trail often follows roads and traverses developed areas along side roads, but tends to be well blazed. Use caution along roadways—some are busy and can be difficult to cross. Trail often rerouted.

Blazes: Orange, but many have faded to a salmon pink color.

Water: Generally plentiful, but expect a lot of exposure to the sun; carry extra containers.

Vegetation: Farmlands and hardwoods; rhododendron prevalent along some streams.

Highlights: Amish heritage, Hammer Creek, covered bridges, Speedwell Forge Lake, old mills, historic houses, Pequea Creek, Susquehanna River Gorge, Tucquan Creek, Wind Cave, House Rock, Holtwood Preserve, Kelly's Run, nice vistas, farmlands, Lock 12 Historic Area.

Maintained by: Lancaster Hiking Club, volunteers.

Contact info:
Lancaster Hiking Club, P.O. Box 7922, Lancaster, PA 17604-7922; website: www.conestogatrail.org.
Lancaster Department of Parks and Recreation (Lancaster County Central Park), 1050 Rockford Rd., Lancaster, PA 17602; phone: 717-299-8215; website: www.co.lancaster.pa.us/parks/site/default.asp.
Holtwood Preserve (Pennsylvania Power and Light), 9 New Village Rd., Holt-wood, PA 17532; phone: 800-354-838; e-mail: pplpreserves@pplweb.com; website: www.pplweb.com/community/enviro_preserves/holtwood.index.htm.
Pequea Creek Family Campground, 86 Fox Hollow Rd., Pequea, PA 17565; phone: 717-285-4587; e-mail: pequeacamp@aol.com.

Maps and guides: Both available for sale, or for free at www.conestoga trail.org.

Trailhead directions:
Northern trailhead: The best parking is for the Horse-Shoe Trail, along PA 501. From the juncture with US 322 at Brickerville, follow US 322 west for 2.1 miles. A parking area and trail sign for the Horse-Shoe Trail will be on the right. Follow this trail west along Pumping Station Road a few hundred yards to the beginning of the Conestoga Trail. Alternatively, follow the same directions along US 322 as above, but travel less than 2 miles west from Brickerville; turn left onto Speedwell Forge Road, and make a quick right onto Pumping Station Road. The trail begins at the Hopewell Iron Forge Monument, with limited parking, on the right.
Southern trailhead (Lock 12 Historic Area): The historic area is located along PA 372, on the west side of the Susquehanna River, about 2 miles east of PA 74 and 7.2 miles west of PA 272 and Buck. Turn onto River Road; a trail parking area is .2 mile farther, on the right. To avoid hiking across the Nor-man Wood Bridge over the Susquehanna River, there is a pull-off area suffi-cient for parking on the south side of PA 372, on the east side of the river, just before or after the bridge.

The Conestoga Trail (CT) connects the Horse-Shoe Trail in the north to the Mason-Dixon Trail to the south, almost traversing the length of Lancaster County. Like the trails it connects, the CT often follows roads and traverses farmlands. The trail passes through several towns and villages; development is common along the trail. Not surprisingly, backcountry camping is limited, as the trail often crosses private property. The southern half of the trail offers the most isolated areas, difficult hiking, and finest scenery. This trail contains many hidden gems that are unexpected in this part of the state. The following description, hiking north to south, is abbreviated.

From the Horse-Shoe Trail, follow roads south and hike underneath the PA Turnpike. For the next 3 miles, the trail passes through scenic woodlands, meadows, and fields. Reach Speedwell Forge Lake and cross the lake over a bridge. Turn left off the road, pass a parking area, and follow the trail along the shore. Pass a parking area and dam, and proceed downstream along scenic Hammer Creek. For the next 6.5 miles, the CT stays in close proximity to this creek, with relatively little road walking. The trail passes through meadows and farmlands; it also intersects roads at various points and crosses the creek via bridges. This is a pleasant section of trail, with Snavely's Mill, about a mile south of Speedwell Lake, and Erb's Covered Bridge, near the southern end of this section.

Cross Cocalico Creek and follow roads to busy PA 772; cross carefully. Follow roads to Cocalico Creek, which you cross again over a scenic covered bridge, built in 1849. Follow roads and cross PA 272. For the next 5 miles, the trail follows roads to PA 23, crossing two more covered bridges. Follow roads for 4 more miles and cross PA 462. Follow roads and streets in Lancaster, cross the Conestoga River, and enter Lancaster County Central Park. This park offers camping, but a reservation and a fee are required. Hike along the creek and pass an outcrop of limestone known as Indian Maiden View, or Indian Rock. Continue to explore this scenic park, passing a side trail to Rock Ford Historic Site and crossing a covered bridge over Mill Creek. Cross back over Mill Creek via a cable bridge and reach busy PA 222; cross carefully.

Enter Buchmiller Park and turn left onto an old railroad grade along Conestoga River. Cross Mill Creek over a railroad bridge. The trail leaves the grade to the left and follow roads, but then it returns to the grade, which it follows for .5 mile before leaving the grade again and following roads to busy PA 324 and New Danville Pike; cross carefully. Turn left on New Danville Pike and follow this road for .3 mile before

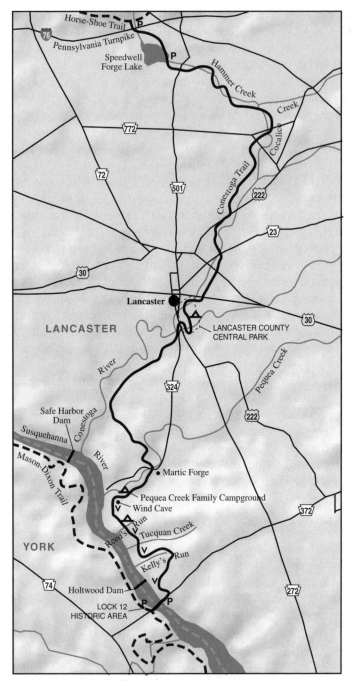

Hike 7: Conestoga Trail

turning left onto Long Lane, which the trail follows for about 4 miles until it reunites with the Conestoga River.

You now begin to hike the southern portion of the CT, regarded as the most beautiful section of the trail. In fact, this section offers some of the most surprising scenery in the entire state, with sweeping views, cascades, a cave, and beautiful glens with streams, boulders, and rhododendron. This portion of the CT is definitely worth backpacking.

Turn left off the road and enter the woods along a small, cascading stream. Climb out of the glen and pass behind a cemetery at the top. Turn left onto Main Street, and continue to follow roads down to scenic Pequea Creek and historic Martic Forge. Cross PA 324 and pass a covered bridge and Pequea Creek Family Campground, offering seasonal campsites for a fee. Continue to hike along the creek downstream. Past the Pequea Boat Club, the trail begins to climb, crossing a road and a small stream. The CT then passes the entrance to Wind Cave, one of the largest tectonic caves in the eastern United States. Tectonic caves are formed by the faulting, separating, and moving of rock layers. Cross small House Rock Run, squeeze through rock outcrops, and climb to House Rock Vista. The trail winds through the glens of Brubaker and Reed's Run, the latter offering a camping area and a blue-blazed trail to the left leading to a spring. Climb from Reed's Run, passing excellent views, and then descend to scenic Tucquan Creek. As you climb away from the creek, you pass more outcrops and reach more vistas, including Pinnacle Vista, where you find parking, seasonal restrooms, and water.

Descend to incredible Kelly's Run, one of the CT's highlights. This stream and its gorge are renowned for their beauty, with boulders and massive rock outcrops, small waterfalls and cascades, and thick rhododendron and hemlocks. Climb out of Kelly's Run Gorge and descend toward the Susquehanna River, with views of Holtwood Dam. Descend to a small stream before climbing steeply to PA 372. Turn right and cross the Norman Wood Bridge over the river. The bridge is nearly a mile long and offers space to walk, but not much. The river features many rock outcrops, ledges, and islands with spires of rocks and cliffs. After crossing the bridge, turn right and enter Lock 12 Historic Area. Here you will find the lock as well as a restored limekiln, remains of a sawmill, race, and dam, and scenic Anderson Run. The CT joins with the Mason-Dixon Trail and ends at River Road.

8. Mason-Dixon Trail

Length: 190-mile linear trail (Pennsylvania segment is about 115 miles long, of which 105 miles are described).

Duration: 14 to 24 days (entire trail).

Difficulty: Easy to moderate.

Terrain: Trail often follows roads through pastoral countryside, small towns, and developed areas. Ascents and descents range from 100 to 400 feet and tend to be gradual, across hilly, rolling terrain, but steep, rocky climbs regularly occur near the Susquehanna River as the trail climbs in and out of several side gorges and glens, and along the river's gorge.

Trail conditions: Trail often follows roads and is generally well blazed, though some blazes may be inconsistent. Because of private landowners, the trail is often rerouted and at times severed. The sections of trail that do not follow roads are generally well maintained. Towns, homes, villages, and other development are a constant experience along the trail.

Blazes: Blue.

Water: Generally plentiful, but expect a lot of sun exposure because of the road walking; carry extra containers.

Vegetation: Farmlands and hardwood forests; rhododendron and hemlocks often found along streams near the Susquehanna River.

Highlights: Appalachian Trail, Gifford Pinchot State Park, Codorus Creek, Codorus Furnace, Susquehanna River Gorge, Otter Creek, Muddy Creek, Oakland Run, fine vistas, scenic countryside, Holtwood Preserve, historic buildings and towns, Lock 12 Historic Area, Conestoga Trail, Peavine Island.

Maintained by: Mason-Dixon Trail System, Inc., volunteers.

Contact info:

Mason-Dixon Trail System, Inc., 719 Oakbourne Rd., West Chester, PA 19382; website: www.angelfire.com/pa2/yorkhikingclub/mdts.html, www.kta-hike.org.

Gifford Pinchot State Park, 2280 Rosstown Rd., Lewisberry, PA 17339-9787; phone: 717-432-5011; e-mail: giffordpinchotsp@state.pa.us; website: www.dcnr.state.pa.us/stateparks/parks/giffordpinchot.asp.

Apollo County Park, Administrative Headquarters, 400 Mundis Race Rd., York, PA 17402-9721; phone: 717-840-7440; website: www.york-county.org/gov/Parks/Apollo.htm.

Otter Creek Campground, 1101 Furnace Rd., Airville, PA 17302; phone: 717-862-3628, 877-33-OTTER; e-mail: ottercreek@ottercreekcamp.com; website: www.ottercreekcamp.com.

Holtwood Preserve (Pennsylvania Power and Light), 9 New Village Rd., Holtwood, PA 17532; phone: 1-800-354-838; e-mail: pplpreserves@pplweb.com;
website: www.pplweb.com/community/enviro_preserves/holtwood.index.htm.
Peach Bottom Nuclear Power Plant, 717-456-4759.

Maps and guides: Both available for sale from Mason-Dixon Trail System, Inc.

Trailhead directions:

Gifford Pinchot State Park: The trail crosses many roads and small parking
areas throughout the park. From Harrisburg, follow I-83 south to Exit 35.
Follow PA 177 south for 6.8 miles to the park office, on the left. The trail
crosses PA 177 at Boat Mooring Area #1, with parking about 1.8 miles
beyond the park office. For other parking areas, consult the park map.
From York, follow PA 74 north for 13 miles to Rossville, and turn right
onto PA 177. Boat Mooring Area #1 is .5 mile farther.

Apollo County Park: From Red Lion, follow Burkholder Road east to New
Bridgeville. Take PA 425 east for 3.5 miles and turn left onto Boyd Road,
following this road for .8 mile. There is a parking lot at the end of the
dirt road.

Otter Creek Campground: From York, follow PA 74 south through Red Lion
and on to Airville. Turn left onto PA 425 north and proceed for 5 miles to
the campground.

Lock 12 Historic Area: The historic area is located along PA 372, on the west
side of the Susquehanna River, about 2 miles east of PA 74 and 7.2 miles
west of PA 272 and Buck. Turn onto River Road; a trail parking area is .2
mile farther on the right.

The Mason-Dixon Trail (MDT) is 190 miles long, of which about 115
miles are in Pennsylvania. It begins at the Appalachian Trail, heads
east through Gifford Pinchot State Park, and then proceeds southeast
along the western shore of the Susquehanna River. The MDT proceeds
through Maryland and Delaware, and then winds back and forth along
the Delaware and Pennsylvania border before ending at the Brandwine
Trail near Chadds Ford. This description covers the western section
between the Appalachian Trail and Maryland border.

Like the nearby Conestoga and Horse-Shoe Trails, the MDT often follows roads through countryside, towns, and developed areas. The trail
has been increasingly forced onto roads and always has to contend
with private property owners. As a result, this trail is often rerouted.
The dedication of the volunteers who keep this scenic trail alive is
impressive. If you live in this section of the state, consider helping out.

The most scenic section is along the Susquehanna River Gorge, where you'll find vistas, the most isolated areas and rugged terrain, beautiful side gorges carved by streams, Codorus Creek, exceptionally beautiful Muddy Creek, and Otter Creek. Backcountry camping along the trail is extremely limited. The description that follows is abbreviated.

To hike the MDT west to east, begin at the Appalachian Trail, near Whisky Springs and Rocky Ridge. Follow roads eastward for almost 7 miles across farmlands and through pastoral scenery, until the trail passes through the small town of Franklintown. Continue eastward, primarily on roads, through woodlands and state game lands for an additional 9 miles to Gifford Pinchot State Park. The trail explores the western and southern portions of the park, then crosses a park road to the campground area, where a reservation and a fee are required if you want to camp. In the park, the MDT follows the Beaver Creek, Lakeside, Ridge, Alpine, and Midland Trails across rolling terrain, with many views of Pinchot Lake. The park provides typical amenities, including parking, picnic facilities, restrooms, and water. Pass the dam that creates Pinchot Lake and follow a road along scenic Beaver Creek. Descend to and cross large Conewago Creek over a bridge. Continue along roads eastward for 7 miles, until the trail crosses over I-83 and enters Strinestown. The trail continues to follow roads across Little Conewago Creek, along Conewago Creek, and toward the Susquehanna River.

Continue to follow roads along the river and a railroad. Cross scenic Codorus Creek, known for its beautiful gorge and whitewater upstream. The road to the right leads to the historic Codorus Furnace. Follow a road and climb away from Codorus Creek. Descend back to the river along North River Drive; pass Wildcat Run, with cascades; and continue along the river to Accomac. Continue along roads for 4 miles to Wrightsville. Follow PA 624 out of Wrightsville and away from the river. The MDT leaves PA 624 along side roads but rejoins with PA 624 near the river. Follow roads along the river for 3 miles to Fishing Creek and its narrow gorge.

The trail now begins to explore the Susquehanna River Gorge. From here to the Maryland border, the MDT offers excellent scenery, with views and beautiful streams with boulders, cascades, and rhododendron. The trail also passes old canal locks, Lock 12 Historic Area, Wallace Run, Mill Creek, Peavine Island, and Muddy Creek. You'll still encounter a lot of road walking and limited camping, but these scenic places should not be missed.

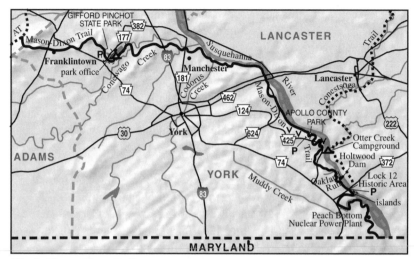

Hike 8: Mason-Dixon Trail

Cross the bridge, leave the road, and climb steeply along the ridge above the river. This is a 300-foot climb over .4 mile. Descend gradually to Green Branch along the river. For the subsequent mile to Cuff's Run, the trail traverses very rocky terrain along the river without the aid of a road. Cross scenic Cuff's Run and make a steep, rocky climb to a rock promontory with excellent views. In this area, the trail had to be rerouted because of landowner problems. The MDT follows a new trail as it descends along rocky terrain on the side of the gorge. Reach Apollo County Park, featuring backcountry camping. Hike along scenic Wilson Run and climb out of the gorge. Traverse the crest of the Susquehanna River Gorge above Safe Harbor Dam. Cross a powerline swath with views, and descend into the glen carved by Boyd's Run. Climb out of the glen to Shenks Ferry Road; cross PA 425 and descend to beautiful Otter Creek, with its scenic gorge. Climb out of the gorge, cross PA 425, and reach excellent Urey Overlook. Descend, cross PA 425 again, and continue on to Otter Creek Campground, offering water, restrooms, showers, and campsites for a fee. Consider hiking the side trail along beautiful Otter Creek, with large boulders, pools, and cascades—a very scenic place.

After passing through the campground, hike along scenic Sawmill Run through state game lands. Follow roads for about 2 miles before descending into the gorge of beautiful Wallace Run, also in state game lands. Follow the run downstream, ascend up a side drainage, follow the contour of the gorge above the run, then descend steeply back to the run. Follow Wallace Run downstream to the Susquehanna River. Hike along the river for almost a mile, pass Holtwood Dam, and then steeply ascend the side of the Susquehanna River Gorge, passing powerline swaths. Descend into the scenic glen of Mill Creek and cross River Road. Mill Run is very beautiful, with thick rhododendron, cascades, boulders, and a waterfall. Reach Lock 12 Historic Area, featuring the lock, a restored limekiln, and remains of a sawmill, dam, and race. This area also marks the southern terminus of the orange-blazed Conestoga Trail.

Cross under PA 372, pass the remains of Lock 13, and hike along the river to scenic Peavine Island, with fascinating cliffs, ledges, and rock outcrops. The river is filled with similar-looking islands, and the scenery is excellent. Reaching the island in high water is difficult, as it is separated by a narrow side channel to the river. Cross back to shore and climb along rock outcrops and ledges. Look out to the river, with its steep-sided gorge and numerous islands with rock outcrops. Hike up to River Road and follow the road as it descends to the Lock 15 Interpretive Park and to the Pennsylvania Fish Commission boat launch with parking. Climb along a road away from the river and follow roads for more than 3 miles to busy PA 74. After .4 mile, head straight off PA 74 onto another road that descends to one of the MDT's highlights, exceptional Muddy Creek. Cross the creek over a bridge and follow it downstream. For the next 4 miles, the trail explores this stream and isolated gorge renowned for its incredible beauty, cascades, boulders, trout fishing, and whitewater rapids. The MDT follows the creek downstream, but ultimately climbs away from the creek and traverses the side of the gorge. Muddy Creek is a favorite of kayakers. The terrain in the gorge is rugged and steep, with sidehills, but it is well worth the effort. One can only hope that Muddy Creek will always remain in its natural state.

Descend from the ridge of the gorge to the river. Follow roads past cottages, climb away from the river, and descend back along roads. Reach Coyne Lock and hike behind Peach Bottom Nuclear Power Plant, passing transmission lines and powerlines. Because of security concerns, backpacking around the power plant area requires prior permission. Call ahead, carry photo identification, and don't be surprised if you are stopped by guards or police. Descend to a creek and climb back out. Follow roads for the remaining 3.5 miles to the Maryland border.

Central Pennsylvania: Ridge and Valley Region

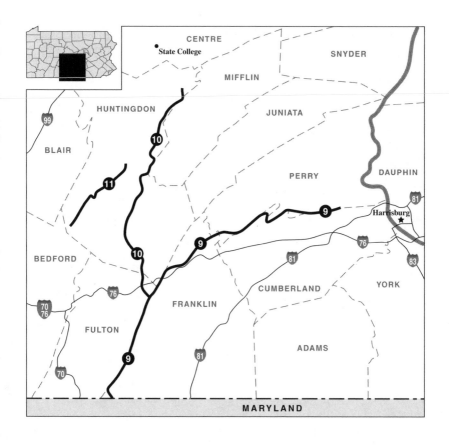

The section of the state features a series of near-symmetrical ridges separated by scenic valleys dotted with small towns and extensive farmlands. The ridgetops have rocky, rugged terrain and numerous outstanding vistas from rock outcrops and talus slopes. The Tuscarora, Link, and Mid State Trails (the Mid State Trail System is covered in the next chapter) are primarily ridgetop trails. Water is limited and can generally be found when the trails descend from the ridges to cross valleys or water gaps. It is important to carry extra containers for water while hiking these trails. The Terrace Mountain Trail follows the ridges and shoreline east of Raystown Lake. If you enjoy isolation and great views, and don't mind rocks, these trails are for you.

9. Tuscarora Trail

Length: 95-mile linear trail (Pennsylvania section).

Duration: 7 to 11 days.

Difficulty: Moderate to very difficult.

Terrain: Primarily a very rocky ridgeline trail. Generally level along ridges. Ascents and descents can be steep and rocky where the trail crosses valleys or gaps and can exceed 1,000 feet.

Trail conditions: Trail generally is established and blazed well, but a few sections may be brushy with inconsistent blazes. There is some road walking. Trail is isolated in sections.

Blazes: Blue.

Water: Because the trail primarily follows ridgetops, extensive sections are dry. Water typically found when the trail descends off the ridge. Carry extra containers.

Vegetation: Ridges are dominated by hardwoods and mountain laurel; hemlocks and pines found along streams; agricultural farmlands where the trail passes through valleys.

Highlights: Excellent vistas, Flat Rock, Colonel Denning State Park, Hemlocks Natural Area, Cowans Gap State Park, isolation, wildlife.

Maintained by: Potomac Appalachian Trail Club (PATC).

Contact info:
Potomac Appalachian Trail Conference (PATC), 118 Park St., S.E., Vienna, VA, 22180-4609; phone: 703-242-0693; e-mail: info@patc.net; website: www.patc.net.
Tuscarora State Forest, R.R. 1 Box 486, Blain, PA 17006; phone: 717-536-3335; e-mail: fd03@state.pa.us; websites: www.dcnr.state.pa.us/forestry/stateforests/forests/tuscarora/tuscarora.htm, www.dcnr.state.pa.us/forestry/hiking/tuscarora.htm.
Buchanan State Forest, 440 Buchanan Trail, McConnellsburg, PA 17233-6204; phone: 717-485-9283; e-mail: fd02@state.pa.us; website: www.dcnr.state.pa.us/forestry/stateforests/forests/buchanan/buchanan.htm.
Colonel Denning State Park, 1599 Doubling Gap Rd., Newville, PA 17241-9756; phone: 717-776-5272; e-mail: coloneldenningsp@state.pa.us; website: www.dcnr.state.pa.us/stateparks/parks/coloneldenning.asp.
Cowans Gap State Park, HC 17266, Fort Loudon, PA 17224-9801; phone: 717-485-3948; e-mail: cowansgapsp@state.pa.us; website: www.dcnr.state.pa.us/stateparks/parks/cowansgap.asp.

Maps and guides: Both available for sale; contact the PATC.

Trailhead directions:

Colonel Denning State Park: From I-81, take Exit 37 onto PA 233 and proceed
north 12 miles to the park. The trailhead is .3 mile before reaching the
park, on the left, at the juncture with Elk Hill Road.

Cowans Gap State Park: From the west along the PA Turnpike, exit at Fort
Littleton and take US 522 north to Burnt Cabins. At Burnt Cabins, US 522
makes a sharp left. Bear right and head straight off US 522; follow this
road for .7 mile. Turn right onto SR 1005 and follow it for almost 5 miles
into the state park. From the east along the PA Turnpike, exit at Willow Hill
and follow PA 75 south for 11 miles to Richmond Furnace. Turn right and
follow Richmond Road into the park. From US 30, turn onto PA 75 north
in Fort Loudon, and proceed 4 miles to Richmond Furnace. Turn left onto
Richmond Road, which leads into the park.

The Tuscarora Trail (TT) is a 250-mile-long side trail to the famed
Appalachian Trail, and it passes through Pennsylvania, Maryland,
West Virginia, and Virginia. Pennsylvania's section of the trail is 95
miles long. The TT leaves the Appalachian Trail at Shenandoah National
Park, follows a route to the west, and rejoins the Appalachian Trail
north of Harrisburg, creating a loop known as the Tuscalachian Loop.

The TT was originally established to provide an alternate route for
the Appalachian Trail, which was being threatened by development and
landowner problems in the late 1960s. Thankfully, the Appalachian
Trail received federal protection and a reroute was unnecessary. Originally, the section of the Tuscarora Trail in West Virginia and Virginia
was known as the Big Blue Trail, and only the section in Maryland and
Pennsylvania was known by the current name. By the 1980s, the TT
was in desperate shape, and there was talk of abandoning it. The
Potomac Appalachian Trail Club (PATC) stepped in, took over the entire
trail system, and named all of it the TT, and volunteers resurrected the
trail. Plans are to construct shelters along the entire length of the trail;
currently there are two. The PATC did an incredible job of transforming
the TT into a first-rate trail that rivals the Appalachian Trail in beauty,
vistas, isolation, wildlife, and difficulty. The description below follows
the trail from north to south.

Section One: Appalachian Trail to Colonel Denning State Park

The northern terminus of the trail is at the intersection of the
Appalachian and Darlington Trails, near the Darlington Shelter and a
spring. Because the northern terminus is not near a road, it can be

reached only by foot. The trail proceeds west along the ridge of Blue Mountain through State Game Lands (SGL) 170 and crosses Deans Gap. A rugged road passes through the shallow gap. Over the next 1.8 miles, the TT traverses the ridge, leaves the state game lands, passes powerline swaths with views, and descends into Sterretts Gap, where it reaches PA 34. Follow PA 34 to the right and descend from the ridge. After .6 mile, the trail bears left onto a driveway, crosses a small stream, and passes through private property for more than a mile before steeply ascending the ridge, where it reaches a nice view of the Cumberland Valley and Carlisle. For the next 5.2 miles, you hike along the ridgetop, with rocky terrain and rolling changes in elevation; the trail occasionally follows old mountain roads and skirts the boundary of SGL 230.

The TT enters Long Gap and turns right on Long Gap Road, following it downhill off the ridge, and passing a private wildlife sanctuary and a small stream. This is a 600-foot descent over approximately a mile. At the bottom of the ridge, the trail turns left onto Polecat Road

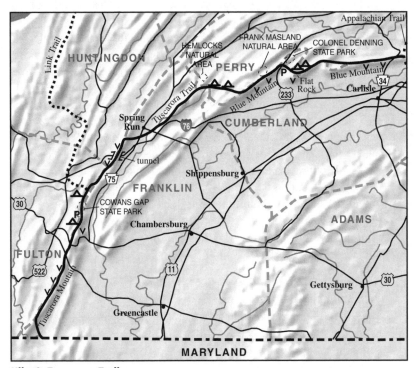

Hike 9: Tuscarora Trail

and follows it for more than 2 miles through pastoral countryside and along a small stream, until it reaches PA 74. Turn left onto PA 74, cross the stream, and turn right onto Greens Valley Road. For the next mile, the trail is mostly level as it passes along roads, farmlands, and private residences. Pick up an old forest road and begin to ascend the ridge, a 1,300-foot climb over almost 3 miles. The ascent is along a small stream. After you reach the top of the ridge, known as Barkley Ridge, you make a short but steep descent into McClures Gap and cross a jeep road. For about 3 miles, the TT follows the ridgetop, with very rocky, rugged terrain and occasional views. Blowdowns may be a problem. Elevation changes along the ridgetop are rolling. Make a minor descent into Berrys Gap, and bear right away from the ridgetop along a forest road. After almost a mile, the TT enters the Tuscarora State Forest and reaches a junction with the Warner Trail, to the right. This trail rejoins the TT in 2.5 miles at a "wagonwheel" trail juncture where five trails meet near Flat Rock. Pass a spring and enter Wildcat Hollow along Wildcat Run. Here you'll find good camping underneath hemlocks. Until now, the TT crossed state game lands and private land, making camping opportunities limited. As a result, backpackers generally use the 23-mile section where the TT traverses the Tuscarora State Forest.

The TT passes the Lehman Trail to the right and bears left, making a 500-foot climb over .6 mile out of Wildcat Hollow. You then reach one of the trail's highlights—spectacular Flat Rock Vista, which offers an incredible panorama of the Cumberland Valley and South Mountain. Flat Rock is about 1,300 feet above the valley. This section of trail is very popular with dayhikers from Colonel Denning State Park. The TT makes a rocky 400-foot descent over .6 mile from Flat Rock back into Wildcat Hollow, where there are potential campsites and water. Make a gradual climb, passing a nice trail shelter, until you reach the "wagonwheel" juncture. From here, Flat Rock Trail makes the descent to Colonel Denning State Park; the TT turns left and makes a rocky 900-foot descent over 1 mile to PA 233 and a parking area. The descent includes switchbacks and a spring.

Section Two: Colonel Denning State Park
to Cowans Gap State Park

Cross PA 233 and Doubling Run. Follow Elk Hill Road and pass a parking area. The trail leaves the road and begins a 1,000-foot climb over 1.3 miles, exiting the state forest and passing through private property with springs and a small stream. You follow various old forest roads as the trail steepens where it nears the ridgetop. Pass a view and reenter the Tuscarora State Forest; cross over the ridgetop and make a 300-foot descent. Bear left near Meadows Road and reascend the ridge. After 2 miles, the trail passes some nice views and an intersection with the Bill Miller Trail to the right; a spring can be found several hundred feet along this side trail. For the next 4 miles, the trail gradually ascends along the ridgetop with rocky terrain, passing numerous vistas. Bear right away from the ridge across level terrain and cross Cowpens Road.

Over the next 9 miles, the trail cuts across the ridges, climbing up and over them; water is also more plentiful. From Cowpens Road, the terrain is level, but after 1.6 miles, the trail begins to descend to Laurel Run, where you'll find potential camping. Cross the run and begin a mild ascent to Three Square Hollow Road. Leaving the road, you begin a steep ascent along an old forest road up Sherman Mountain. As you near the top, the trail steepens and follows switchbacks. This is a climb of about 400-feet climb over .4 mile. At the top, the TT turns left onto Spotts Road and follows the relatively flat ridge as the road diminishes. Bear right and descend off the ridgetop; at first the descent is steep, but it becomes more manageable. This is a 500-foot descent over .5 mile. Turn right on a forest road, cross Second Narrow Road, and pass a wetland. Begin a mild climb over a low ridge and descend to Shaeffer Run. Cross the run and Couch Road. Begin a steep 300-foot climb over .2 mile up Amberson Ridge, and then return to Couch Road. Turn right onto the road and follow it for about .2 mile. Bear left off the road and begin a mild ascent to the top of Amberson Ridge. In typical fashion, the trail soon makes a steep, rocky descent off the ridge and passes through hemlocks. The TT follows switchbacks and becomes less steep; this is an 800-foot descent over .5 mile. Cross Fowler Hollow Run, with good camping, and make a short climb across an old forest road. The trail passes Fowler Hollow Shelter, featuring a stone hearth and a spring.

The trail follows an old railroad grade and passes seasonal springs. Bear right and leave the grade to begin a steep, rocky ascent up Rising Mountain. The TT climbs 600 feet over .4 mile. The trail levels near the top and bears right to meet Hemlock Road. To the right (northwest) 200 feet is the Hemlocks Natural Area, featuring old-growth hemlocks in a narrow ravine and Patterson Run, a good stream. Because there is no water for the next 11 miles, it is imperative that you fill all your containers. Leave the road and begin a gradual climb along a logging road. After a mile, reach the crest of Rising Mountain and pass the Stewart Narrows Trail to the left; this trail descends into a glen with a small stream. The TT bears right and follows the ridgetop of Knob Mountain. For the next 9.5 miles, the terrain is very rocky, with blowdowns, rock outcrops, and several excellent vistas of the surrounding ridges and valleys. There are no water sources. Along the way, the trail passes junctures with Mountain Road and Catholic Path; the last 4 miles before PA 641 is private property. At the end of Knob Mountain, the trail descends off the ridgetop across rocky terrain, an 800-foot descent over about a mile. Pass seasonal springs and reach PA 641. The small village of Spring Run, with phone, grocery store, and restaurant, is .8 mile north on PA 641.

The TT crosses scenic Path Valley via roads for the next 4 miles. Fill your containers again at the streams in the valley, as there are no water sources for the next 8 miles, until the trail nears Aughwick Creek. The trail begins to ascend the ridge along a dirt jeep road; this is a 1,000-foot climb over about a mile. For the next 3 miles, follow the ridgetop, with rocky, rugged terrain and numerous outstanding vistas from rock outcrops and talus slopes. After crossing Fannettsburg–Burnt Cabins Road (SR 4004), the trail begins to descend off the ridge via old forest roads, a total of 600 feet over almost 2 miles. Enter the Buchanan State Forest and cross small streams, passing the Ellisic Trail and joining the Allen Trail; camping is permitted in the state forest. Cross Aughwick Creek and Allens Valley Road. Turn left on historic Forbes Road Trail and pass a juncture with the Link Trail to the right, a 72-mile-long trail that heads north to Greenwood Furnace State Park and the Mid State Trail. For the next 2 miles, the trail is level with a gentle incline, passing several springs and camping. Enter scenic Cowans Gap State Park, cross the dam, and pass near the beach. No backcountry camping is allowed in the state park, but you can camp in the camping area and use the showers for a fee. A public phone is available near the park office. Fill water bottles at the park.

Section Three: Cowans Gap State Park to Maryland Border

Pass the juncture of Allens Valley, Richmond, and Aughwick Roads. Cross Aughwick Road and pass through picnic area. Begin to climb the ridge via switchbacks, which can be steep at times. The trail ascends 600 feet in .8 mile. For the next 3 miles, the trail gradually ascends along the ridge with rocky terrain, outcrops, and occasional views. Begin a 400-foot climb over .5 mile to the top of Big Mountain, the highest point on the trail, at almost 2,500 feet. Past a grassy area where a fire tower used to stand (this is a dry campsite), you reach exceptional Big Mountain Vista, a rock outcrop overlooking Path and Cumberland Valleys. This vista surpasses Flat Rock because of the varied terrain: numerous sharp ridges rising to the north, interspersed with deep, pastoral valleys. For the next 1.8 miles, follow Tower Road (open to vehicles) to paved Aughwick Road. The trail follows Aughwick Road to the left for almost a mile, passing homes, before reaching US 30 and a parking area on the north side of the road. Be careful crossing US 30, as it is on top of the ridge, at a bend, and can be busy. Pass to the left of Tuscarora Summit Inn (primarily a bar) and cross under powerlines. To the right is a hang-gliding platform with an excellent vista to the west. For the next mile, the trail follows the ridgetop, with views and possible dry camping, and straddles the boundary of the Buchanan State Forest. Cross PA 16 just east of the ridgetop; to the west, at the top of the ridge, is another excellent vista.

For the next 11 miles, the TT continues to follow the ridgetop of Tuscarora Mountain, with rocky terrain, ledges, outcrops, and numerous excellent views. There are no water sources along the trail, but side trails lead to reliable springs. Much of the trail is in State Game Lands (SGL) 124, where camping is not permitted. Three miles from PA 16, you pass the Alice Trail to the left, which leads to a good spring 1.2 miles from the TT; this trail descends from the ridge to PA 456. Three miles farther to the left is Hells Hill Trail, which also descends from the ridge and features a spring after about a mile. Two miles farther is a yellow-blazed trail, which descends the ridge to the left for a mile to a seasonal spring. This yellow-blazed trail forms a loop with a blue-blazed trail. Follow the ridge for 4 miles, then begin to descend the east side of Tuscarora Mountain, a 1,500-foot descent over 2.5 miles. During the lower half of the descent, the trail passes a few springs. Turn right, then left on Furnace Road, and leave SGL 124. Cross PA 456 and continue straight on Forge Road. Cross Little Cove Creek and continue following Forge Road. Turn left on Little Cove Road, turn left on a jeep road, cross a small stream, and ascend Coon Ridge. Here you reach the Pennsylvania-Maryland border. The TT continues south through Maryland, West Virginia, and Virginia, ending at Shenandoah National Park and the Appalachian Trail.

10. Link Trail

Length: 72-mile linear trail.

Duration: 5 to 8 days.

Difficulty: Moderate to very difficult.

Terrain: Ridgetops are very rocky but tend to offer rolling hiking. Ascents and descents can be long, rocky, and steep, with 300- to 1,300-foot climbs where the trail descends from the ridges into gaps or valleys. Trail occasionally follows old grades. Extensive road walking between Three Springs and Blacklog Mountain.

Trail conditions: Trail is generally established and blazed sufficiently, but parts are brushy and unestablished, particularly between Mapleton and Three Springs, where blowdowns might be a problem. There is road-walking between Three Springs and Blacklog Mountain.

Blazes: Orange.

Water: Unevenly distributed. Ridgetops are generally dry, so carry extra containers. Water generally available when the trail descends to gaps or valleys. There is no water between Greenwood Furnace and Martins Gap, a distance of about 11 miles.

Vegetation: Ridgetops usually have hardwoods with thickets of mountain laurel, rhododendron, and blueberries. Occasional old-growth hemlock groves on the ridges. Rocky Ridge Natural Area has rare wildflowers.

Highlights: Greenwood Furnace State Park, Cowans Gap State Park, excellent vistas, rock formations, Rocky Ridge Natural Area, Hunters Rock, sinkholes, Thousand Steps, isolation, Jacks Narrows, Juniata River, Stone Valley Vista, Sausser's Stonepile, Butler Knob Vista, Throne Room Vista, Hall of the Mountain King, old-growth hemlock groves, historic areas.

Maintained by: Link Trail Hiking Club, Keystone Trails Association.

Contact info:
Link Trail Hiking Club, 336 Hillsdale Ave., Lewistown, PA 17044-1236
Keystone Trail Association, P.O. Box 129, Confluence, PA 15424-0129; e-mail: info@kta-hike.org, linktr@kta-hike.org; website: www.kta-hike.org/link_trail.htm.
Buchanan State Forest, 440 Buchanan Trail, McConnellsburg, PA 17233-6204; phone: 717-485-9283; e-mail: fd02@state.pa.us; website: www.dcnr.state.pa.us/forestry/stateforests/forests/buchanan/buchanan.htm.
Rothrock State Forest, P.O. Box 403, Rothrock Lane, Huntingdon, PA 16652; phone: 814-643-2340; e-mail: fd05@state.pa.us; website: www.dcnr.state.pa.us/forestry/stateforests/forests/rothrock/rothrock.htm.
Greenwood Furnace State Park, R.R. 2 Box 118, PA Rte. 305, Huntingdon, PA 16652-9006; phone: 814-667-1800; e-mail: greenwoodfurnacesp@state.pa.us; website: www.dcnr.state.pa.us/stateparks/parks/greenwoodfurnace.asp.

Cowans Gap State Park, HC 17266, Fort Loudon, PA 17224-9801;
   phone: 717-485-3948; e-mail: cowansgapsp@state.pa.us;
   website: www.dcnr.state.pa.us/stateparks/parks/cowansgap.asp.

Maps and guides: Currently in publication.

Trailhead directions:

Greenwood Furnace State Park: From US 322 and points east, take the
   Reedsville/PA 655 exit. Follow PA 655 to Belleville, where you turn right
   on PA 305 and follow it 7 miles to the park. The park is 5 miles east of
   McAlvey's Fort, along PA 305. Park at the lot near the park office.

Thousand Steps: This trailhead is located 1.8 miles west of Mount Union,
   along US 22; parking is on the left. The Thousand Steps are also 6 miles
   east of Mill Creek and 11 miles east of Huntingdon, along US 22.

Three Springs: From Three Springs, proceed west on SR 2022 for 1.1 miles
   toward Saltillo, turn right onto a game commission dirt road, and drive
   up to the parking area. From Saltillo, proceed east on SR 2022 for .6 mile
   toward Three Springs.

Cowans Gap State Park: From the west along the PA Turnpike, exit at Fort
   Littleton and take US 522 north to Burnt Cabins. At Burnt Cabins, US 522
   makes a sharp left. Bear right and head straight off US 522; follow this
   road for .7 mile. Turn right onto SR 1005 and follow it for almost 5 miles
   into the state park. From the east along the PA Turnpike, exit at Willow Hill
   and follow PA 75 south for 11 miles to Richmond Furnace. Turn right and
   follow Richmond Road into the park. From US 30, turn onto PA 75 north
   in Fort Loudon, and proceed 4 miles to Richmond Furnace. Turn left onto
   Richmond Road, which leads into the park. The Link Trail does not actually
   reach Cowans Gap State Park, but ends at its juncture with the Tuscarora
   Trail, about 3 miles north of the park.

The Link Trail (LKT) was first established in the late 1970s, but
because of maintenance problems, landowner problems, and
underuse, the Keystone Trails Association considered abandoning it.
But a man named Mike Sausser insisted on the trail's preservation,
and as a result of his determination, the LKT exists today and has even
begun to attract interest among backpackers. Joe Healey, Joe Clark,
and Richard Scanlon have also provided invaluable assistance to this
trail. In 2002, the Link Trail Hiking Club was formed to help ensure the
trail's survival. The Link Trail is so named because it connects the Mid
State Trail System to the Tuscarora Trail. The trail is known for its isolation and exceptional vistas and is one of the most scenic and rugged
trails in the state. If you're looking for a beautiful and challenging trail
offering many scenic features, this is the trail for you. The description
below follows the trail from north to south.

Section One: Greenwood Furnace State Park to US 22

With its many scenic features, continuity, and accessibility, this section of the LKT attracts the most backpackers, though you likely will have the trail all to yourself. The northern trailhead is located in historic, scenic Greenwood Furnace State Park. Make sure you carry plenty of water, as there is no water source between the state park and Martins Gap. Pass the quaint Stone Valley Church and climb gradually along old forest roads under hemlocks, pines, and hardwoods. Follow the switchbacks up the northern flank of Stone Mountain. The climb is not very steep or difficult, but the terrain becomes increasingly rocky. The LKT levels off as it traverses the ridge of the mountain, with occasional short climbs. You'll soon reach beautiful Stone Valley Vista, offering an expansive view of the ridges, valleys, and the lake at Greenwood Furnace State Park. The vista is a 900-foot climb over 2 miles from the state park. This incredible vista is just a taste of many others to come along the trail.

The LKT continues along the ridgetop, passing the blue-blazed Turkey Trail to your right. This trail descends steeply to Turkey Hill Road and the state park. For about 7 miles, follow the rocky ridge of Stone Mountain. You'll pass through incredibly scenic old-growth hemlock forests, a powerline offering views from both sides of the mountain, and several other vistas from talus slopes. The hemlocks soon diminish and hardwoods predominate, as do the rocks. There are no established campsites, but some rock-free areas allow dry camping. As you near Allensville Road, the LKT passes Sausser's Stonepile, an exceptional expansive vista. Follow the ridgetop past Hawk Watch, a platform for watching raptors; this area is a popular flyover. Do not camp on the platform.

Soon thereafter, the trail drops from the ridge, crosses Allensville Road, and begins a 1,000-foot descent to Martins Gap. The descent is steep in sections and often follows old forest roads. As you near the bottom, seep springs appear in years with normal rainfall. Possible campsites become more available, including one attractive meadow to your left. The LKT bears to the right and crosses Frew Road. If it's a dry year, hike Frew Road to your right, keeping an eye on the stream off to your left until there is water.

Cross Frew Road and enter the Rocky Ridge Natural Area, a place known for its rare wildflowers and unique rock formations. Cross a powerline swath and follow the ridge past more rock outcrops. Bear left and gradually descend to Frew Road. At the end of Frew Road, there is a small stream. An unblazed trail ascends to your right along a private-property line. This trail leads to Hunters Rock, one of the most impressive rock formations in the state, with massive spires of sandstone, jumbled boulders, crevasses, and a small cave. Cross the end of Frew Road, pass a campsite, and follow the trail as it bears right. You'll pass seep springs, a scenic grove of hemlock, potential campsites, and a series of sinkholes. Stinging nettles may be a problem through this section. For about the next 7 miles, the trail is fairly level, with no significant ascents or descents as it traverses the western flank of Stone Mountain under hardwoods and around the occasional sinkhole. In midspring, redbuds blooming along this section are particularly nice. Cross PA 655 and Saddler Creek. Although Saddler Creek looks clean, it contains runoff from farms.

Pass through private property and begin a 1,300-foot climb to the crest of Jacks Mountain. During the climb, the trail passes a spring and a cabin, and enters State Game Land 112 and then Rothrock State Forest. At the top is a hardwood forest with a thick understory of mountain laurel. Pass a vista and continue to the end of an access road to a communications tower. This road, with occasional blue blazes, leads to an excellent spring and rejoins with the LKT near the top of the Thousand Steps, near a dinkey house used to house and repair trains that transported ganister, a fine-grained quartzite quarried here. The LKT reenters the forest and descends across rocky terrain underneath old-growth hemlocks and thick mountain laurel. Now begins a series of long, gradual switchbacks along old quarry roads. At the end of one switchback is an excellent vista of the Juniata River valley. The trail reaches a bench along the mountain and turns left. As you near the Thousand Steps, vistas and rock outcrops begin to appear. The trail passes in front of a quarry and scrub pines as you hike along the rim of Jacks Narrows, a 1,300-foot-deep water gap, then arrive at the dinkey house. The blue-blazed trail to your left leads to an excellent spring, about .3 mile away. Continue to the top of the famous Thousand Steps. There actually are about 1,100 steps, which have been placed to create a staircase across numerous talus slopes and give views of impressive Jacks Narrows. In the summer, you'll see numerous small lizards along the steps. The steps were used by workers every day to reach the mountaintop quarry; the men must have been in excellent shape.

At the bottom of the steps, the LKT bears right onto an old grade; a trail continues down to US 22, where there is parking. The spring

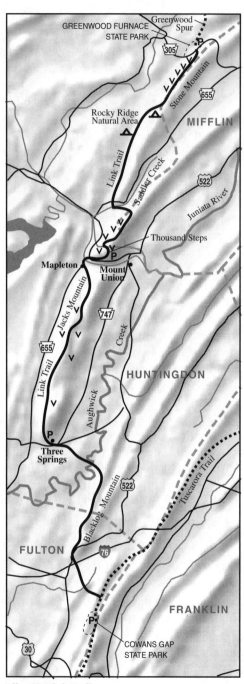

Hike 10: Link Trail

along this side trail, although crystal clear and cold, may be contaminated with PCBs. Follow this level grade above US 22 for about 1.3 miles, with several views. The trail also passes rock outcrops and rugged glens with cliffs. The LKT reaches US 22 and a hotel. Be careful crossing the highway here, as it is busy and at a curve.

Section Two: US 22 to Three Springs

After crossing the highway, descend through woodlands to Mapleton. Turn right at a road and pass a community park. Cross the new bridge over the Juniata River and enter Mapleton, a small town with public phones and a little general store. The LKT passes through Mapleton, with infrequent blazes, and then begins another difficult ascent up Jacks Mountain along Scrub Run. Part of the trail here may be unestablished, and the ascent is steep and very rocky in sections. Upon entering watershed lands, you'll come upon a No Trespassing sign that forbids hiking; however, hikers and backpackers are permitted to pass through these lands. Bear right at the top of the mountain and begin a descent, passing pipeline swaths and Singer Gap Creek. The trail is fairly level for about a mile, until it begins to climb through open hardwoods to Silver Mine Knob. At the top is a register; a side trail to your right leads to Throne Room Vista, one of the finest in the state, with 180-degree views of the surrounding ridges, valleys, and Jacks Narrows to the north. The LKT follows the crest of the knob and passes rock outcrops to your left, overlooking Orbisonia. The terrain becomes very rocky as the trail traverses Hall of the Mountain King, a massive talus slope in the saddle between Silver Mine and Butler Knobs. Excellent views can be had from both sides of the mountain. Notice the blueberry bushes once you reenter the forest. For the next mile, the trail passes through Rothrock State Forest, where camping is permitted but there are no water sources. The terrain is level through hardwoods. Upon reaching the forest road, the trail follows it to the right. Follow the road straight for .3 mile to incredible Butler Knob Vista, a fire tower, and communication towers. When I was here last, hikers were able to climb the rickety fire tower and see the excellent 360-degree view from the top. Return to the trail.

The road descends from Butler Knob and passes cabins. Watch where the road enters state game lands and look to your right for Deeter's Spring, which usually runs year-round. Continue to follow the road for about a mile, cross over a small stream, and turn right onto gated Butler Road. The LKT follows this road for about .7 mile before turning right and entering the forest. Begin a gentle climb to the ridgeline. The terrain becomes increasingly rocky. Bear left upon reaching the ridge and follow it for about 1.5 miles. Turn left at a sign for Hoopers Gap Vista, which is just off the trail, and descend into Hoopers Gap, where you can find water. The gap is scenic, with a nice stream, hemlocks, and sizable hardwoods. Cross the stream and climb out of the gap over increasingly rocky terrain. Bear left on a forest road, and then bear left again onto Butler Road. Follow the road as it climbs over the ridge, with nice views from the top looking north. Descend along the road, with more views to the south. This is a long descent that steepens as you near the bottom. Pass a gate and parking area, and reach SR 2022 between Three Springs and Saltillo. The LKT is difficult to backpack from here to the southern trailhead near Cowans Gap State Park because of road walking, limited campsites, extensive areas of private land, and landowner problems.

Section Three: Three Springs to Tuscarora Trail and Cowans Gap State Park

Follow SR 2022 left to the small town of Three Springs. Pass through Three Springs, and then turn right onto SR 2004. Follow this road for about 7 miles, until you reach Meadow Gap and State Game Lands (SGL) 81. Climb up Blacklog Mountain, and follow the crest across rocky terrain with forest dominated by hardwoods. You are treated to occasional views and outcrops. After 3 miles, you reach Ramsey Path, a blue-blazed trail to your right; the LKT continues south but is cut off at the end of Blacklog Mountain because of landowner problems. The Ramsey Path descends into a scenic gap with boulders and rock outcrops; springs can also be found here. Descend to SR 1011 and turn left on the road. Follow the road for about 3 miles, until you reach Fort Littleton and US 522. Turn left and follow US 522 for about 2.5 miles, until the trail turns right and goes through a culvert under the PA Turnpike. Ascend the mountain along a small stream and enter the Buchanan State Forest. Descend to the Tuscarora Trail, about 3 miles north of Cowans Gap State Park.

11. Terrace Mountain Trail

Length: 25-mile linear trail (when completed).

Duration: 2 to 3 days.

Difficulty: Moderate.

Terrain: Trail often follows old grades, with gradual changes in elevation. Rocky in sections. Most significant climbs are located along the northern half; most ascents and descents are gradual.

Trail conditions: Trail is generally established and blazed well. Entire trail is not yet completed.

Blazes: Blue.

Water: Generally plentiful.

Vegetation: Hardwoods predominate, with understory of mountain laurel; occasional groves of hemlock, rhododendron, and pine; a few open glades and meadows.

Highlights: Raystown Lake, Tatman Run, Trough Creek State Park, Trough Creek Wild Area, lakeside vistas, Raystown Branch of the Juniata River.

Maintained by: Volunteers, Keystone Trails Association.

Contact info:
Rothrock State Forest, P.O. Box 403, Rothrock Lane, Huntingdon, PA 16652; phone: 814-643-2340; e-mail: fd05@state.pa.us; website: www.dcnr.state.pa.us/forestry/stateforests/forests/rothrock/rothrock.htm.
Trough Creek State Park, R.R. 1 Box 211, James Creek, PA 16657-9302; phone: 814-658-3847, e-mail: troughcreeksp@state.pa.us; website: www.dcnr.state.pa.us/stateparks/parks/troughcreek.asp.
Raystown Lake (Army Corps of Engineers), R.D. 1 Box 222, Hesston, PA 16647; phone: 814-658-3405; e-mail: Raystown.WEB@nab02.usace.army.mil; website: www.raystown.nab.usace.army.mil.
Paradise Point/Peninsula Camp, Lake Raystown Resort, 814-658-3500.

Maps and guides: Guide is available on the Raystown Lake website.

Trailhead directions:
Weaver's Bridge (southern trailhead): This trailhead is located north of Saxton. From PA 26, turn onto PA 913 east and drive through Saxton. After 3 miles, turn left onto SR 3007. At the top of a hill, turn right onto SR 3003, and descend to Weaver's Bridge, a mile total from PA 913. The trail begins at the gate before crossing the bridge. There is a trail sign, but parking is limited, as you are not permitted to block the gate.
Tatman Run: From Huntingdon, proceed south on PA 26 for 14.6 miles. Turn left onto PA 994; after 4.6 miles, turn left on Tatman Run. Drive .8 mile down this road until it crosses the trail. Parking is on the right.

Trough Creek State Park: From Huntingdon, proceed south on PA 26 for 14.6 miles. Turn left onto PA 994; after 5.2 miles, turn left onto SR 3031. Proceed 1.7 miles to the park. In the park, pass the office, and turn left onto Trough Creek Drive. Follow this road to its end at a picnic area, through which the trail passes. Contact the park in advance about leaving your car overnight.

John Bum Road: Follow the same directions to the park office in Trough Creek State Park. Turn right at the park office, cross Trough Creek, and head straight, avoiding Trough Creek Drive to the right. Proceed straight onto Tar Kiln Road, drive through Youth Forestry Camp No. 3, and after a mile from the park office, turn left onto John Bum Road. Follow this road for 4 miles to the intersection with Fink Road. A parking area is on the left. This was the former northern trailhead, and you'll still find occasional faded blue blazes on the gated Fink Road, to the left. You can follow this road down to the trail, which is currently being extended northward to Corbin's Island. In the future, the Terrace Mountain Trail may no longer follow this segment of Fink Road, but it does provide convenient access.

The Terrace Mountain Trail (TMT) explores the shores and mountains east of beautiful Raystown Lake, one of the most scenic manmade lakes you'll find anywhere. The trail is currently being extended northward to Corbin's Island and will be about 25 miles in length when completed. Besides backpacking, the Raystown Lake region offers great opportunities for boating, swimming, fishing, canoeing, camping, and dayhiking.

To hike the TMT from south to north, begin at the southern trailhead, located at Weaver's Bridge, near the Weaver Falls Access Area. The trail is level for the first .5 mile, as it follows near the shore of the lake along a gated road. Begin a gradual ascent. Return to the shore along the steep slope of Terrace Mountain. Begin another climb that ascends 500 feet and is steep in sections along the slope of Terrace Mountain. Pass an intersection to Putt's Camp, to your left. This Boy Scout facility may be used by hikers needing water or restrooms, but camping by the general public is not permitted. Continue the climb for .4 mile, and then the trail descends along the slope of Terrace Mountain, dropping 900 feet over 1.25 miles to Peninsula Camp. A trail to the left descends .25 mile to Paradise Point/Peninsula Camp, a fee campground operated by Lake Raystown Resort that can be reached only by boat or by hiking. Over the course of the next mile, the TMT ascends and passes behind the Lake Raystown Resort. Soon thereafter, it crosses PA 994, which is 7 miles from Weaver's Bridge.

Descend to and cross scenic Tatman Run, one of two streams that cut through Terrace Mountain to empty into Raystown Lake, the other being beautiful Trough Creek. Climb the bank on the other side and cross the access road to Tatman Run Access Area, which is located .25 mile to the left, along the lake. This access area has drinking water, picnic facilities, restrooms, parking, and a beach area. Descend to a pipeline swath and the lake. The trail subsequently climbs along the slope of the mountain; the next 1.6 miles of trail feature rocky and rugged terrain, with a nice vista of the lake. Descend back to shore

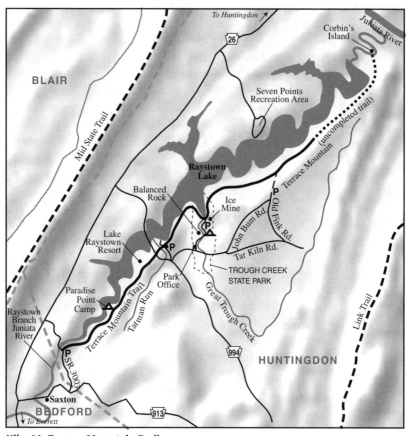

Hike 11: Terrace Mountain Trail

and follow an old, level grade for almost 3 miles to Trough Creek State Park. The trail offers many views of Raystown Lake along the shore.

Trough Creek State Park is one of the TMT's highlights and one of Pennsylvania's most scenic state parks. Here Great Trough Creek has carved a rugged gorge through Terrace Mountain. The creek is renowned for its great beauty, fine fishing, whitewater rapids, and rugged gorge with views, cliffs, and rock outcrops. The state park has geological features such as Balanced Rock, Raven Rock, and Copperas Rock. Rainbow Falls is a small, scenic cascade along Abbot Run. The park is also home to the Ice Mine, which emits cold air in the summer, and several historic sites, including Savage Forge and Paradise Furnace. Most of these features can be reached only from side trails off the TMT; it is well worth taking time to explore Trough Creek State Park.

Upon entering the park, follow the TMT across the bridge over Great Trough Creek and through the picnic area, where you'll find drinking water and restrooms. Bear left onto the park road and pass the Ice Mine. The state park's camping area is .2 mile to the right along the road; and a fee is required. The TMT follows an old paved road above an inlet of Raystown Lake; talus slopes can be seen above the trail to the right. Descend gradually to the shore, where the road disappears into the lake. The TMT enters the rocky woods to the right. The trail is mostly level as it follows the contour of the lower slopes of Terrace Mountain, with rock outcrops, boulders, and ledges. After almost 2 miles, begin a gradual ascent up the side of Terrace Mountain along an old logging road. Climb 600 feet over a mile to Old Fink Road. The TMT originally turned right onto this road and climbed .3 mile to end at the intersection with John Bum Road.

The TMT is currently being extended northward. The trail now turns left onto Old Fink Road and descends toward the lake. The trail will then proceed northward along the slope above the lake, pass the dam, and descend along the Raystown Branch of the Juniata River. This beautiful river offers great fishing, tubing, and canoeing and is often home to bald eagles. The trail is anticipated to end near Corbin's Island Access Area, on the other side of the river.

Mid State Trail System

At more than 260 miles in length, the Mid State Trail (MST) is the longest in the state and the centerpiece of Pennsylvania's extensive backpacking trail system. The trail begins along the Pennsylvania-Maryland border and currently ends at the West Rim Trail, in the Pine Creek Gorge, just a few miles north of Blackwell. It is being extended north to the New York border and may ultimately join the Finger Lakes Trail and North Country Trail. The MST also features two spur trails that make for great backpacking trips as well: the Greenwood and Reeds Gap Spurs.

The MST showcases the state's panoply of terrains: high ridgelines, water gaps, wide river valleys, plateaus, glens, canyons, and gorges. The trail originally began in the town of Water Street and proceeded north to Blackwell. In the late 1990s, the MST was extended south along ridgelines to the Maryland border. Along the way, it eclipsed the Appalachian Trail as the longest trail in the state.

A determined group of volunteers, organized as the Mid State Trail Association, maintain the MST. Beginning with just a few miles of trail in 1968, they have created a superb backpacking trail system. One man, however, is deserving of special recognition. Tom Thwaites has been a driving force behind the MST and the Keystone Trails Association. Thwaites has selflessly spent countless hours helping maintain, preserve, and protect dozens of Pennsylvania's trails over the past thirty years. He is also the respected author of the 50 Hikes series, covering trails in eastern, central, and western Pennsylvania. These hiking guides introduced many people, including me, to the beauty and trails of

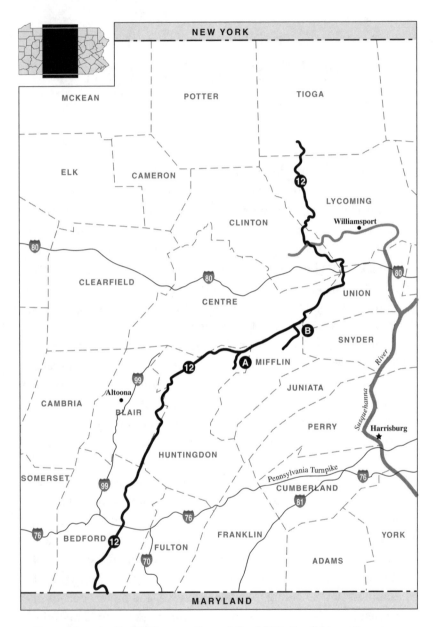

Pennsylvania. In 2002, a section of the MST, the first section ever established near Big Flat Laurel, south of State College, was dedicated in his honor, a fitting tribute to a man who has done more for Pennsylvania's trails than any other person.

🏃🥾 12. Mid State Trail

Length: 260-mile linear trail.

Duration: 4 to 7 weeks.

Difficulty: Moderate to very difficult.

Terrain: From the Maryland border to Bear Meadows Natural Area, the trail follows extensive ridgetops with very rocky terrain. The terrain is often level or rolling on the ridgetops, but ascents and descents are rocky and steep where the trail drops to cross water gaps. From Bear Meadows Natural Area to the West Branch of the Susquehanna River, the trail traverses the Seven Mountains region and spends less time along the ridgelines as it climbs in and out of glens and valleys carved by streams. Many climbs are steep and rocky. From the West Branch of the Susquehanna River to the northern terminus at the West Rim Trail, the trail has both level periods of hiking along the tops of plateau and steep climbs as it traverses the glens, gorges, and canyons of many streams. Ascents and descents range from 200 to 1,400 vertical feet.

Trail conditions: Trail is generally blazed well, though sections may be unestablished. Trail is often rerouted. Many stream crossings, often without bridges.

Blazes: Orange; side trails blue.

Water: From the Maryland border to Bear Meadows Natural Area, the trail primarily follows dry ridgetops with limited and seasonal water sources; carry extra containers. From Bear Meadows to US 322, water sources are more common, with several springs and streams. From US 322 to Poe Paddy State Park, the trail again follows dry ridgetops but also passes along streams. For the remainder of the trail, there are typically sufficient sources of water.

Vegetation: Mostly northern hardwoods and oak, especially at higher elevations and along the ridgetops. Generally a thick understory of mountain laurel and lowbush blueberries. Hemlocks, pines, and rhododendron often found along streams and in wetter environments.

Highlights: Martin Hill Wild Area, Sweet Root Natural Area, Lower Trail, Little Juniata Natural Area, Little Juniata River, Big Flat Laurel Natural Area, Bear Meadows Natural Area, Detweiler Run Natural Area, Thickhead Wild Area, Penn Roosevelt State Park, Poe Valley State Park, Poe Paddy State Park, Penns Creek, The Hook Natural Area, R. B. Winter State Park, Halfway Run Natural Area, Ravensburg State Park, West Branch of the Susquehanna River, Woolrich Factory Outlet, Pine Creek Gorge, Little Pine State Park, Bark Cabin Natural Area, Wolf Run Wild Area, Gillespie Point, Pine Creek Trail, Jerry Run Falls, Bohen Run Falls, Pine Creek, scenic mountain streams, excellent vistas, fine campsites, isolation, wildlife, diverse terrains and habitats, gorges, glens, and canyons.

Maintained by: Mid State Trail Association, Keystone Trails Association, volunteers.

Contact info:
Mid State Trail Association, P.O. Box 167, Boalsburg, PA 16827; websites: www.dcnr.state.pa.us/forestry/hiking/midstate.htm, www.kta-hike.org.
Rothrock State Forest, P.O. Box 403, Rothrock Lane, Huntingdon, PA 16652; phone: 814-643-2340; e-mail: fd05@state.pa.us; website: www.dcnr.state.pa.us/forestry/stateforests/forests/rothrock/rothrock.htm.
Buchanan State Forest, 440 Buchanan Trail, McConnellsburg, PA 17233-6204; phone: 717-485-9283; e-mail: fd02@state.pa.us; website: www.dcnr.state.pa.us/forestry/stateforests/forests/buchanan/buchanan.htm.
Bald Eagle State Forest, Box 147, Laurelton, PA 17835; phone: 570-922-3344; e-mail: fd07@state.pa.us; website: www.dcnr.state.pa.us/forestry/stateforests/forests/baldeagle/baldeagle.htm.
Tiadaghton State Forest, 423 E. Central Ave., S. Williamsport, PA 17702; phone: 570-327-3450; e-mail: fd12@state.pa.us; website: www.dcnr.state.pa.us/forestry/stateforests/forests/tiadaghton/tiadaghton.htm.
Tioga State Forest, One Nessmuk Lane, Wellsboro, PA 16901; phone: 570-724-2868; e-mail: fd16@state.pa.us; website: www.dcnr.state.pa.us/forestry/stateforests/forests/tioga/tioga.htm.
Penn Roosevelt State Park, c/o Greenwood Furnace State Park, R.R. 2 Box 118, PA Rte. 305, Huntingdon, PA 16652-9006; phone: 814-667-1800; e-mail: greenwoodfurnacesp@state.pa.us; website: www.dcnr.state.pa.us/stateparks/parks/pennroosevelt.asp.
Poe Valley State Park, c/o Reeds Gap State Park, 1405 New Lancaster Valley Rd., Milroy, PA 17063-9735; phone: 814-349-2460, 717-667-3622; e-mail: reedsgapsp@state.pa.us; website: www.dcnr.state.pa.us/stateparks/parks/poevalley.asp.
Poe Paddy State Park, c/o Reeds Gap State Park, 1405 New Lancaster Valley Rd., Milroy, PA 17063-9735; phone: 717-667-3622; e-mail: reedsgapsp@state.pa.us; website: www.dcnr.state.pa.us/stateparks/parks/poepaddy.asp.
R. B. Winter State Park, 17215 Buffalo Rd., Mifflinburg, PA 17844-9656; phone: 570-966-1455; e-mail: rbwintersp@state.pa.us; website: www.dcnr.state.pa.us/stateparks/parks/rbwinter.asp.
Ravensburg State Park, c/o R. B. Winter State Park, 17215 Buffalo Rd., Mifflinburg, PA 17844-9656; phone: 570-966-1455; e-mail: rbwintersp@state.pa.us; website: www.dcnr.state.pa.us/stateparks/parks/ravensburg.asp.
Little Pine State Park, 4205 Little Pine Creek Rd., Waterville, PA 17776-9705; phone: 570-753-6000; e-mail: littlepinesp@state.pa.us; website: www.dcnr.state.pa.us/stateparks/parks/littlepine.asp.

Maps and guides: Both available for sale. Trail also shown on free Rothrock, Bald Eagle, and Tiadaghton State Forest maps.

Trailhead directions:

Water Street (Lower Trail): From Huntingdon, take US 22 west for 9 miles. After crossing the Frankstown Branch, make a sharp right on SR 4014 to Alfarata. Follow this road for .2 mile to a parking area on the right for the Lower Trail (a rail-trail). From the west, follow US 22 east for less than a mile from the PA 45/453 juncture, and make the next left to the Lower Trail.

Little Juniata Natural Area: From Huntingdon, take US 22 west for 7 miles and turn right onto PA 305 east. Drive .5 mile to Alexandria. Turn left at the stop sign, leaving PA 305. Drive .6 mile and turn right onto PA 4004. Follow this road to Barree and cross the Little Juniata River. After crossing the river, make the next left and drive .6 mile to a gravel parking area. PA 305 is about 3 miles east of the PA 45/453 juncture with US 22.

Jo Hayes Vista (PA 26): This trailhead is located at Jo Hayes Vista, at the top of Tussey Mountain, along PA 26. It is 2 miles south of Pine Grove Mills and 24 miles north of Huntingdon. Ample parking is located along the road.

Penn Roosevelt State Park: This is a small, isolated park. From the juncture of PA 144 and US 322 at Potters Mills, proceed east on US 322 less than a mile. Turn right onto Crowfield Road and follow for 6 miles to the park.

Poe Valley and Poe Paddy State Parks: These parks are located in an isolated area of the Seven Mountains. No road that leads to these parks is entirely paved. From the juncture of PA 144 and US 322 at Potters Mills, proceed east on US 322 for about 1.5 miles. Turn left onto a dirt forestry road and follow for 10 miles to Poe Valley State Park. To reach Poe Paddy, continue an additional 3.5 miles on Poe Valley Road.

Hairy Johns Picnic Area: This trailhead is located along PA 45, 4 miles east of Woodward and 16 miles west of Mifflinburg.

R. B. Winter State Park: The park is located east along PA 192, 28 miles east of Centre Hall and 16 miles west of Lewisburg. A parking area is located along Halfway Lake near the dam.

Ravensburg State Park: The park is located along PA 880, 8 miles south of Jersey Shore and 8 miles north of Carroll, from Exit 192 off I-80.

Little Pine State Park: From US 220, take the Pine Creek exit and proceed north onto PA 44. After 10.8 miles, at Waterville, turn right onto SR 4001 and proceed 3.4 miles to the park. Turn right into the campground area and park at the second car lot.

Blackwell: Blackwell is 5.3 miles west on PA 414 from PA 287 at Morris, and 16 miles west on PA 414 from US 15. A parking area is on the left before you cross the bridge over Pine Creek. The parking area is about 6 miles east of Cedar Run along PA 414.

Despite its length and scenery, the MST has largely been overlooked by backpackers. With continued support and maintenance, it is poised to become one of the Mid-Atlantic's premier trails. The trail currently connects with Maryland's Green Ridge Trail and eventually may extend into New York, possibly connecting with the Finger Lakes Trail and North Country Trail. When this is completed, the MST will become a nationally significant trail. The description below is from south to north.

Section One: Maryland Border to Water Street (Southern Extension)

The 90-mile southern extension of the MST begins at the northern terminus of the Green Ridge Trail at the Maryland border and proceeds north to Water Street, the traditional southern trailhead of the MST. This section is known for its isolation, extremely rocky ridgetop hiking, exceptional views, and limited water along the ridgetops. The southern portion of this section, where the trail traverses Buchanan State Forest and camping is permitted, is suitable for backpacking. Camping is not permitted along most of this section of the MST, because it is forbidden on state game lands, so most of this challenging section cannot be backpacked.

From the Mason-Dixon line, the trail follows a township road for .5 mile, until it enters Buchanan State Forest to the right. Cross a forest road and begin a gradual ascent around the northern flank of Ragged Mountain. Bear right onto gated Collins Road and cross a small stream. Bear right onto Stuckey Road and reach the state forest boundary at Elbinsville Road, on which you turn left. Follow this road for .6 mile to Covered Bridge Road; turn left and follow this road for more than 2 miles. The road climbs over Polish Mountain and descends into Town Creek's valley. Cross scenic Town Creek over the Hewitt Covered Bridge. Reach the small village of Hewitt and turn right onto Town Creek Road; follow this road .4 mile to PA 326. Follow PA 326 for 1.8 miles, until the MST turns right and follows the Karns Trail through a private farm pasture; if anyone is home, please let them know you are passing through. Climb gradually along the edge of the pasture, near a small stream, and enter Buchanan State Forest.

Begin a 600-foot climb over .7 mile to the intersection of the Gap Trail, along which are campsites and a side trail to a spring. The MST's climb becomes steeper as it ascends 400 feet over .5 mile to the crest of Tussey Mountain. The trail has a special relationship with Tussey

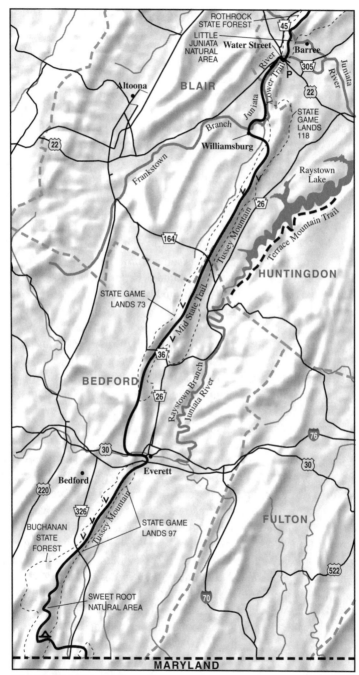

Hike 12: Mid State Trail

Mountain, following along the top or side of this ridge for 120 miles. You also will have a special relationship with this mountain, either cursing its rocks and rugged terrain or reveling in its awesome views. For the next 4.3 miles, the trail follows the rounded crest of Tussey Mountain along an old forest road, with level or rolling terrain. Cross paved Beans Cove Road; a spring exists 400 feet to the left along this road. The trail now follows Martin Hill Road for a mile, until it bears left along a powerline. Pass a view to the east and climb steeply to the summit of Martin Hill. Turn left onto Tower Road and pass a fenced-off fire tower. At 2,720 feet in elevation, Martin Hill is the highest point along the MST; unfortunately, there are no views at the summit.

Proceed on Evitts Mountain Road and turn right onto Basin Trail. The trail makes a very steep, rugged descent, totaling 500 feet over .3 mile. Cross Martin Hill Road and continue the descent, which becomes more mild as the trail drops almost 400 feet over .5 mile. The trail reaches a small stream and spring. You are now in the Sweet Root Natural Area, where camping is prohibited. The terrain is rocky. Ascend gradually, and then descend to Tarkiln Trail and a small stream. Turn right and proceed downstream into Sweet Root Gap. The natural area is known for its old-growth forest, rare species, and steep, rocky, and rugged terrain. Unfortunately, the old-growth hemlocks have been devastated by the woolly adelgid. Bear left and gradually climb along Sweet Root Run. Bear right onto Garlic Trail, leaving the natural area and entering state game lands. Gradually descend into Rainsburg Gap, and pass a small stream in the gap. After several stream crossings, the trail reaches and crosses PA 326.

The next segment, between PA 326 and Everett, is incredibly challenging and scenic. This segment is about 16 miles long and is very isolated. It is extremely rocky and rugged, with outcrops and ledges, and it features several outstanding vistas that will take your breath away. This is a wilderness ridgetop trek. Not surprisingly, it is also very dry, with no reliable water sources directly along the trail. This is probably the most difficult section along the entire MST. After completing this segment, you will either love or hate Tussey Mountain and its knife edges, but you will surely have come to respect this mountain.

Gradually climb to the crest of Tussey Mountain along old forest roads. The trail follows the rocky ridgetop for more than 2 miles, with several vistas, rock outcrops, and ledges. The trail descends gradually and follows the bench along the west side of Tussey Mountain for another mile or so before gradually ascending back to the ridgetop.

Follow the rocky, rugged ridgetop for more than 3 miles, with excellent vistas and rock outcrops that often require scrambling. The terrain is very rugged and scenic. The MST again descends gradually to the left, dropping back to the bench along the west side of the mountain. After about a mile, you reach a state game land access road. To reach a water source, follow this road to the left down the mountain for .7 mile; otherwise, follow the trail as it continues along the side of the mountain and passes through two small glens with seasonal springs. Ascend steeply back to the ridgetop. Follow the ridgetop for more than 2 miles across very rugged terrain and past exceptional vistas. The trail often traverses the sheer rock outcrops across the ridgeline.

Descend steeply off the ridgetop to the left, once again reaching the bench along the side of the mountain. The trail comes to an access road and follows it for less than a mile, then begins an increasingly steep descent off Tussey Mountain and into the water gap carved by the Raystown Branch of the Juniata River. At the bottom, turn right onto Ashcom Road; follow the roads and streets through Earlston and pass under the PA Turnpike. Cross the bridge over the Raystown Branch of the Juniata, and follow the streets through Everett, which features restaurants and food stores where you can resupply. Head west out of Everett along old grades and roads. Pick up Mount Dallas Road and follow it until you reach Snake Spring Valley Road (SR 1005); turn right. Follow this road for almost 8 miles, as it gradually ascends into a bucolic farm valley encased by Tussey Mountain to the east and Evitts Mountain to the west. This extended road walk is necessary because private property prevents placing the trail along the crest of Tussey Mountain. At the head of the valley, the road's incline steepens. Leave the road to the right and follow the trail as it ascends an embankment. Reach a state game land access road and follow it to the right, passing a parking area. Follow this road for about a mile, passing another parking area before the gate. Bear left and once again follow the crest of Tussey Mountain for 4.5 miles. Here the terrain offers easier hiking than south of Everett, with few vistas. Begin a gradual descent to scenic Yellow Creek and PA 36 in Loysburg Gap.

Yellow Creek is a sizable stream, and crossing it during high water can be very difficult. The trail turns right on PA 36. Be careful hiking along this road, which can be busy and has curves; you may want to hike on the outside of the guardrail. Pass a large pull-off area along the road, which can be used for parking, and turn left, entering State Game Lands (SGL) 73. Begin a steep 500-foot climb over .5 mile, passing a corner of the state game lands boundary, and gradually descend into Maple Run's valley, crossing seasonal streams. After a mile, the trail begins to ascend for .5 mile, then gradually descends to scenic Maple Run, a reliable water source. Ascend gradually over a mile in proximity to Maple Run; climb out of the valley through a narrowing gap. The MST levels and in .5 mile reaches a dirt township road, on which it turns left and follows for .3 mile. Turn right into a parking area and gradually ascend along a gated road. After a mile, pass a gate and bear left on a dirt access road, and descend gradually. After .5 mile, you reach a paved road, on which the trail follows to the right and climbs gradually. At the top of the ridge, the MST turns left and leaves the paved road. Follow an access road as it gradually descends and levels off along the western bench of Tussey Mountain. After 2 miles, the trail descends into a shallow glen, where a seasonal spring can be found in a culvert. The trail continues to be level or rolling, with no views, for more than 3 miles farther before it ascends and reaches PA 164 with parking. Be very careful crossing this road, as it is at a bend.

Follow a pipeline swath and turn left to ascend the ridge. After .5 mile, pass a nice view to the east. The trail follows the rocky ridge of Tussey Mountain for 1.5 miles before reaching a pipeline swath offering great views to the east and west. Drop from the ridge to the left, descending 400 feet over .5 mile, until the trail levels along the western bench of Tussey Mountain. Continue along the level and rolling bench for more than 4 miles. The MST then bears right and climbs back to the ridgeline of Tussey Mountain. For the next 4.4 miles, the trail follows the crest of Tussey Mountain, with very rocky terrain, several scenic vistas, and dry conditions. When you reach Tussey Mountain Road, bear left on the road and descend off the mountain. A relocation is planned here, with MST following the western flank of Tussey Mountain for 3 miles, then dropping down to Williamsburg.

The trail follows a road off the mountain, crosses Clover Creek, and in another 2 miles reaches Williamsburg. Pass through the town on its streets until you reach the southern parking area of the Lower Trail, a beautiful bike path along an old grade that follows the Frankstown Branch of the Juniata River. The MST follows the 12-mile Lower Trail in its entirety and is unblazed. Camping is not permitted. While hiking this bike path, you pass remains of a canal and old iron operations. Near the northern end of the Lower Trail, you enter a canyon with fine scenery. This section ends when you reach the parking area at the northern end of the Lower Trail, near the village of Water Street.

Section Two: Water Street to US 322
(Seven Mountains Region)

Water Street was the former southern terminus of the MST, until it was extended southward. It continues to serve as the traditional southern trailhead of the MST, because camping restrictions make it difficult to backpack the southern extension. This section reveals the true beauty of the MST as it traverses the heart of the famed Seven Mountains region. The trail passes incredible vistas, rocky ridgelines, four beautiful natural areas—Little Juniata, Big Laurel Flat, Bear Meadows, and Detweiler Run—and scenic, isolated Penn Roosevelt State Park.

Cross Alexandria Road and begin a steep climb of 400 feet over .3 mile. The trail levels off and begins a gradual descent along the eastern flank of Short Mountain. Pick up a quarry road and continue the gentle descent until the trail nears the Little Juniata River. There were plans to construct a ford across the river, but for now you must follow the blue-blazes along the railroad tracks, turn left and pass through Barree, turn left again and cross the bridge over the Little Juniata River, and then make the next left and hike .7 mile along the road into the main parking area of the natural area. The Little Juniata is one of the MST's highlights. The river has carved a rugged 1,100-foot deep water gap through Tussey Mountain. It is one of the few such water gaps in Pennsylvania not traversed by a road or highway, although a busy railroad does pass through the gap. During World War II, soldiers were stationed here to protect the railroad tunnels and viaducts from sabotage, as they were crucial to the war effort. The Little Juniata River is great for tubing and is one of the finest trout streams in the Mid-Atlantic region. It was here that I caught my first trout with a fly. It is only fitting that this beautiful river and water gap are now protected as a natural area.

Fill all your containers here, because water is scarce on the ridge of Tussey Mountain. The trail begins a steep 1,000-foot climb over .7 mile up the rim of the water gap. The MST levels off at a bench with a few views and evidence of past quarrying. Continue the remaining climb of 400 feet over .5 mile to the top of Tussey Mountain, where you are treated to a phenomenal view to the southwest from a talus slope. Follow the rocky, level ridgetop for 1.4 miles, until the MST reaches the blue-blazed Rainbow Trail to the left. This side trail descends very steeply to Colerain Road, Indian Lookout, and Colerain Picnic Area along PA 45. From here until PA 26, blue-blazed side trails occasionally descend steeply to the left; they typically lead to water sources. In another .6 mile, cross Colerain Road. For the next 8 miles

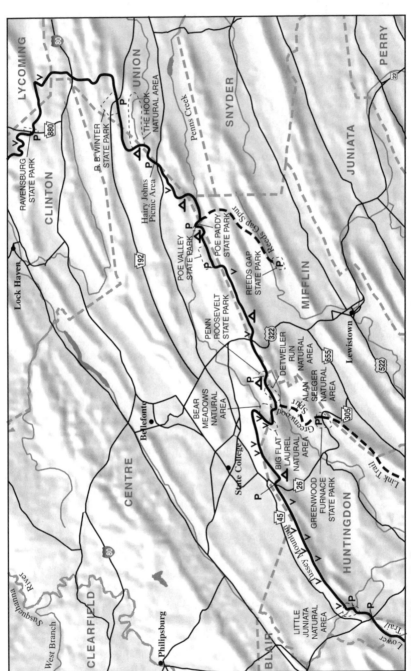

Hike 12: Mid State Trail

to Pennsylvania Furnace Road, follow the very rocky ridgetop of
Tussey Mountain; the terrain is rolling or level. You pass several excellent vistas, including Stone Towers Overlook and Top of Promontory.
One noteworthy section, before the MST crosses the Ewing Path, is an
extensive talus slope offering a series of great views to the northwest.
Although rocky and rugged, the awesome views and isolation make
for a great backpacking experience.

Cross Pennsylvania Furnace Road and follow an old forest road to
the site of a former fire tower. Continue to follow the rocky ridgetop,
with occasional views. In 1.5 miles, cross Indian Steps Trail. This trail
to the right leads down the side of the mountain over several stone
steps; it is not known who constructed them. Continue along the
ridgetop for 2 miles, with more views, until the trail crosses PA 26,
with a large parking area, and reaches Jo Hays Vista overlooking State
College. The blue-blazed Jackson Trail continues to follow the rocky
ridgeline with views; this 2.8-mile trail rejoins the MST and can be
used as a shortcut if you don't need water or camping. The MST turns
right and descends 700 feet over .8 mile into the valley carved by
Shaver Creek. At the bottom, the blue-blazed Ironstone Loop joins
from the right; turn left and proceed gradually up the valley for 1.8
miles, passing springs and campsites; Shaver Creek is off to your right.
The trail begins an ascent, leveling off along the side of the mountain
before making a steep 400-foot climb over .3 mile to the ridgeline of
Tussey Mountain; Jackson Trail joins from the left.

For the next 4 miles, the trail follows the rocky, rugged ridgetop of
Tussey Mountain, with several fine views. Cross the Sand Spring Trail,
which you can follow a mile to the left to Sand Spring. Soon thereafter,
a cross-country ski trail meets the MST from the right. Pass a gate and
cross Laurel Run Road. Then follow another dirt road for .6 mile to the
Little Flat fire tower, in a spruce grove with partial views to the north.
Enter thick mountain laurel and follow the rocky crest of Fourth
Mountain for 2 miles across rocky terrain, with several nice vistas off
to your left. The spectacular Indian Wells Vista offers a tremendous
panorama of Bear Meadows and the surrounding mountains. Tunnel
through thick mountain laurel and pass a blue-blazed side trail to the
right, leading to reliable Keith Spring and a view .2 mile away. Continue through the thick laurel of Big Flat Laurel Natural Area. Cross
the junction of North Meadows and Gettis Roads.

Descend steeply toward Bear Meadows; the MST soon turns right,
but a blue-blazed trail descends to water and the natural area. The

MST gradually ascends along the flank of the mountains and crosses the blue-blazed Gettis Trail in a shallow gap. Ascend over a knob of Thickhead Mountain and descend to Bear Meadows Road. Cross the road and descend 400 feet over .5 mile, and you reach Bear Meadows Road once again. Turn left on the road and follow it for .3 mile, until the trail bears right, leaving the road and making a short, steep ascent to beautiful Detweiler Run and the Greenwood Spur. Here you'll find reliable water and small campsites. The MST turns left and for the next 2.8 miles proceeds upstream along Detweiler Run, a highlight of the trail. Here you pass through the Detweiler Run Natural Area, with thick rhododendron and primeval old-growth forest—a truly beautiful place. Tunnel through thick rhododendron and hemlocks. Campsites can be found at a pipeline swath. Eventually the rhododendron diminish and hardwoods predominate. The MST turns right and makes a short, rocky climb away from Detweiler Run.

At the top, cross gated, grassy Thickhead Mountain Road. After a short period of level hiking, begin a steep and rocky descent to Penn Roosevelt State Park, dropping 500 feet over .6 mile. Penn Roosevelt is a small, beautiful, isolated state park offering a small lake, primitive campground, parking, and water. There is no park office, so if you want to camp here, you must self-register and pay a fee. A Civilian Conservation Corps camp was located here in the 1930s and was one of twelve African-American camps in Pennsylvania. A monument stands in honor of those who served. The MST climbs out of the state park, ascending 500 feet over .8 mile up Broad Mountain. Pass Trico, where Mifflin, Centre, and Huntingdon Counties meet. The trail is level or rolling for 1.5 miles, as it descends gradually into a saddle and passes the Muttersbaugh Trail. This side trail descends .7 mile to the right and reaches Muttersbaugh Gap, where reliable water can be found. The MST follows the crest of Bald Mountain, with views for a mile, then descends steeply to a grassy old forest road. Gradually descend to US 322, passing Twin Springs and a small stream. The MST goes through a culvert under US 322. The highway does not offer suitable trailhead parking.

Section Three: US 322 to Hairy Johns Picnic Area (PA 45)

This section offers numerous views, scenic streams, isolation, gorges, and glens, making the MST one of the finest trails in the state. Because the MST spends relatively little time along the ridgetops, and crosses against the grain of the ridges, water sources are more frequent.

Begin a steep, rocky climb up Long Mountain, passing side trails to the left that lead to the roadside rest area along US 322. Reaching the crest of the mountain, you pass Big Valley Vista, offering a beautiful view of the Laurel Creek Reservoir and Milligan Knob. This vista is featured on the cover of the MST's 2001 *Guidebook, 10th edition*. For the next 1.3 miles, follow the level crest of Long Mountain, passing occasional views to the south. Begin a steep and very rugged 450-foot descent over .5 mile into Stillhouse Hollow. Bear right onto Stillhouse Hollow Road and cross Lingle Stream. Follow the road for .4 mile, and turn left along an old grade by Greens Valley Stream. For the next 4.5 miles, the MST gradually ascends Greens Valley along the stream, with campsites and water. At the head of the valley, reach the crest of Front Mountain and cross the Siglerville-Millheim Pike, a dirt forest road often used by the local Amish population.

For the next mile, the trail is level; headwaters to Panther Creek are off to your left. The trail turns left, crosses Panther Creek, and begins a steep 350-foot descent over .4 mile into Little Poe Valley. Cross Little Poe Creek and turn right on an old forest road. The trail gradually descends 1.5 mile down the valley; the creek is off to your right. The MST turns left and makes a short ascent to the crest of Little Poe Mountain, where it turns right along the ridgetop. Hunters Path descends straight ahead .4 mile to Poe Valley State Park, which features a lake, beach, seasonal water and telephone, and campsites for a fee. The MST follows the crest of Little Poe Mountain and descends to Little Poe Creek and Road. Then it begins a 600-foot climb over .7 mile to the rocky, rugged ridgetop of Long Mountain, offering several nice views. The trail then steeply descends via switchbacks 600 feet over .6 mile to scenic, isolated Poe Paddy State Park, offering parking, restrooms, water, telephone, and shelters and campsites for a fee. The blue-blazed Reeds Gap Spur joins from the right. Nearby is beautiful Penns Creek, known for its incredible green drake hatches in spring and fine trout fishing. The creek twists and turns through its rugged gorge.

Cross Big Poe Creek and follow the road for .4 mile past cabins. The trail turns right and crosses Penns Creek via an old railroad bridge. The trail then enters a 200-foot tunnel through Paddy Mountain. For the next 3 miles, follow the level, wide railroad grade, with views of Penns Creek and the surrounding mountains. Bikes and horses are also permitted on this grade. Turn left, leaving the grade and climb along a private property line. Descend to and cross scenic Cherry Run. When you reach Cherry Run Road, turn left and follow the road for .8 mile, until the MST makes a sharp left onto Old Mingle Road. The trail then makes a sharp right and climbs into a scenic glen, with hemlocks and a small, cascading stream. Here you will find nice campsites. Climb gradually out of the glen through mountain laurel, pass a cabin off to your left, and cross Rupp Hollow Road. Ascend more steeply along an old forest road to the top of Thick Mountain. After a short period of level hiking, you pass a partial view to the north overlooking Woodward.

Descend gradually to the headwaters of Bear Run, where you'll find seep springs. The MST makes a sharp left turn and begins a gradual and increasingly rocky climb back to the crest of Thick Mountain, where there are nice views to the north and south from talus slopes. The trail then makes a short, steep descent to Woodward Road, with a spring to your right. Level and rolling terrain follows for almost 2 miles. You then pass the blue-blazed Bear Gap Trail to your right, which leads to camping in .2 mile and water in .3 mile. In another 1.3 mile, you cross PA 45 and reach the Hairy Johns Picnic Area, named after John Voneida, a hermit who once lived here. If you park at the picnic area, be sure to notify Bald Eagle State Forest personnel.

Section Four: Hairy Johns Picnic Area
(PA 45) to R. B. Winter State Park

Pass through the picnic area and a spring; begin a gradual ascent that steepens as the trail reaches the crest of Winklebleck Mountain. This is a 600-foot climb over a mile from the picnic area. At the top, pass a view and follow the ridgetop of the mountain to the right. Descend off the mountain and cross Sheesley Run. When you reach Stony Run Road, turn right, passing Cinder Pile Spring to your left. Follow the road for a short distance before the trail turns left, leaving the road, and begins a steep 350-foot climb over .4 mile to the top of Buffalo Mountain. The trail levels and passes the headwaters of Buffalo Creek. The MST makes a short, somewhat steep descent and crosses a gated forest road. Beginning here, for about a mile, the trail is the western boundary of The Hook Natural Area, the largest in Pennsylvania; as a result, no camping is permitted to the east of the trail. The trail descends into a shallow hollow, passing the seasonal headwaters of the North Branch of Buffalo Creek. Climb gently and reach the ridge of Sharpback Mountain. A steep but short descent follows through hemlocks, and the trail crosses Pine Creek, with camping to the right.

Cross Pine Creek Road before the trail begins a steep 300-foot climb over .3 mile to the crest of Buck Ridge. The trail passes an intermittent stream and climbs gradually to Stover Run Road. Descend on the road, passing Horse Path Spring. Follow the road for .5 mile, until you reach the switchback, where the MST bears right. For the next 4 miles, the terrain is rolling as the trail follows Brush Mountain. The trail passes two hollows, where springs can be found. Descend gradually to PA 192 and R. B. Winter State Park. This scenic park features a lake, parking, telephone, water, restrooms, and camping for a fee. Contact the park office if you plan to leave a car here overnight.

Section Five: R. B. Winter State Park
to Ravensburg State Park

This isolated stretch of trail continues the roller-coaster climbs and descents over the tangled ridges that dominate the terrain in this section of the state. There are generally sufficient water sources along this section. The MST often crosses, and at times follows, sections of the red-blazed Central Mountains Shared-Use Trails System, an interconnected 120-mile trail network open to hikers, horseback riders, and mountain bikers.

Cross PA 192, pass near a scenic stone dam, and cross a paved park road. The trail gradually ascends Bake Oven Mountain and crosses a pipeline swath with views. Continue along the ridge; off to your left is Halfway Run Natural Area. The trail crosses Boyer Gap Road underneath hardwoods and begins a gradual ascent toward Sand Mountain. The trail turns left and crosses Sand Mountain Road, then reaches a gated fire tower.

Descend 400 feet over .5 mile into a valley carved by Spruce Run. Gradually ascend the valley before the trail turns right and crosses the run with campsites. Climb gradually out of the valley, entering a hollow before the MST turns left to make a slight ascent to the ridge of Naked Mountain. Descend from the ridge into a scenic gap, with a spring and potential camping. Continue the descent, which steepens, as the trail enters the scenic valley carved by White Deer Creek, a sizable scenic stream with campsites nearby. Cross the creek over a footbridge, climb to and cross White Deer Creek Road, and begin a steeper 320-foot climb over .5 mile into another glen with water. The trail crests and gradually descends to another dirt forest road. Continue the easy descent to paved Sugar Valley Narrows Road and turn left, following the road as it crosses over I-80.

The MST follows the road .2 mile farther, then it bears right onto Zimmerman Road. The trail quickly turns left to gradually ascend along the side of a hill. The terrain levels as you cross an old forest road and begin a 400-foot climb over .5 mile to Tea Knob. Descend gradually from the knob, cross Zimmerman Road again, and make a short climb over a ridge. Descend more steeply to a pipeline swath, which the trail follows to the left. Pass a blue-blazed side trail and Gas Line Spring, with camping, to your left. Continue to follow the swath across a small stream and, soon thereafter, Mohn Mill Road. Over another mile of rolling terrain, follow the swath across Pipeline Road. Bear right, leaving the road and swath, and descend slightly to Fourth Gap Road, which the trail crosses. Cross a small, seasonal stream and begin a 360-foot climb over .5 mile to South White Deer Ridge; the climb steepens as you near the top. Bear right along the ridge and pass a nice view to the south; the terrain is rocky and rugged.

Leave the ridge to the left and cross Walters Road. Now you begin an 800-foot descent over .9 mile to Cove Road. This is a long, taxing descent that is steep in sections. Cross Cove Road and descend to White Deer Hole Creek. Cross the creek and ascend the other side of the valley; turn left onto an old grade. After .6 mile, turn left onto Dunbar Road, followed by a right turn along White Deer Hole Creek, and pass a spring. Begin a gradual 700-foot climb over 1.3 miles up this rocky valley. Cross Kalbfleish Road as well as a pipeline swath. The trail then passes the site of a fire tower and follows the level crest of White Deer Ridge, with views north into Nippenose Valley. Nippenose is a unique geologic feature—a limestone valley almost completely encircled by mountains. Virtually all the streams that enter the valley from the surrounding mountains disappear into a labyrinth of caves in the valley's floor. These streams resurface as the state's largest spring to form Antes Creek, which passes through a water gap and empties into the West Branch of the Susquehanna River.

The trail drops 660 feet over a mile; the descent is steep in sections. Cross the juncture of Kalbfleish, Krape, and Sand Spring Roads. Gradually ascend, pass Sand Spring, and follow the edge of the plateau, along the state forest boundary. Make a steep 350-foot descent over .3 mile into Ravensburg State Park. This trail turns right onto PA 880, then leaves it to follow scenic Rauchtown Run to the right. It rejoins with PA 880, passing a parking area on the other side of the road. To your left is Castle Rock, an impressive rock formation with spires of sandstone. Ravensburg is a small park located in a narrow gorge surrounded by rock outcrops and talus slopes. It features campsites for a fee, water, restrooms, parking, and picnic facilities.

The park is managed by R. B. Winter State Park, so staff are not always present. If you plan to park here, contact R. B. Winter State Park in advance. Pass Thousand Steps Trail off to the right; unlike the Thousand Steps located along the Link Trail, most of these steps are missing. Follow Rauchtown Run downstream, pass the park office, and cross PA 880.

Section Six: Ravensburg State Park to Woolrich Factory Outlet

The MST follows the Falling Springs Trail for a short distance before it bears right and skirts the side of the plateau along an old grade. The trail continues to follow the curve along the flank of the plateau and stays near the state forest boundary. It crosses Shaw Mountain Road and descends to a small stream with camping. Then it turns left and begins a steep climb to the top of the plateau along a small stream. This is a 400-foot climb over .4 mile. At the top, the MST turns right and begins a mild ascent, followed by a slight descent. Bear right onto Ramm Road and follow it over a mile along the crest of Nippenose Valley, with one view of the valley. Turn left, leaving the road, and follow the state forest boundary again; the trail turns right and crosses Bixel Road, a gated forest road. A gradual 400-foot descent over .9 mile follows, as the trail enters a glen carved by small Yarns Run, where campsites and water can be found.

Turn left and begin a 600-foot climb over a mile to Round Top; the climb becomes more steep at the top. The trail curves around to the north side of the summit, where talus slopes offer an excellent vista to the north over the valley and Pine Creek. The West Branch of the Susquehanna River flows 1,100 feet below. A long and at times steep 900-foot descent over a mile follows as the trail drops into the rugged, scenic glen of Henry Run. Climb up the other bank; the trail follows a series of roads down to the West Branch of the Susquehanna. Pass a historical sign for Fort Horn and follow a road along the river. As you near the bridge, pass the former site of a Delaware Indian village. Scramble up a road embankment and cross the river along SR 1005. Turn right off the bridge and continue to follow roads, passing ruins of the Pennsylvania Canal. The remaining 2 miles of trail to the Woolrich Factory Outlet follows roads and passes through sections of private property. It is possible that the MST may end up completely on roads here as a result of development. Follow roads to the Woolrich Factory Outlet.

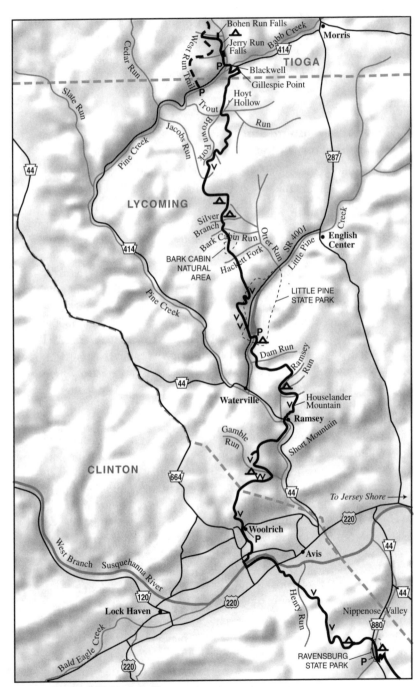

Hike 12: Mid State Trail

Section Seven: Woolrich Factory Outlet
to Little Pine State Park

The trail follows roads and passes through private property. After .2 mile, you hike through private land with a No Trespassing sign, which does not apply to hikers. For the next mile, the trail gradually ascends through fields and more private property; pass through as quickly and discreetly as possible. Climb a ridge and the trail enters the small glen of a stream; climb up the side of the glen. Soon thereafter, the MST enters the Tiadaghton State Forest. Cross over the crest and gradually descend into the glen of Big Spring Branch. Proceed upstream, pass Big Spring to the right, and cross Big Spring Road.

The remainder of the MST traverses the Pine Creek Gorge region, one of Pennsylvania's most scenic areas. Not surprisingly, this is also one of the most—if not *the* most—scenic section of the MST. I have always heard backpackers praise this section of trail, and it's easy to see why. Here you will find the incredible Pine Creek Gorge, countless side glens and gorges, beautiful mountain streams, excellent camping, incredible views, waterfalls, and isolation. It is here that the trail transforms from a rocky ridge trail to a plateau trail. Here the MST is not as rocky, but the ascents and descents are steeper and longer, separated by periods of level hiking. Water is also more available. When backpackers think of Pine Creek, they often think of the more popular West Rim or Black Forest Trails; however, it is the MST that truly showcases the splendor of this region.

The trail is level for .7 mile, then descends into Gamble Run's gorge. This is a steep 900-foot descent over .9 mile, with great views. The trail turns left and continues the descent to beautiful Gamble Run. Cross the run and follow it upstream, passing pools, cascades, and nice campsites. The MST turns right and ascends the side glen of Schultz Fork; this is a steep 800-foot climb over .7 mile. At the top, a blue-blazed trail to the left leads to an exceptional vista of Gamble Run's gorge and Pine Creek Gorge; watch for rattlesnakes. Climb out of the glen and pass a spring and possible camping. A mild ascent follows, and the trail crosses Bull Run Road. Begin a steep 800-foot descent over .8 mile into the Pine Creek Gorge, passing boulders and rock outcrops. Turn abruptly left and follow an old grade more gradually down the side of the gorge, crossing small streams.

Continue the descent and cross Bonnell Run. The trail levels along Pine Creek and enters Camp Kline. Pass through the camp and join the rail-trail. At the Bonnell Flats canoe camping area to the left, backpackers can also camp. Cross Pine Creek along a scenic old railroad bridge and enter the village of Ramsey. Turn right onto PA 44 and follow it for a few hundred feet. Cross the road and begin the long, hard climb up Houselander Mountain, with several switchbacks. Pass through the glen of a seasonal stream with cascades. Continue to climb along rock ledges and outcrops. This is a 1,300-vertical-foot climb. At the top, the trail levels through thick mountain laurel and meets a forest road; a blue-blazed trail joins from the left. The MST used to continue along PA 44 for more than a mile before climbing Houselander Mountain, with several excellent vistas; the trail was rerouted in 2001 to avoid the long, dangerous road walk along PA 44.

The MST makes a rocky descent, and thereafter ascends into a shallow glen with a small stream. Continue the gradual ascent out of the glen, bear left, and after .5 mile of level hiking, pass a side trail to a vista of the gorge. Begin to descend steeply into the rugged, rocky glen of a side stream to Ramsey Run. The MST descends 700 feet over .7 mile to scenic Ramsey Run; bear right and follow Ramsey Run upstream along an old grade, with water and nice campsites at a fork in the glen. The run has many cascades. Gradually climb 800 feet over 1.8 miles up Ramsey Run's glen, cross Ramsey Road, and cross the top of the plateau. Bear left on an old forest road for a mile of level hiking; it was here that I saw my first bear while backpacking. When you reach the edge of Little Pine Creek Gorge along an old grade, keep an eye out for the blazes, because it's easy to keep following the grade and miss the trail turning off it to the right. The MST then descends steeply 1,100 feet over .9 mile to Dam Run, a small tributary to Little Pine Creek. Cross Dam Run Road and beautiful Dam Run with cascades and a swimming hole. The MST is level and rolling the remaining 2.5 miles to Little Pine State Park, but it follows a narrow sidehill along the steep bank above Little Pine Creek. Along the way, you have to tunnel through pine saplings underneath hemlocks and white pines. There are potential campsites at Parker Hollow Run and along Little Pine Creek, if you are willing to descend to it. Upon entering the state park, pass through the campground and cross a bridge over Little Pine Creek below the dam. Follow the park road and cross SR 4001. Little Pine is a beautiful state park offering parking, water, campsites for a fee, restrooms, and a telephone.

Section Eight: Little Pine State Park
to Blackwell and the West Rim Trail

This final section explores the plateau, streams, and glens several miles to the east of Pine Creek. The MST does not rejoin with Pine Creek until Blackwell. Unlike the previous section, the terrain is more moderate, following old grades and forest roads, with sections of flat and rolling hiking and gradual changes in elevation. The biggest climbs are at the beginning and end of this section. The MST crosses many streams and springs, and there are numerous potential campsites. This section of trail is also very isolated.

Cross SR 4001 and begin a steep 1,000-foot climb over 1.4 miles along the edge of the canyon. Pass a few views of the canyon. Reach the top of the plateau, with level hiking. The trail soon turns right and descends steeply into Wildcat Hollow; this is an 800-foot descent over .6 mile. Cross Love Run and turn left onto Love Run Road and Trail. After .3 mile, turn right off the road and climb to a nice view and a juncture with Panther Run Trail. Begin an initially steep 400-foot climb over .7 mile back up to the plateau. The trail levels and crosses Schoolhouse Road. Descend gradually into a small hollow with a stream. The trail crosses Hackett Fork and ascends the bank to cross Hackett Road.

The trail is level, then gradually descends to Ott Fork; cross this small stream and enter Bark Cabin Natural Area, with its old-growth hemlocks. Camping is not permitted in the natural area. Climb gradually and then descend gradually to Bennys Run. Follow the level contour of the plateau and cross Bark Cabin Run. Climb gradually up the plateau, cross an old forest road, and descend gradually to Silver Branch, with nice campsites. In typical fashion, a gradual climb ensues, then by level hiking, until the trail descends gradually into another glen with a small stream and campsites. The MST turns left and is level for more than a mile before crossing Okome Road. Enter Wolf Run Wild Area and descend gradually to the headwaters of Sebring Branch, with campsites. Climb gradually out of the glen, cross Barrens Road, and pass through a saddle in the plateau.

The trail continues to be level as it enters another glen and crosses a stream. Begin a gradual, mile-long ascent to the crest of Oregon Hill, with a nice view to the north. The MST initially drops steeply into another glen, a 500-foot descent over .7 mile. At the bottom, turn right above the stream; proceed downstream along an old grade. Cross Brown Fork and climb up to Brown Fork Road, a rough jeep road. Turn left onto the road and follow it for .6 mile. Turn right off the road and gradually ascend into a side glen, until the trail turns left at the top of the plateau. The MST follows rolling terrain for a mile and begins a long, gradual descent to scenic Brown Fork and Trout Run. Cross Brown Fork, then turn right to descend and cross Trout Run. Turn right to ascend Hoyt Hollow with a nearby waterfall. Continue the gradual ascent up the hollow to the source of the small stream. Cross over the top of the level plateau, and descend gradually into scenic Ashworth Hollow, with a small stream and campsite. At the bottom, turn right and follow an old grade above Big Run. Cross the run and Big Run Road; begin a gradual climb into Brill Hollow, along Brill Run. Turn left, cross the small run, and ascend more steeply to the summit of Gillespie Point, with nice views of Pine Creek Gorge. This was a 700-foot climb over a mile from Big Run Road. Gillespie Point's peak is unique in an area dominated by plateaus. The following descent is much more steep than the ascent, the trail dropping 800 feet over .8 mile to Babb Creek and the small town of Blackwell, with restaurant and hotel. Pass through town and reach a parking area to the left with restrooms, water, and telephone. Here you will find the scenic Pine Creek bike trail, Pine Creek with fine canoeing and fishing, and Pine Creek Gorge.

Cross the bridge and turn right. The trail begins to follow a steep, narrow sidehill above Pine Creek. The climb becomes more moderate as the trail traverses the side of the gorge. Enter the scenic glen of Jerry Run Falls, a 30-foot waterfall along a small stream. Cross above the falls and pick up an old grade. A blue-blazed side trail descending to the right goes down to Pine Creek and Bohen Run. It offers exceptional campsites beneath pine trees right next to Pine Creek. The MST gradually ascends along the grade and enters the beautiful, rugged, hemlock-draped glen carved by Bohen Run. Far below is gorgeous Bohen Run Falls, a narrow 60-foot waterfall. To the left, the blue-blazed side trail rejoins. Continue the ascent of Bohen Run up this beautiful glen. Soon the run, with scenic cascades, joins the trail. The MST inconspicuously ends at its juncture with the West Rim Trail along Bohen Run. Small campsites are nearby.

12a. Greenwood Spur

Length: 6.7-mile linear trail.

Duration: 1 to 2 days.

Difficulty: Moderate.

Terrain: Often rocky, with long ascent and descent over Broad Mountain.

Trail conditions: Trail is established and well blazed.

Blazes: Blue.

Water: Generally plentiful, but no reliable source on top of Broad Mountain.

Vegetation: Hemlocks and impressive rhododendron; hardwoods and mountain laurel common on Broad Mountain; old-growth forest.

Highlights: Greenwood Furnace State Park, views from Greenwood Fire Tower, Alan Seeger Natural Area, Detweiler Run Natural Area, old-growth forest, thick rhododendron.

Maintained by: Mid State Trail Association, Keystone Trails Association, volunteers.

Contact info:
Mid State Trail Association, P.O. Box 167, Boalsburg, PA 16827
Rothrock State Forest, P.O. Box 403, Rothrock Lane, Huntingdon, PA 16652; phone: 814-643-2340; e-mail: fd05@state.pa.us; website: www.dcnr.state.pa.us/forestry/stateforests/forests/rothrock/rothrock.htm.
Greenwood Furnace State Park, R.R. 2 Box 118, PA Rte. 305, Huntingdon, PA 16652-9006; phone: 814-667-1800, 888-PA-PARKS; e-mail: greenwoodfurnacesp@state.pa.us; website: www.dcnr.state.pa.us/stateparks/parks/greenwoodfurnace.asp.

Maps and guides: Both included in the Mid State Trail guide, which can be purchased from the Mid State Trail Association.

Trailhead directions:
Greenwood Furnace State Park: From US 322 and points east, take the Reedsville/PA 655 exit. Follow PA 655 to Belleville, where you turn right on PA 305 and follow it 7 miles to the park. The park is 5 miles east of McAlevys Fort, along PA 305.

The Greenwood Spur (GS) is a short trail that offers a lot of history and scenery, including two of the state's finest natural areas, Alan Seeger and Detweiler Run. It is becoming increasingly popular because it offers a great one-night trip. The GS is also a very strategic trail, connecting the Link Trail and Greenwood Furnace State Park to the Mid State Trail (MST). From here it is possible to hike south to the Appalachian Trail or north to Pine Creek Gorge, and maybe someday to the Finger Lakes Trail and the North Country Trail in New York.

Heading south to north, the trail begins in beautiful Greenwood Furnace State Park, also the northern trailhead for the Link Trail and once the location of a prosperous community that smelted iron from charcoal furnaces. The surrounding region contained the necessary ingredients of water, plentiful wood, limestone, and high-grade ore. Many historic sites are within the park, including one preserved stack, ruins of other stacks, a cemetery, the Iron Master's Mansion, and the scenic Stone Valley Church. The park has several excellent dayhikes, and campsites and showers are available for a fee. With beautiful mountain scenery and so many hiking and backpacking trails, this is a great park to visit.

From the park office, follow Broad Mountain Road past the preserved stack and over the East Branch of Standing Stone Creek. To be safe, fill your water bottles for your climb over Broad Mountain. The GS turns right, leaving the road and passing through meadows and hemlocks. Cross a small stream and continue east, passing a register. Turn left and begin the long ascent up Broad Mountain; a 1,300-foot climb over 2.5 miles. The ascent is gradual but increasingly steepens, and you begin to pass old charcoal flats. About .3 mile into the climb, you pass a good campsite on a charcoal flat on the left; about 300 feet farther west is a good spring. Continue to climb the increasingly steep terrain, with switchbacks. The trial often follows old forest and wagon roads. As you near the top, the ascent becomes more gradual. Upon reaching Seeger Road, turn right and follow for a short distance before turning left along the Telephone Trail and its powerline swath. If hiking here on a hot, sunny day, you may come across a rattlesnake, as I did the first time I hiked this trail.

You then reach the top of Broad Mountain and the Greenwood Fire Tower, which can be climbed and affords exceptional views, especially to the east. An open, grassy glade surrounds the tower and offers a nice campsite, but with no water source. The GS bears left and enters the forest along the Johnson Trail. Here you'll find thick mountain laurel, hardwoods, and hemlocks. At first the descent is gradual, but it soon becomes very steep, with switchbacks. The total descent is 1,400 feet over 1.8 miles. Cross Seeger Road and descend straight down. The ravine to the right usually has a running spring. The descent becomes more gradual through a scenic hemlock forest, until you cross Seeger Road once again and enter the exceptional Alan Seeger Natural Area,

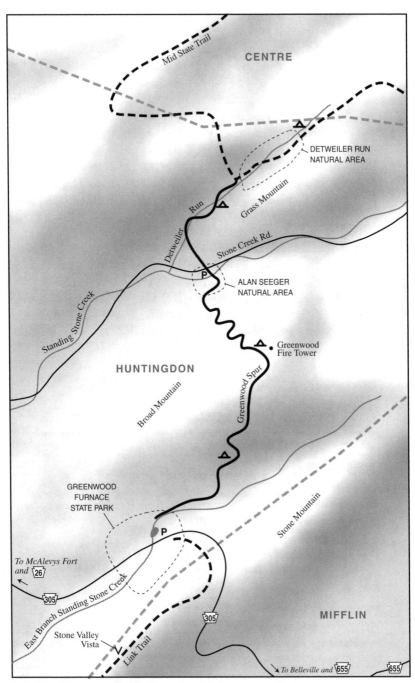

Hike 12a: Greenwood Spur

which features old-growth forest, massive trees, thick rhododendron tunnels, and scenic Standing Stone Creek. Camping and blazes are prohibited in the natural area, but the trail is clearly established and signed. This is a great place to take a break and explore.

After passing through the natural area, cross Stone Creek Road, and the blazes reappear. Follow an old grade through hardwoods until you near beautiful Detweiler Run, with its thick hemlocks and tunnels of rhododendron. The remainder of the GS follows the run upstream until it meets the MST. Cross the stream, pass behind a cabin, then cross the stream again. The trail crosses the stream yet again; this juncture may be confusing because the blazes are hard to see. A few campsites can be found here before the trail meets the MST. To the left, the MST climbs to Detweiler Road, and to the right, it enters the exceptional Detweiler Run Natural Area, with scenery similar to that of Alan Seeger. The MST follows Detweiler Run almost to its source (about 3 miles from the northern end of the GS), with thick rhododendron and hemlocks in an isolated setting. It's a beautiful place to explore.

A great weekend backpacking trip is to hike the MST from PA 26 to Detweiler Run Natural Area, and then follow the GS to Greenwood Furnace State Park. These trails offer great views and scenery, with a very convenient shuttle along PA 305 and PA 26.

12b. Reeds Gap Spur

Length: 13.85-mile linear trail.

Duration: 1 to 2 days.

Difficulty: Moderate to difficult.

Terrain: Terrain is often very rocky and steep; the trail cuts across ridges and valleys, requiring several climbs. Ascents and descents range from 200 to 1,100 feet.

Trail conditions: Blazes may be faded and infrequent. Trail is unestablished and brushy in many sections, so long pants are advisable. Isolated hiking.

Blazes: Blue.

Water: Generally sufficient, but there is no water between Reeds Gap and Bear Gap, so carry sufficient containers.

Vegetation: Valleys and gaps dominated by hemlocks, pines, and rhododendron; ridges dominated by oaks, hardwoods, and mountain laurel.

Highlights: Isolation, scenic mountain streams, hemlocks and mountain laurel, Penns Creek, Reeds Gap State Park, Poe Paddy State Park, rock outcrops, extensive talus slopes.

Maintained by: Formerly maintained by the Mid State Trail Association.

Contact info:
Mid State Trail Association, P.O. Box 167, Boalsburg, PA 16827
Bald Eagle State Forest, Box 147, Laurelton, PA 17835; phone: 570-922-3344; e-mail: fd07@state.pa.us; website: www.dcnr.state.pa.us/forestry/ stateforests/forests/baldeagle/baldeagle.htm.
Reeds Gap State Park, 1405 New Lancaster Valley Rd., Milroy, PA 17063-9735; phone: 717-667-3622; e-mail: reedsgapsp@state.pa.us; website: www.dcnr.state.pa.us/stateparks/parks/reedsgap.asp.
Poe Paddy State Park, c/o Reeds Gap State Park, 1405 New Lancaster Valley Rd., Milroy, PA 17063-9735; phone: 717-667-3622; e-mail: reedsgapsp@ state.pa.us; website: www.dcnr.state.pa.us/stateparks/parks/poepaddy.asp.

Maps and guides: Both included in the Mid State Trail guide, which can be purchased from the Mid State Trail Association.

Trailhead directions:
Reeds Gap State Park: From the Milroy exit along US 322, the park is 7 miles. Follow road signs to the park.
Poe Valley and Poe Paddy State Parks: These parks are located in an isolated area of the Seven Mountains. No road that leads to these parks is entirely paved. From the juncture of PA 144 and US 322 at Potters Mills, proceed east on US 322 for about 1.5 miles. Turn left onto a dirt forest road and follow for 10 miles to Poe Valley State Park. To reach Poe Paddy, continue an additional 3.5 miles on Poe Valley Road.

The Reeds Gap Spur (RGS) connects Reeds Gap State Park to the Mid State Trail at Poe Paddy State Park. This scenic trail is isolated, rarely hiked, and located within the Bald Eagle State Forest. Almost the entire trail is within beautiful Mifflin County, with its sizable Amish population, impressive valleys, steep ridges, and numerous caves. This trail offers a taste of the Seven Mountains and the state's beautiful ridge and valley region. Unfortunately, the Mid State Trail Association may abandon the RGS and no longer maintains it. If you would like to help maintain this short, demanding trail, contact Reeds Gap State Park or Bald Eagle State Forest.

Heading south to north, the trail begins in Reeds Gap State Park and New Lancaster Valley, one of several valleys throughout the region that are separated by nearly uniform ridges. Follow the access road and ascend into Reeds Gap; to your right is small Reeds Gap Run. At the park boundary, pass the Flicker Path to your left and the Blue Jay Trail to your right. Enter the woods along the remnants of an old logging road, then enter scenic Reeds Gap, with large boulders, rock outcrops, hemlocks, rhododendron, and cascades. The trail bears right and then left as it ascends along a small stream with a few small campsites. The trail turns right on Knob Ridge Road, following the road for .25 mile. Get as much water as you can here, because there will be no water sources for almost 6 miles before descending into Bear Gap.

Bear left off the road and follow an old forest road up to High Top. This is a 750-foot climb over .7 mile, and the trail becomes increasingly steeper as you near the top. At High Top, bear right onto a jeep road; the summit has satellite and microwave towers. For the next 5 miles, the RGS follows the crest of Thick Mountain. The terrain is level but often rocky. Turn left where the trail drops from the ridgetop into Bear Gap; High Top Trail continues straight along the ridgetop. Like Reeds Gap, Bear Gap is rugged, with large boulders, talus slopes, hemlocks, and a small stream that often disappears under the numerous rocks. The trail descends along an old forest road, and the surrounding terrain is very rocky. The descent becomes more moderate as you leave Bear Gap and pass some possible campsites near Bear Gap Run. Continue your descent through Chestnut Gap, with more potential camping and rock outcrops, and cross Bear Gap Run. The trail passes hemlocks, rhododendron, and a hunting camp to your right, then reaches Bear Gap Picnic Area along Red Ridge Road. No camping is permitted at the picnic area.

Bear left onto Treaster Valley Road and cross the bridge over scenic Treaster Run. Bear right onto an old forest road and proceed east. For the next 1.8 miles, the terrain is level as the RGS heads upstream along Treaster Valley; hemlocks and rhododendron become more common. Turn right onto Old Camp Road, pass a hunting camp, and cross Strong Mountain Road. Campsites can be found along Treaster Run, but you can hear the occasional car on Treaster Valley Road off to the right.

The trail turns left and follows the Long Path up and over Treaster Mountain. This is a 300-foot climb over .25 mile that becomes steeper as you ascend, and the terrain is rocky. Descend to Little Weikert Run, with potential camping. This run may become dry during drought. Cross the run and begin a steep, rocky climb over Strong Mountain, a 360-foot climb over .3 mile. Descend again to Weikert Run, a scenic

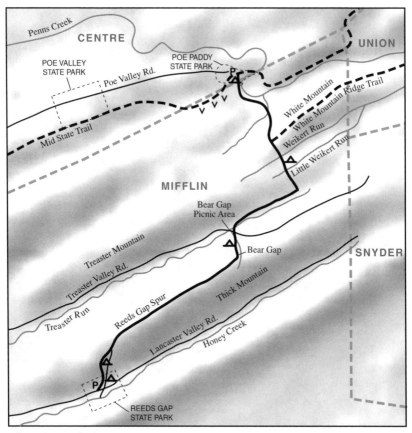

Hike 12b: Reeds Gap Spur

stream with potential camping. Unlike the climb, this is a 600-foot descent over .6 mile. Cross the stream, cross Longwell Draft Road, and in typical fashion, climb another ridge. The southwest flank of White Mountain stands before you—a very steep, rocky, 750-foot climb over .6 mile. At the top, you pass the White Mountain Ridge Trail to your right; this isolated trail explores the impressive thickets of mountain laurel that cover White Mountain, a worthwhile trip in June when the laurel is in bloom. Now begins a 1,100-foot descent over about 1 mile. At first the descent is very steep and rocky, but it gradually becomes more manageable. Near the bottom, you pass a cabin and cross scenic Swift Run. Bear right onto Swift Run Road and follow it through the run's water gap, with talus slopes, rock outcrops, and rhododendron. The road bears left high above beautiful Penns Creek. Cross Panther Creek and enter Poe Paddy State Park, with restrooms, piped water, and phone. This park also features trail shelters and campsites close to Penns Creek, but you must pay a fee to use them. Penns Creek is known for its excellent trout fishing and incredible fly hatches, and it's a popular stream for tubing and even kayaking when the water is high enough. The rugged scenery that surrounds Poe Paddy is very beautiful. The RGS ends at its juncture with the Mid State Trail at Poe Paddy.

North-Central Pennsylvania: Pine Creek Gorge and the Allegheny Plateau

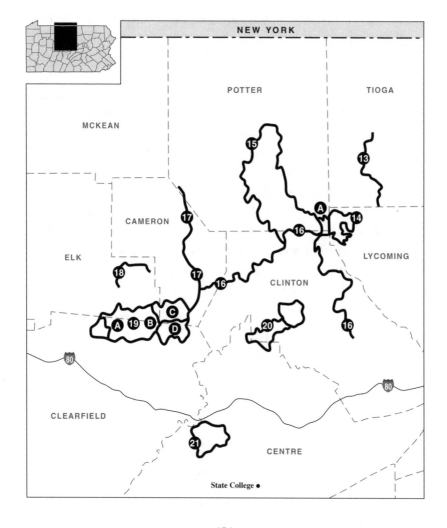

North-central Pennsylvania features the most isolated and expansive forestlands between New York City and Chicago, with more than a million acres of state-owned land, great natural beauty, numerous backpacking trails, countless dayhiking opportunities, plentiful wildlife, and sylvan isolation. In other words, this is one of the great backpacking destinations in the eastern United States.

The trails here explore the vast Allegheny Plateau, with steep climbs and descents through hollows, glens, gorges, and canyons carved by streams. These climbs and descents are separated by periods of level hiking where the trails traverse the top of the plateau. If you are looking for isolation, this is the place for you.

Here you'll find the awesome Pine Creek Gorge. At 50 miles in length and reaching nearly 1,400 feet deep, this gorge is the greatest of any in the eastern United States. Pine Creek was one of the original rivers to be considered for the National Scenic Rivers system; it is currently a state scenic river. This great stream features fine fishing, canoeing, mild whitewater, and incredible scenery. One of the nation's most scenic rails-to-trails straddles Pine Creek for much of its length. Many side streams enter Pine Creek amid beautiful waterfalls and cascades. Two of Pine Creek's famed tributaries, Slate and Cedar Runs, feature great trout fishing, their own impressive gorges, and unmatched scenery.

These numerous backpacking trail systems are your ticket to explore this region's expansive, wild, and incredible natural beauty.

🚶🚶 13. West Rim Trail

Length: 30.5-mile linear trail.

Duration: 2 to 3 days.

Difficulty: Moderate.

Terrain: One significant climb of 1,100 feet from the southern trailhead, where the trail ascends the plateau. Mostly level or rolling, often with mild descents into shallow hollows or glens of side streams to the gorge. Elevation changes on the plateau range from 50 to 300 feet and are typically mild. Trail often follows old forest roads. Several rock outcrops along trail. The northern end of the trail features a more gradual slope than the southern end.

Trail conditions: Trail is established and well blazed. Can be rocky and wet in sections. Stinging nettles are a problem in a few places.

Blazes: Orange; side access trails blue.

Water: Generally plentiful during years with normal precipitation; some small streams may dry up during drought.

Vegetation: Northern hardwoods dominate, with understory of mountain laurel; hemlocks and white pines more prevalent near streams; occasional red pine plantations and open meadows.

Highlights: Pine Creek Gorge, Pine Creek, excellent vistas, Colton Point State Park, Barbour Rock, small mountain streams, off-trail waterfalls, nice campsites

Maintained by: Tioga State Forest, volunteers.

Contact info:
Tioga State Forest, One Nessmuk Lane, Wellsboro, PA 16901; phone: 570-724-2868; e-mail: fd16@state.pa.us; websites: www.dcnr.state.pa.us/forestry/stateforests/forests/tioga/tioga.htm, www.dcnr.state.pa.us/forestry/hiking/westrim.htm, www.kta-hike.org.
Pine Creek Outfitters, R.R. 4 Box 130B, Wellsboro, PA 16901; phone: 570-724-3003; e-mail: pinecrk@clarityconnect.com; website: www.pinecrk.com.

Maps and guides: Both available for sale; free map also available from Tioga State Forest.

Trailhead directions:
Southern terminus (Blackwell and Rattlesnake Rocks): Blackwell is 5.3 miles west on PA 414 from PA 287 at Morris, and 16 miles west on PA 414 from US 15. Rattlesnake Rocks is an additional 2 miles west of Blackwell on PA 414, or about 4 miles east of Cedar Run.
Northern terminus: Follow US 6 west from Wellsboro for 11 miles to Ansonia, and make a left after Twin Pine Tavern onto Colton Road. Follow for .6 mile to parking on left.

The popular West Rim Trail (WRT) traverses the west rim of the spectacular Pine Creek Gorge, one of the largest and deepest of any in the eastern United States. Most people hike from south to north, leaving their cars in Ansonia and hiring a shuttle from Pine Creek Outfitters to the south trailhead at Rattlesnake Rocks. Expect company on this trail during summer, fall, and holiday weekends.

You may also choose to begin this hike from Blackwell along the Mid State Trail (MST), where you will pass beautiful Jerry Run Falls, Bohen Run Falls, and Bohen Run. There is an excellent campsite along Pine Creek, accessed by a blue-blazed side trail. The MST joins the WRT at the top of Bohen Run's glen.

Beginning at the Rattlesnake Rocks trailhead, cross PA 414 and pass through a field. Enter the forest near Lloyd Run, a small, scenic stream. You'll find a trail register, nice campsites, and sizable white pines. The WRT now begins the long and increasingly steep ascent up Lloyd Run's glen, with white pines and hemlocks. As the trail nears the top of the plateau and the head of the glen, the terrain becomes steeper, with rock outcrops. This is a 1,100-foot ascent over 1.6 miles, by far the most difficult section of the WRT. At the top, the trail becomes level, following old forest roads, and crosses West Rim Road. Begin a slight descent to small Jerry Run and follow the edge of the run's glen until you reach a vista of the gorge, Blackwell, and Gillespie Point. Proceed north and begin a gradual descent to Bohen Run and the northern terminus of the Mid State Trail, the longest trail in the state. Here you'll find water and a small campsite. Bohen Run features nice waterfalls and cascades along the MST. Virtually every small stream the WRT crosses has beautiful waterfalls as it descends to Pine Creek. Because the terrain into the gorge is so steep and treacherous, it is impossible to route the WRT near these waterfalls.

Cross Bohen Run and begin a mild ascent up a small side stream. The trail reaches the edge of Bohen Run's glen and passes a partial vista. Turn left away from the glen and continue north, passing rock outcrops and a small open area. Descend gradually to the head of Dillon Hollow, a small stream with camping. The trail crosses the stream, turns right, nears the edge of the gorge, and then turns left and heads north for .5 mile. It then bears left and begins a gradual descent to Steel Hollow, with water and camping. The blue-blazed Steel Trail joins from the left; this .6-mile-long trail accesses West Rim Road. Cross the stream, bear right, and begin a gradual climb out of Steel Hollow. The WRT bears left near the edge of the gorge; a short side

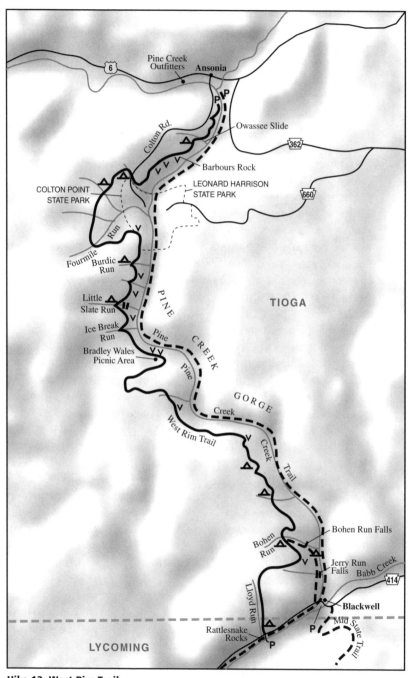

Hike 13: West Rim Trail

trail to the right leads to a vista of the gorge and Pine Island Run on the east rim. After another mile, the trail makes another gradual descent into Gundigut Hollow. The blue-blazed Gundigut Trail, a .5-mile-long access trail to West Rim Road, joins from the left.

The WRT turns right and gradually ascends out of Gundigut Hollow to the gorge rim, with views from rock outcrops. Turn left and ascend along the rim for .4 mile, and then bear right and make a gradual descent. The trail levels off and crosses seasonal streambeds for a mile before reaching another fine vista, rock outcrops, and Falling Springs the highest waterfall in the gorge, at several hundred feet. The waterfall can be seen from below along Pine Creek, but it is fed by a very small stream that disappears in summer. The trail begins a mild descent and leaves the rim. Descend and cross Good Springs Run, a seasonal stream. The trail follows a sidehill along the hollow and again crosses the stream with campsites. Begin a gradual climb away from Good Springs Run and ascend the plateau. After a mile, the trail circumvents a wet beaver meadow and crosses Fahnestock Run, a tributary to Cedar Run. Turn right onto West Rim Road and follow it for .5 mile, then turn right off the road and pass a good spring.

The trail passes along a spruce plantation, winds through a mixed-hardwood forest, and picks up an old forest road. Descend to Straight Creek, with campsites. Cross the creek and climb to the Bradley Wales Picnic Area, with several great vistas of the Pine Creek Gorge. The northern half of the WRT from Bradley Wales is more scenic, with several excellent vistas and beautiful hemlock-shaded glens.

Parking and water are available at the picnic area. For the next mile, the trail descends gradually to Ice Break Run, only to turn right and climb out of the glen back to the gorge rim with a nice vista. The blue-blazed Ice Break Trail, a .7 mile connector trail to Painter-Leetonia Road, joins from the left. In typical fashion, the trail begins another gradual descent, passing a vista, along the steep glen carved by Little Slate Run, a beautiful stream with waterfalls and cascades downstream. Cross the run, where you'll find water and excellent camping. The WRT gradually climbs away from the run and once again returns to the rim of the gorge. Follow the rim closely, passing views and crossing tiny Tumbling Run, a seasonal stream. Return again to the rim with more fine vistas, before bearing left to gradually descend to Horse Run, with water and camping. Ascend gradually out of the hollow to the rim, with another nice vista of the gorge, and bear left again to begin another gradual descent to Burdic Run. The blue-blazed Siemans Trail joins from the left; a nice campsite is off to your left. This .7-mile trail connects with Painter-Leetonia Road and with the WRT, offering a 2-mile shortcut. Potential camping can be found .2 mile along Siemans Trail, to your left. To your right, Burdic Run plunges down the gorge, creating an 80-foot waterfall along the gorge wall; it is very difficult to reach this waterfall.

Cross and ascend from Burdic Run and return to the rim. For the next mile, the trail is mostly level. Reach a vista of the gorge and Fourmile Run's steep, rugged glen. This is a glen of fantastic beauty, with several waterfalls, deep pools, thick hemlocks, and plentiful trout. President Teddy Roosevelt enjoyed fishing and staying at a cabin along Fourmile Run. The WRT does not access the glen; instead, the trail goes around it. Here the trail begins a big semicircle where it leaves the rim and circumvents Fourmile Run's glen and Colton Point State Park. Leave the rim of the glen and begin a mild ascent, following old forest roads, for about 1.3 miles, reaching Painter-Leetonia Road and Siemans Trail. Cross the road and descend via switchbacks to Thompson Hollow Road. Follow the road for about .4 mile; to your left is Fourmile Run. The WRT makes a 350-foot ascent over .5 mile, and then a steeper descent to Painter-Leetonia Road. Cross the road and make another steep but short descent to the Right Branch of Fourmile Run. Ascend and cross Colton Road. The trail follows the run upstream along an old forest road and passes a campsite.

Bear right away from the stream and begin a mild 160-foot ascent over .5 mile. Begin a mild descent to the headwaters of Rexford Branch, and then a short ascent to Deadman Hollow Road. The WRT is level for the next .6 mile but begins a gradual descent to Bear Run, with camping and water. Pass through a red pine plantation and cross Colton Road. To the right is the Colton Point State Park boundary; you can follow the road to the right to several nice vistas and the popular but difficult Turkey Trail, which descends to Pine Creek and passes near scenic waterfalls along Rexford Branch. No camping is permitted in the state park.

Cross Bear Run; off the trail, this stream features incredible waterfalls farther down in its steep glen. The trail bears to the left and follows the rim of the gorge, with several spectacular vistas. Be very careful, as the trail is close to the precipitous rim. The famous Barbours Rock offers a final, exceptional view. The blue-blazed Barbour Rock Trail connects the trail to Colton Road; it is a popular dayhike. Begin a 400-foot descent over .5 mile to Owassee Slide, a small stream. Here you'll find camping, water, and a 50-foot waterfall downstream. *Owassee* is the Iroquois word for rapids and is also the name of Pine Creek's most significant Class II + rapid. The WRT leaves Owassee Slide and begins a gradual descent along the side of the gorge, passing seasonal Matson Spring. Then it crosses Owassee Road and winds through Strap Mill Hollow, with its small stream. The northern trailhead is along Colton Road, opposite the forestry building, with plentiful parking.

14. Black Forest Trail

Length: 42-mile loop.

Duration: 2.5 to 4 days.

Difficulty: Very difficult.

Terrain: Rocky, rugged, and steep terrain. Numerous ascents and descents, ranging from 200 to 1,200 feet. Periods of level hiking across the plateau tops. Many stream crossings.

Trail conditions: Trail is established and well blazed. Brushy in sections. Stinging nettles are a problem in summer months along streams in gorges and glens. Many stream crossings without bridges.

Blazes: Orange; side trails blue.

Water: Generally plentiful.

Highlights: Exceptional vistas of Pine Creek and Slate Run Gorge, scenic mountain streams, cascades, small waterfalls, Naval Run Falls, beautiful campsites, gorges, and glens.

Vegetation: Plateaus dominated by oaks and other northern hardwoods, with thick understory of mountain laurel. Spruce plantations, hemlocks, and pine are plentiful, especially along streams.

Maintained by: Tiadaghton State Forest, volunteers.

Contact info:
Tiadaghton State Forest, 423 E. Central Ave., S. Williamsport, PA 17702; phone: 570-327-3450; e-mail: fd12@state.pa.us; websites: www.dcnr.state.pa.us/forestry/stateforests/forests/tiadaghton/tiadaghton.htm, www.dcnr.state.pa.us/forestry/hiking/black.htm, www.kta-hike.org.

Maps and guides: Can be purchased from Tiadaghton Forest Fire Fighters Association.

Trailhead directions:

PA 44 (Ruth Will Cross-Country Ski Trail): From US 220, take the Pine Creek
exit onto PA 44 north and follow for 30 miles. A parking area will be on the
right for the Ruth Will Cross-Country Ski Trail; the Black Forest Trail crosses
PA 44 just to the south. This trailhead is also 12.1 miles north of Haneyville
from the PA 44 and PA 664 juncture, along PA 44. Parking is plentiful.

PA 44 (Big Dam Hollow Road): The trail crosses PA 44 along the Lycoming and
Tioga County line, 35.2 miles north of US 220. Parking is very limited along
the road, and the trail sign is easy to miss.

Slate Run: From US 220, take the Pine Creek exit and proceed north onto PA
44 to Waterville. Just north of Waterville, bear right onto PA 414 and follow
to Slate Run. Turn left into this small village and cross Pine Creek. Turn right
and follow this road for about .5 mile to a small parking area on the right
in a pine plantation. Parking is very limited.

The Black Forest Trail (BFT) was the first trail I ever backpacked. I
borrowed my law school roommate's tent, filled my pack with
tuna and crackers, met a friend at the trailhead, and proceeded to have
an awesome—but exhausting—time. This trail taught me several les-
sons. One was not to pack cans of tuna. Canned tuna is great at home,
but it's heavy and cumbersome to carry and offers little in the way of
much-needed carbohydrates. Also, I should have chosen an easier trail
for my first trip. The BFT is widely considered to be Pennsylvania's
most difficult trail, with rocky terrain, numerous steep descents and
ascents without switchbacks, and several stream crossings. Yet the
BFT is popular because it one of the most beautiful trails in the Mid-
Atlantic, rewarding backpackers with excellent scenery for their effort.
Here you'll find breathtaking vistas of Pine Creek Gorge and the
canyons, gorges, and glens carved by Slate Run and other tributaries.
You'll also find isolation among scenic mountain streams, numerous
cascades, and abundant wildlife. When I reached one incredible vista
of Slate Run's spectacular gorge from a rock outcrop, I realized that all
of the effort and hard work had been worth it.

The Black Forest Trail is an extensive system with numerous side
and connector trails, plus trails connecting to the Susquehannock,
West Rim, and Donut Hole Trails.

There is limited parking at the BFT's traditional trailhead along
Slate Run Road. Descend through a pine plantation and reach the loop
above Slate Run. You can begin hiking in either direction, but this
description begins to the right, or counterclockwise. Continue to

descend until you reach Slate Run. This beautiful stream is known for its scenery, trout, and Class III whitewater rapids. Camping is no longer permitted where the BFT fords the run. Be careful crossing Slate Run in high water, as there is no bridge (though the construction of one is planned). After crossing, the trail bears left and begins a 1.8-mile-long ascent gaining 1,200 feet in elevation. This ascent is often steep and rocky. Near the top is a great vista from an old quarry of Slate Run Gorge. The climb begins to level off as you near the top of the plateau, dominated by hardwoods and mountain laurel.

After another mile, you pass a good spring just off the trail to your right. Level hiking continues for .75 mile farther, then the BFT suddenly makes a sharp right. Pay attention to the blazes; this turn can be easy to miss because the established Algerine Trail continues straight. For the next 3.5 miles, the BFT explores the plateau, passing exposed caprock ledges and an occasional vista when the trail nears the side of the gorge. You then reach a dry campsite and an excellent vista of Slate Run before making a very steep, rocky descent to Red Run. There are no switchbacks. Red Run is a small, scenic stream with cascades and boulders. After passing the juncture of Red Run's two branches, the BFT proceeds downstream, passing nice campsites. Follow a railroad grade to the right where the trail passes over Morris Run, amid cascades and small waterfalls. Descend to Slate Run, cross the bridge, and begin another ascent. This ascent climbs 800 feet over 1.5 miles, passing Slate Run Road and a few vistas. Near the top of the plateau, pass the Chestnut Ridge Trail to your left and follow the edge of the plateau, with more vistas of the gorges and glens of Slate Run. The BFT enters a hollow and passes a small seasonal stream with camping. For the next 3 miles, the trail follows the top of the plateau, with level terrain and more vistas. The trail intersects the Sentiero de Shay Trail and reaches PA 44.

Begin a descent along County Line Branch and again intersect the Sentiero de Shay Trail. During periods of high water, it is advisable to follow that trail because of numerous stream crossings along the BFT. For the next 2 miles, the BFT descends into a scenic glen with plentiful campsites along beautiful County Line Branch and its tributaries. Follow the trail left as it makes a 500-foot climb up the plateau via switchbacks. The next 1.5 miles of the trail offers level hiking underneath hardwoods and through meadows, until the BFT drops into a small glen, crosses a small stream with camping, and climbs back out. Follow the edge of the plateau, with more views and open meadows. The

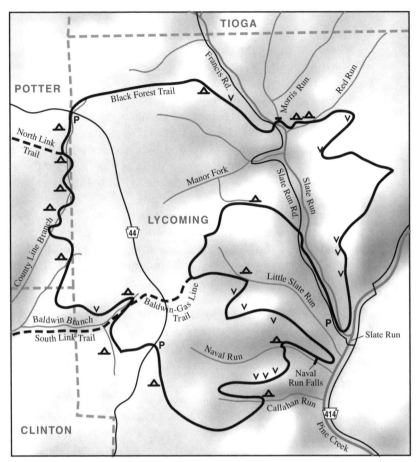

Hike 14: Black Forest Trail

trail turns left and follows the top of the plateau, passes more vistas, and descends into another glen along a small stream with camping. Follow an old railroad grade along the side of the glen, until the trail returns to another small stream with more campsites. The BFT turns left, climbs gradually out the glen, and crosses PA 44.

The trail now follows Trout Run Road for .3 mile, with views of Naval Run's gorge. Then turn right off the road and begin a gradual descent, passing a reliable spring to your left and the headwaters of Trout Run with camping. Cross the intersection of Boyer Mill and Trout Run Roads, and begin a gradual ascent and level hiking before reaching Big Trail Road, with a view of Callahan Run's gorge. Begin your descent along a scenic tributary of Callahan Run. The BFT leaves the stream and ascends the side of the gorge, then descends and returns to the stream via an old skid trail. Continue to head downstream until you reach the juncture with Callahan Run. Here you'll find camping and scenic cascades. An unblazed trail continues downstream to Pine Creek. Turn left and ascend along Callahan Run for 1.3 miles before reaching a saddle in the ridge between Callahan and Naval Runs. The BFT turns right, following the ridge for 1.3 miles, with scenic views of Naval and Callahan Runs' gorges and Pine Creek Gorge. The trail reaches Hemlock Mountain, with more vistas of beautiful Pine Creek, then begins a 1,000 foot descent of .8 mile to Naval Run; thankfully, there are switchbacks.

Upon reaching Naval Run, pass the intersection with Naval Run Trail, which follows scenic Naval Run downstream along the southern bank, and access Naval Run Road near Pine Creek, almost a mile away. The BFT crosses Naval Run and campsites, then turns right and heads downstream. The trail stays about 100 feet above Naval Run. After .6 mile, the trail passes scenic Naval Run Falls, which is about 20 feet high and plunges into a pool. Continue downstream for a short distance before turning left to begin a 800-foot climb via switchbacks over .75 mile. Near the top, pass the Gas Line Trail to your right. The BFT bears left and ascends the flank of the ridge, passing more vistas of Pine Creek and Naval Run while following the crest of the ridge. Begin a gradual ascent to the plateau. Near the top, pass the Frank Herald Trail to your right; this trail descends rapidly to Naval Run Road along Pine Creek. For 1.3 miles, the BFT traverses the plateau, with vistas of Naval Run gorge, Hemlock Mountain, and Pine Creek; you also pass a side trail to scenic White Birch Vista.

The BFT meets the blue-blazed Baldwin–Gas Line Trail and turns right, making a gradual descent into Slide Hollow. The descent steepens, and the trail crosses a small stream. Begin climbing switchbacks back up to the ridge, a 200-foot climb. Turn right and begin to descend steeply into Little Slate Run's gorge, passing scenic vistas along the ridgeline. The trail descends 600 feet over .5 mile to Little Slate Run. Intersect Slide Hollow and turn left, heading upstream along Little Slate Run. This is a scenic area with hemlocks and campsites near the stream. After following Little Slate Run for almost .5 mile, the trail turns left and climbs into a side hollow as you once again ascend the plateau.

At the top of the plateau, turn right onto Manor Fork Road and reenter the forest at the intersection of Pine Hollow Road. Here you follow an old railroad grade through red pine trees. Descend slightly into a small hollow and return to the plateau before making a steep, rocky descent into Foster Hollow. You'll find camping where the two forks of the hollow meet; blue-blazed Foster Hollow Trail joins from the left. The BFT bears right and begins to ascend the other fork. Upon reaching the plateau again, pass a pond with camping and a leased campsite. Cross the top of the plateau before reaching the edge. Now begin a steep 1,000-foot descent over .7 mile along a ridgeline, passing vistas of Slate Run Gorge. Follow the switchbacks off the ridgeline and descend to Slate Run Road. The trail crosses the road and turns right, following downstream along Slate Run for 1.4 miles. The run is typically out of sight and flows far below the trail, yet the scenery is excellent. Upon completing the loop, turn right and hike the trail to your car along Slate Run Road.

15. Susquehannock Trail System

Length: 85-mile loop.

Duration: 5 to 9 days.

Difficulty: Moderate to difficult.

Terrain: Many glens and hollows. Numerous ascents and descents, ranging from 200 to 1,100 feet; most gradual but some steep. Trail often follows old forest roads and railroad grades, but there are rocky stretches.

Trail conditions: Trail is generally well blazed but may be unestablished and brushy in sections. Stinging nettles may be a problem along some streams. Many stream crossings without bridges. Sometimes rocky and wet. Passes through isolated regions.

Blazes: Orange; side trails blue.

Water: Plentiful; trail passes and crosses several streams and springs.

Vegetation: Northern hardwoods predominate on tops and slopes of plateaus; hemlocks, spruces, and pines often along streams; understory of blueberries, mountain laurel, and ferns. Meadows and glades also occur along the trail.

Highlights: Denton Hill, Lyman Run, Patterson, and Ole Bull State Parks, scenic streams, fine camping, vistas, isolation, wildlife, Hammersley Wild Area, Hammersley Fork and Pool, stargazing, deep forests.

Maintained by: Susquehannock Trail Club, volunteers.

Contact info:

Susquehannock Trail Club, P.O. Box 643, Coudersport, PA 16915

Susquehannock State Forest, P.O. Box 673, Coudersport, PA 16915-0673;
    phone: 814-274-3600; e-mail: fd15@state.pa.us; websites:
    www.dcnr.state.pa.us/forestry/stateforests/forests/susquehannock/
    susquehannock.htm, www.dcnr.state.pa.us/forestry/hiking/
    susquehannock.htm, www.kta-hike.org.

Lyman Run State Park, 454 Lyman Run Rd., Galeton, PA 16922;
    phone: 814-435-5010; e-mail: lymanrunsp@state.pa.us;
    website: www.dcnr.state.pa.us/stateparks/parks/lymanrun.asp.

Ole Bull State Park, HCR 62, Box 9, Cross Fork, PA 17729-9701;
    phone: 814-435-5000; e-mail: olebullsp@state.pa.us;
    website: www.dcnr.state.pa.us/stateparks/parks/olebull.asp.

Prouty Place State Park, c/o Lyman Run State Park, 454 Lyman Run Rd., Galeton,
    PA 16922; phone: 814-435-5010; e-mail: lymanrunsp@state.pa.us;
    website: www.dcnr.state.pa.us/stateparks/parks/proutyplace.asp.

Patterson State Park, c/o Lyman Run State Park, 454 Lyman Run Rd., Galeton,
    PA 16922; phone: 814-435-5010; e-mail: lymanrunsp@state.pa.us;
    website: www.dcnr.state.pa.us/stateparks/parks/patterson.asp.

Maps and guides: Both available for sale from Susquehannock Trail Club;
the trail is also shown on the Susquehannock State Forest map.

Trailhead directions:

Northern trailhead: The northern trailhead, also known as the Northern Gateway, is located along US 6, 36.4 miles west of Wellsboro and 8.5 miles east of Coudersport, near Denton Hill Ski Area and State Park. Turn off US 6, and follow the paved road for .1 mile past the forest office to the overnight parking area to the right.

Lyman Run State Park: At the light in Galeton along US 6, proceed south on SR 2002 for 5.3 miles, then turn right onto Lyman Run Road. Follow for 2 miles to the park office and parking area along the dam. Follow the Lyman Run Trail to connect with the Susquehannock Trail System.

Cherry Springs Vista: A parking area is available at this excellent vista along PA 44, 13 miles south of Sweden Valley. The trail crosses PA 44 a few hundred feet down the road.

Ole Bull State Park: The park is located along PA 144, 17.5 miles south of Galeton and 26 miles north of Renovo. The parking area has a trail and information sign.

Cross Fork: This small town is located about 12 miles north of Renovo, along PA 144. Turn right into the town and cross Kettle Creek. Drive for .2 mile and turn right onto a street to the state forestry maintenance buildings, where there is parking and an information sign.

Patterson State Park: This tiny state park is located 6.5 miles south of Sweden Valley, along PA 44. The trail passes through this park, but parking is limited.

The Susquehannock Trail System (STS) was first established in 1966 and has become synonymous with isolated wilderness backpacking, exploring the heart of Pennsylvania's undeveloped north-central region. The STS is one of Pennsylvania's oldest and most venerable backpacking trails. The late Bill Fish was the trail's founder, and a plaque has been erected in his honor.

An added bonus of the STS can be found not on the land, but in the heavens. With little development, the region has become popular with stargazers, as you'll understand if you camp in a meadow or glade on a clear night.

Like the Donut Hole Trail to the south, the STS traverses terrain with numerous ascents and descents, and few long hikes along the flat plateau tops. This gives the trail a roller-coaster effect. The plateau has been heavily dissected by streams and creeks, creating numerous hollows, glens, and gorges.

The hiking descriptions below follow the trail clockwise from the northern trailhead.

Section One: Northern Gateway to Ole Bull State Park

From the Susquehannock State Forest Office, hike the .7-mile blue-blazed connector trail to the STS loop. This connector trail follows rolling terrain along an old forest road, crosses a small stream, and mildly ascends to the loop. At the beginning of the STS loop, the trail is blazed orange; turn left to begin the loop. The trail is level and rolling for 2.3 miles as it crosses behind Denton Hill State Park and ski area and passes a side trail to a vista. A mild descent follows for .7 mile, then the STS crosses Thompson Road. You hike rolling terrain for more than a mile, until the trail bears right and descends into Jacobs Hollow; the initial descent is about 300 feet over a mile. For the next 2 miles, the trail gradually descends into this scenic hollow, with several stream crossings (some without bridges), hemlocks, a small run, open meadows, and nice campsites. Cross Lyman Run Road; about a mile to the left (east) is Lyman Run State Park, with camping, phone, restrooms, showers, swimming, and picnic areas. Cross beautiful Lyman Run over a footbridge. This is a fine trout stream with hemlocks and great campsites. Begin a challenging climb of 500 feet over .7 mile up the plateau. The ascent is steep and rocky in places and passes a few springs.

Level hiking ensues for almost 2.7 miles as the STS crosses over the plateau; the trail may be wet in sections. Begin a steep 400-foot descent over .7 mile off the plateau along a seasonal stream. Turn left onto

Sunken Branch Road, and then turn right on West Branch Road as you cross over the West Branch of Pine Creek. Bear left off the road, pass a hunting camp, and begin a steep climb into another hollow with a small seasonal stream and seep springs. This ascent is 500 feet over .5 mile and is affectionately known as "Cardiac Climb." At the top, pass a blue-blazed side trail to the right leading to a vista. Level and rolling hiking follows for more than 2 miles, until the STS crosses PA 44 and

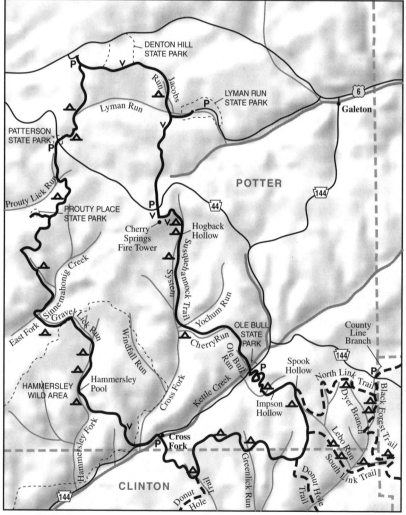

Hike 15: Susquehannock Trail System

reaches the Cherry Springs Fire Tower. An excellent view to the south can be reached by hiking PA 44 to the right (west) several hundred feet. The fire tower still stands, but you are no longer permitted to climb it. This is one of the highest points of the STS, at 2,475 feet in elevation.

Descend 700 feet over a mile into Hogback Hollow. Over the next 4 miles, the STS gradually descends into this hollow along a scenic stream. Along the way, you'll find old beaver dams, open meadows, hemlocks, and several great campsites. Sections of the trail are wet, and there are stream crossings. The trail turns right onto Short Run Road, following it for a short distance, then turns left off the road and follows Cross Fork Creek. Follow the creek downstream for 1.4 miles, cross it via a bridge, and continue downstream. Bear left into Cherry Run's glen along an old grade. Good camping can be found along the run. For nearly 1.5 miles, the STS gradually climbs 500 feet along small Cherry Run; the climb steepens near the top. At the top of the plateau, bear right onto Hungry Hollow Road, and follow it for .25 mile before turning left. Rolling terrain ensues for .7 mile before the STS begins an 800-foot descent over 1.5 miles into the glen of Ole Bull Run. The descent is steep in places as the trail follows the small run downstream; small campsites are along the run. Pass a short side trail to Ole Bull Vista to the right.

Enter isolated Ole Bull State Park, the STS's Southern Gateway, and cross beautiful Kettle Creek via a bridge. The park features parking, campground, restrooms, water, public phone, picnic facilities, and short dayhiking trails. The park is named after a famous Norwegian violinist who tried, along with a group of his countrymen, to settle the area in the 1850s.

Section Two: Ole Bull State Park to Cross Fork

This section is an ideal weekend trip, because there is a convenient shuttle between Ole Bull State Park and Cross Fork along PA 144. Cross PA 144 and begin a 1.75-mile climb ascending almost 1,000 feet. Though long, the climb tends to be gradual, with switchbacks, and offers one vista of Ole Bull State Park. When you reach the top of the mountain where the STS levels off, notice the hardwood forest and understory of mountain laurel. Now begin an 800-foot descent over a mile into Impson Hollow. This descent has switchbacks and is steep in sections. As you near the bottom of the hollow, you pass a few small campsites. At the bottom is a small stream; bear left up Impson Hollow along an old forest road. Begin ascending upstream, through pine plantations and meadows. This 600-foot climb over almost a mile becomes steeper as you ascend. At the top of the plateau, bear left onto Twelve Mile Road. Follow the road for .1 mile, then turn right off the road. Begin a moderate descent into Spook Hollow, named for the deep, dark spruce and pine plantations through which the trail passes. Hike fast and don't look back!

The STS continues its gentle descent through Spook Hollow, passing through more plantations, open meadows, and a pipeline swath along a small stream. The trail meets Big Spring Road and passes a juncture with the blue-blazed North Link Trail to the left; this 8.5-mile-long trail connects with the Black Forest Trail. Turn off the road, pass a camp road, and follow an old grade. Watch the blazes through this section. The STS leaves the grade and moderately ascends to the plateau. Join the Rattlesnake Trail across rolling terrain, with short ascents and descents. After 1.4 miles, pass a juncture with the blue-blazed South Link Trail to the left; this 6-mile-long trail also accesses the Black Forest Trail. Together with the STS, these four trails create a great weekend loop. In another .7 mile, the STS reaches Fork Hill Road. It turns right and follows the road for .7 mile, until the STS joins with the Donut Hole Trail (DHT) for the next 8.7 miles.

The STS turns to the right, leaving Fork Hill Road. The trail is level for .6 mile, then descends steeply to the Left Branch of Young Womans Creek. This is a 700-foot descent over .5 mile down Morgan Hollow, the steepest section of the trail, with switchbacks and rocky terrain; exercise care. Cross the creek, with camping, and climb to Left Branch Young Womans Creek Road. Turn left on the road and follow it for .25 mile, until the trail turns right and ascends into Long Hollow along a small seasonal stream. This is a gradual climb of 700 feet over a mile. Climb over the plateau and descend 500 feet over .7 mile along Bobsled Run to scenic Greenlick Run. The STS turns right and proceeds upstream, following the run for about a mile. Then it turns left, leaves the run, and begins a mild ascent, then descent, to Little Greenlick Run. Cross the run and a road with the same name. For the next 1.2 miles, the trail is level or rolling as it follows forest roads and grades before turning left along a pipeline swath. Follow the swath for almost a mile as it descends to Osborne Branch, mildly ascends, and then descends to Scoval Branch. Here the trail turns left and follows the small creek downstream to Osborne Branch. Follow Osborne Branch downstream for more than a mile into a deepening gorge with nice scenery and camping.

The STS now leaves the DHT, bearing right and gradually ascending up Porter Branch. Cross a pipeline swath and continue the climb. Bear left and follow the trail up Green Timber Hollow, with hemlocks and mountain laurel. Climb gradually out of the hollow and over the crest of the plateau, crossing pipeline swaths. Cross Shephard Road and begin a gradual descent into the glen carved by Lieb Run; this is an 800-foot descent over 1.5 miles. During the descent, the STS typically follows grades along the side of the glen. Reach the small village of Cross Fork, with parking, stores, motels, and phones.

Section Three: Cross Fork to Prouty Place State Park

The highlight of this section is the Hammersley Wild Area, the largest roadless area in the state, the epitome of wilderness in Pennsylvania. The STS is the only established backpacking trail through this famed wild area. After passing through Cross Fork, and a short period of road walking along PA 144, the STS turns right into the Hammersley Wild Area; for the next 10 miles, the trail does not cross a single road, not even the omnipresent dirt forestry roads. An added bonus is that for most of these miles, the trail follows the beautiful Hammersley Fork, with great campsites. This is a unique and far too rare area in Pennsylvania, and the premier highlight along the STS.

Begin a 1.4-mile, 1,000-foot ascent featuring a nice vista of the surrounding plateau and deep canyons. Upon reaching the top of the plateau, the trail is level or rolling for 1.3 miles, as it passes through mountain laurel underneath oaks. Dry campsites can be found here. Pass a small stream and seep springs as the trail begins its descent into Elkhorn Hollow. The trail drops almost 700 feet over a mile through the hollow, traversing rocky, wet terrain and some steep slopes. Small campsites can be found in the scenic hollow. The STS bears right at beautiful Hammersley Fork, with more campsites. Hike upstream to the Hammersley Pool, a deep swimming hole fed by a cascade. This beautiful place is a popular campsite and is suffering from overuse; please treat it with respect so that others can continued to enjoy it.

Follow Hammersley Fork upstream for about 5 more miles, often along old railroad grades that rise above the stream. There are several wet stream crossings and many fine campsites along the Hammersley Fork and at the junctures of side streams and hollows. The terrain is easy, and often wet, as the trail gradually climbs to the source of the stream. The climb steepens as the trail ascends a saddle between mountains and crosses McConnell Road. Hammersley Vista is along the road to the right.

Now begins a 2-mile, 700-foot descent into scenic Gravel Lick Hollow, along a small stream. At first the descent is moderately steep, but it becomes more gradual as the trail moves deeper into the hollow. After about a mile from Gravel Lick Road, pass Duffy's Campsite, a beautiful spot along the stream that can hold several tents. Continue to descend gradually until the trail reaches the end of the hollow and crosses onto private property, where camping is not allowed. Turn right and follow a grade through meadows and several wet areas. Proceed upstream along the East Fork of the Sinnemahoning Creek, a large stream with fine camping on state forest land. In another mile, the trail passes a house, bears left, and crosses the creek over a bridge.

Turn right onto East Fork Road. Bear left off the road and begin another climb with switchbacks up the plateau. Begin a steep 500-foot ascent over .6 mile to a ridge with old flagstone quarries. The STS then begins a gradual 400-foot descent over .7 mile into Stony Run's glen. For the next 1.3 miles, the trail follows this small run upstream, with nice campsites. As the trail gradually climbs along the run to its source, the terrain becomes steeper. Climb 400 feet over .6 mile until the trail reaches the top of the plateau with rolling terrain. The STS makes a sharp right and begins a descent to Wild Boy Run, covering 500 feet in a mile. At first the descent is gradual, but it becomes steeper into the glen, where nice camping can be found. Turn left up the glen of a side stream and begin to ascend 300 feet over .5 mile. The terrain levels at the top of the plateau, and the trail crosses Wild Boy Road. Rolling terrain ensues for .7 mile, until the trail crosses Rock Ridge Road.

Cross the road and begin a gradual descent for a mile along the contour of the plateau. As you enter Prouty Lick Run's glen, the trail steepens, but it becomes more gradual as it nears the stream. Nice camping can be found where the two branches of the run meet. A blue-blazed side trail to the left descends along the small run for .5 mile to Prouty Place State Park, with camping, water, and parking.

Section Four: Prouty Place State Park
to Northern Gateway

Climb 600 feet over .8 mile out of the glen and cross Prouty Lick Road near the top. For the next mile, follow the crest of the plateau along rolling terrain, passing rock outcrops and a nice vista of the surrounding plateau and Prouty Run's gorge. Bear left and begin a 550-foot descent over .8 mile into Hockney Hollow, which is fed by a seasonal stream. Bear right and descend into Ford Hollow, with nice camping along a small stream. Bear right again and begin a gradual climb along a grade up the glen of a small stream; this is a 600-foot ascent over 1.3 miles that becomes steeper as you near the crest of the plateau. At the top of the plateau, bear left along level terrain and enter Patterson State Park, with camping, parking, pit toilets, and water.

Cross PA 44 and begin a 300-foot descent over .7 mile into a hollow. Bear left along the West Branch of Pine Creek, with nice campsites. Follow the small creek gradually upstream for about a mile to its source. A steeper climb ensues as the trail passes through a saddle between the plateau and crosses Sunken Branch Road. The trail then descends 450 feet over .7 mile down Splash Dam Hollow; at first the descent is steep, but it becomes more gradual. Follow Splash Dam Run downstream, with nice campsites; you may catch a glimpse of beavers, which inhabit the run. The STS turns left and proceeds up a side hollow carved by a seasonal stream. Climb 500 feet over a mile to the top of the plateau. Upon reaching the top, as the trail passes its highest elevation, 2,545 feet, it traverses rolling terrain. Begin a mild descent and cross Lyman Road. The trail is level for the last mile, where it completes its loop.

15a. STS–Link–BFT Loop

Length: 25-mile loop encompassing 2.3 miles on the Susquehannock Trail System (STS), 6 miles on the South Link Trail (SLT), 8 miles on the Black Forest Trail (BFT), and 8.5 miles on the North Link Trail (NLT).

Duration: 2 to 3 days.

Difficulty: Moderate.

Terrain: Ascents and descents range from 200 to 700 feet. Periods of level and rolling hiking across plateau. Old railroad grades often followed.

Trail conditions: Trails are generally well blazed, but some sections may be brushy. Stinging nettles can be a problem along some streams. Often wet and boggy. Many stream crossings without bridges. Isolated hiking.

Blazes: STS and BFT, orange; NLT, blue rectangles; SLT, blue circles.

Water: Generally plentiful; the trail passes and follows numerous streams.

Vegetation: Northern hardwoods with understory of mountain laurel and ferns found along mountaintops and plateau; hemlocks, spruce, and pines primarily along streams; open meadows and glades along trail.

Highlights: Scenic mountain streams, isolated hiking, wildlife, old railroad grades, nice campsites, spruce and hemlock forests.

Maintained by: Volunteers.

Contact info:
Susquehannock Trail Club, P.O. Box 643, Coudersport, PA 16915
Susquehannock State Forest, P.O. Box 673, Coudersport, PA 16915-0673; phone: 814-274-3600; e-mail: fd15@state.pa.us; websites: www.dcnr.state.pa.us/forestry/hiking/susquehannock.htm, www.kta-hike.org.

Maps and guides: Map and guide included with the STS guidebook, available for sale.

Trailhead directions: The most convenient access is at the juncture of PA 44 and Big Dam Hollow Road. The Black Forest Trail crosses PA 44 along the Lycoming and Tioga County line, 35.2 miles north of US 220; parking is limited and the trail sign is easy to miss. There is space along PA 44 to park.

The North Link Trail (NLT) and South Link Trail (SLT) are two connector trails between the Susquehannock Trail System (STS) and the Black Forest Trail (BFT). Together these four trails make an ideal weekend loop that offers a lot of isolation along scenic streams with nice campsites and verdant spruce and hemlock forests. This loop often follows old railroad grades, some of impressive size. These grades were constructed to transport lumber during the logging era almost a hundred years ago.

Hiking counterclockwise from the BFT, depart from PA 44, and proceed south on the BFT for a mile as it gradually descends to the headwaters of County Line Branch, with several stream crossings. Turn right onto the NLT at a sign for the Cou-Dyer Trail, and begin a gradual 250-foot climb over .5 mile. Gradually descend and cross Dyer Road near a cabin. Continue the descent to Dyer Run; bear right and follow the run upstream along old grades for almost a mile, with nice campsites along the run. The NLT bears left and crosses Robinson Road. After a slight ascent, begin a moderate 350-foot descent over .7 mile to Lebo Road. Turn right on the road for a short distance, then turn left and descend to Lebo Run. Cross the run and follow the trail as it ascends to an old railroad grade, once used by the North Bend and Kettle Creek Railroad. Most of the remainder of the NLT follows this grade along the circuitous contour of the plateau. Along the way, you'll notice deep cuts into the side of the plateau and fills across side hollows and drainages to keep the level 3 percent grade. This grade was constructed by Italian laborers with pick and shovel more than a century ago.

After 1.5 miles from Lebo Run, the trail descends from the grade and crosses Big Trestle Run. Continue to follow the level contour of the plateau for 3 miles, until the trail makes a gradual descent to Big Spring Road and joins with the STS. Turn left onto the STS, which you will follow for about 2.3 miles. The STS turns off the road, passes a camp road, and follows an old grade. Watch the blazes through this section. The STS leaves the grade and moderately ascends to the

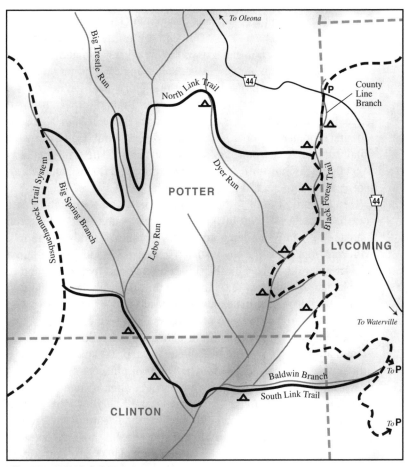

Hike 15a: STS–Link–BFT Loop

plateau. Join the Rattlesnake Trail across rolling terrain with short ascents and descents. After 1.4 miles, pass a juncture with the blue-blazed SLT to the left, also known as Wildcat Trail. The SLT descends 700 feet over a mile into a hollow; the descent is steep in sections, and the glen features hemlocks and cascades along a small stream. At the bottom, turn right onto Lebo Road and continue along the SLT on the Lebo Trail. Follow a grade downstream along scenic Lebo Run for about 2 miles, usually staying on the right side of the stream. This is a beautiful section of trail, with hemlocks and several nice campsites. The surrounding gorge is almost 800 feet deep. Sizable Lebo Run begins to braid, and the trail crosses the run without bridges. This stream crossing is difficult in high water.

The SLT climbs an embankment away from Lebo Run and follows a sidehill along the steep slope. Descend to County Line Branch and cross the lawn of a hunting camp. Follow a grassy road across two stream crossings with bridges. Reach Robinson Road. Turn right on the road and cross Baldwin Branch. After the bridge, bear left and pass a hunting camp. Follow a grade up Baldwin Branch into an isolated gorge. For the next 1.5 miles, the SLT follows Baldwin Branch closely, crossing it numerous times without a bridge. The trail may be brushy. Small campsites can be found along the stream. The trail gradually ascends upstream, until it bears right up a small side hollow and makes a steep, rocky 150-foot ascent to the BFT.

Turn left onto the BFT; the remainder of the hike will follow this trail back to PA 44. The BFT follows a grade along the side of the plateau and gently descends to the headwaters of Baldwin Branch, with camping. Cross the small stream and begin a gradual climb up a side hollow to the plateau. The trail bears left and reaches the top of the plateau. For the next 2.6 miles, the trail is mostly level and often follows the edge of the plateau, with vistas from open glades. Descend from the plateau into the glen of a small stream with campsites. Cross the stream and climb back to the plateau. Level hiking ensues for more than a mile before the BFT makes a steep 500-foot descent of .5 mile down to County Line Branch. The trail proceeds for 2.5 miles upstream along scenic County Line Branch, often using old grades. There are numerous stream crossings without bridges, so this section may be difficult in high water. This section of trail features several nice campsites, often at the intersection of side streams and side hollows.

Pass the NLT to the left and continue the gradual ascent upstream with more campsites for a mile to PA 44.

16. Donut Hole Trail

Length: 90-mile linear trail.

Duration: 7 to 9 days.

Difficulty: Moderate to difficult.

Terrain: Numerous ascents and descents, ranging from 200 to 1,200 feet. Often steep and demanding, with flat or rolling terrain where trail crosses the plateau. Old forest roads and grades are often followed.

Trail conditions: Maintenance may be a problem along sections of this trail. Some sections may have inconsistent blazes and are unestablished. Many stream crossings without bridges. Few established campsites. Isolated hiking. Stinging nettles can be a problem along some streams.

Blazes: Orange.

Water: Generally plentiful; the trail passes and follows numerous streams.

Vegetation: Northern hardwoods with understory of mountain laurel and ferns found along mountaintops and plateaus, hemlocks, pines, and rhododendron primarily along streams; open meadows and glades occur along trail.

Highlights: Scenic mountain streams, isolated hiking, wildlife, views, Hyner Run State Park, Kettle Creek State Park, deep forests.

Maintained by: Volunteers, Keystone Trails Association.

Contact info:
Sproul State Forest, HCR 62, Box 90, Renovo, PA 17764;
phone: 570-923-6011; e-mail: fd10@state.pa.us; websites:
www.dcnr.state.pa.us/forestry/stateforests/forests/sproul/sproul.htm,
www.dcnr.state.pa.us/forestry/hiking/donut.htm, www.kta-hike.org.
Hyner Run State Park, P.O. Box 46, Hyner, PA 17738-0046;
phone: 570-923-6000; e-mail: hynerrunsp@state.pa.us;
website: www.dcnr.state.pa.us/stateparks/parks/hynerrun.asp.
Kettle Creek State Park, 97 Kettle Creek Park Lane, Renovo, PA 17764-9708;
phone: 570-923-6004; e-mail: kettlecreeksp@state.pa.us;
website: www.dcnr.state.pa.us/stateparks/parks/kettlecreek.asp.

Maps and guides: Free map available from Sproul State Forest; no guide available.

Trailhead directions:
Farrandsville: From US 220, take the Lock Haven/PA 120 exit. Turn right onto PA 120 off the ramp and follow straight through Lock Haven. Where PA 120 turns left, proceed straight across the bridge on PA 664. After crossing the bridge, make an immediate left onto SR 1001. Follow this road for 5.3 miles along the river to Farrandsville. Cross the railroad tracks and continue straight through the small town on Farrandsville Road, passing a massive,

impressive old iron furnace stack. This road becomes a dirt road and descends to a parking area at Lick Run; there is no trail sign. The parking area is 1.4 miles from the railroad.

Hyner Run State Park: From Renovo, follow PA 120 east for 6 miles. Turn left onto Hyner Run Road (SR 1014) and proceed for 2 miles. Turn left and enter the park.

Kettle Creek State Park: The trail passes through the Lower Campground, located 6 miles north of Westport and PA 120 along SR 4001. A parking area is on the right along Summerson Run.

Jericho: There isn't a trail sign, parking area, or established trailhead at the trail's western terminus in Jericho. The trail simply begins along Jericho (Jerico) Road; you'll notice orange blazes on the telephone poles. Heading west on PA 120 from Renovo, Jericho Road is the last right before crossing the First Fork of Sinnemahoning Creek and entering Sinnemahoning.

The experienced backpacker looking for an isolated trail will appreciate the lonely Donut Hole Trail (DHT). Few trails can compare with its expansive isolation, deep-woods experience, and the opportunity to witness wildlife. The DHT follows a rough upside-down U between Farrandsville and Jericho. The northern portion of the trail also follows the beautiful Susquehannock Trail System. Considering the length of this trail, the shuttle between Farrandsville and Jericho is made convenient by PA 120. Although it's not along the trail, I strongly suggest you visit Hyner View State Park, which offers incredible views of the West Branch of the Susquehanna River and surrounding mountains. The hike is described heading east to west (Farrandsville to Jericho).

Section One: Farrandsville to Hyner Run State Park

The parking area is in State Game Lands 89, along beautiful Lick Run. Enjoy this stream now, because the DHT does not follow it. The trail follows a level jeep road or grade for .3 mile through impressive hemlock groves and rhododendron thickets. The trail follows and crosses an old railroad grade and appears to pass what looks like a railroad grade wall. At a Y, the grade, popular with bike riders, proceeds straight, while the DHT bears left and ascends. This is a 400-foot climb over .3 mile. For the next 2.2 miles, the trail gradually ascends along level or rolling terrain as it follows the edge of the gorge carved by Lick Run, a designated state scenic river. Enter a glen and cross the headwaters of a small side stream. Bear right and return near the edge of Lick

Run's gorge. The DHT follows the edge of the gorge upstream for the next mile before turning left, then right, and ascending to Carrier Road.

Cross the road and descend to the headwaters of a small tributary to Ferney Run. The trail bears right and leaves the glen of this tributary as it follows the edge of the plateau above Ferney Run's 1,000-foot-deep gorge. Pass a vista of the gorge and maintain the same elevation as the trail enters the glen of another small stream, which you cross. Continue to follow the contour of the plateau and cross another tributary. Follow the tributary upstream, bear left, and ascend to the plateau. Level hiking ensues for almost a mile, then the trail follows an old forest road and crosses Ferney Run. After a quick ascent, turn left onto Oak Ridge Road, which you take for about .7 mile. Turn right off the road and begin a slight descent into a glen that increasingly steepens. This glen has been carved by a small, scenic run; this is a 700-foot descent over .7 mile. At the bottom of the glen, turn right onto Kingston Road. Follow the road for about a mile and cross Rattlesnake Run; be sure to fill your water bottles here. The DHT makes a 200-foot ascent, levels off for .5 mile, and then begins a steep climb of 600 feet over .3 mile to the top of the plateau.

For about the next 4 miles, the trail is level as it crosses over the plateau, often following old forest roads and grades. The trail then

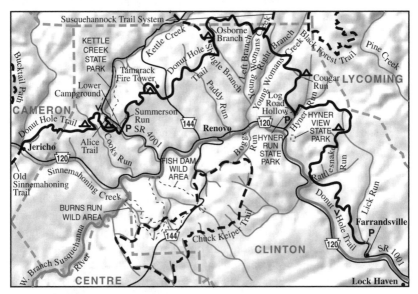

Hike 16: Donut Hole Trail

makes a 500-foot descent over .5 mile into Rattlesnake Run's gorge. Bear left and follow this scenic run upstream for 1.4 miles, with three stream crossings and nice campsites. The trail turns right and gradually climbs away from the run, crosses over the plateau, and mildly descends to West Branch and Lick Run. Cross both streams and ascend slightly to the plateau for almost 3 miles of level hiking, then the DHT picks up an old forest road and crosses Lick Run again. Turn right on another old forest road and follow it for a mile. Bear right onto Ritchie Road and cross Hyner Mountain Road. The trail passes underneath powerlines and crosses another forest road, then bears left and traverses the rolling top of the plateau for 2 miles. You now begin a 900-foot descent over .9 mile into the scenic glen of Bear Pen Hollow. The trail follows a small stream down the glen and turns left on Hyner Run Road. Follow the road for more than a mile to scenic Hyner Run State Park, with a pool, restrooms, water, phone, park office, and campsites. Hyner Run is a fine trout stream.

Section Two: Hyner Run State Park
to Kettle Creek State Park

Turn right off the road, pass under powerlines, and begin to ascend up scenic Log Road Hollow, with its small stream. This ascent is 800 feet over 1.3 miles and can be rocky and rugged. At the top of the plateau, the DHT bears right along Flat Ridge Trail, an old forest road. Leave the old forest road, and after .7 mile of level hiking, pass a juncture with the Long Fork Trail, which descends Long Fork Hollow to Hyner Run Road. After another mile of level hiking, make a short descent to Abes Fork Road and cross Abes Run. The trail switchbacks up the side of the glen and reaches the plateau again. Cross over the level plateau for almost a mile, then make a steep 350-foot descent to scenic Cougar Run. Turn left and follow the run upstream as you gradually ascend out of the glen up to the plateau and Dry Run Road. Cross the road and follow old forest roads for 1.5 miles. The DHT descends 500 feet over .4 mile into the glen of a seasonal stream. Meet Seven Mile Run and follow it downstream for a mile, then turn right and climb to Seven Mile Road. Turn left on the road and follow it for .7 mile to Right Branch Young Womans Creek Road, on which you turn left and cross Young Womans Creek, a famous trout stream. Pass a monument commemorating the first land purchase for the state forest. The DHT leaves the road, turns right, and enters the scenic glen of Bull Run. Follow the run upstream for 1.8 miles, until the trail turns left and climbs steeply along a side stream. At the top, the trail turns right on Fork Hill Road at a juncture with the Shingle Hollow Trail. Follow the road for .8 mile to the DHT's juncture with the Susquehannock Trail System (STS).

The DHT and the STS turn to the left, leaving Fork Hill Road; the STS also continues to the right along the road. For the next 8 miles, these two trails follow the same route—a section of trail that forms the southern end of the STS's loop and the northern end of the DHT's upside down U.

The DHT is level for .6 mile before descending steeply to the Left Branch of Young Womans Creek. This is a 700-foot descent over .5 mile. Cross the creek and climb to Left Branch Young Womans Creek Road. Turn left on the road and follow it for .25 mile, until the trail turns right and ascends into the glen along a small seasonal stream. This is a gradual climb of 400 feet over .8 mile. Climb over the plateau and descend 500 feet over .7 mile to scenic Greenlick Run. The DHT turns right and proceeds upstream, passing potential campsites and hemlocks. The trail follows the run for about a mile. Turn left, leave the run, and begin a mild ascent, then descent, to Little Greenlick Run. Cross the run and a road with the same name. For the next 1.2 miles, the trail is level or rolling as it follows forest roads and grades, then it turns left along a pipeline swath. Follow the swath for almost a mile as it descends to Osborne Branch, mildly ascends, and then descends to Scoval Branch. At Scoval Branch, the trail turns left and follows the small creek downstream to Osborne Branch. Follow Osborne Branch downstream for more than a mile into a deepending gorge with nice camping and scenery.

The STS departs the DHT to the right before reaching Manning Hollow Trail. The DHT continues to follow Osborne Branch downstream for almost another mile, with potential camping and isolated scenery. The trail turns right and leaves Osborne Branch to begin a climb up Merriman Hollow. The ascent becomes increasingly gradual and rises 500 feet over a mile. Near the top, follow an old forest road to Pfoutz Valley Road. Turn right on the road and follow it for .7 mile as it descends toward McNerney Run. Leave the road to the left and descend to the run, along which the trail follows downstream for 1.4 miles. McNerney Run joins Paddy Run, which the DHT crosses. Climb up to Pfoutz Valley Road. Turn right and follow the road for almost a mile, until the trail leaves the road to the left and climbs to the plateau, a 300-foot climb over .3 mile. The trail crosses the plateau over rolling and level terrain.

Cross Hensel Fork Road and two pipeline swaths, then turn right and follow a third swath for .6 mile. Turn left and leave the swath, proceeding south for almost a mile to the headwaters of Pong Hollow. Over the next mile, the DHT passes junctures with three short trails: Boone Road Trail, Sandy Trail, and Left Fork Trail. Bear right and gradually descend to Drury Run and PA 144. Cross both the run and the highway and begin a gradual 1.5-mile ascent to the Tamarack Fire Tower. From the tower, the trail descends steeply, about 600 feet in .7 mile, to Left Fork. Cross and gradually climb from Left Fork, then descend along Long Hollow to Right Fork. Cross small Right Fork and begin a 500-foot climb over .8 mile. For the next 1.4 miles, the trail crosses the top of the plateau, with mild terrain. Pass the Spicewood Trail and the headwaters of Spicewood Run. More level and rolling hiking follows for 1.8 miles, until the DHT begins its descent along scenic Summerson Run, with sections of sidehill hiking. Summerson Run has carved an attractive glen, with rhododendron and small cascades. Follow the run downstream for about 2 miles to a small parking area along SR 4001, a convenient trailhead for hiking the DHT.

Section Three: Kettle Creek State Park to Jericho

Cross the road and enter the Lower Campground of Kettle Creek State Park, where you will find a phone, water, restrooms, and campsites for a fee. This is a scenic campground along beautiful Kettle Creek, with a small dam, pond, and swimming area. The trail fords Kettle Creek below the dam. Kettle Creek is a large stream, and fording it in high water is dangerous. During periods of high water, you have to hike 1.2 miles north along SR 4001 toward Kettle Creek State Park, until the road crosses Kettle Creek. Right after the bridge, turn left onto Alice Trail. This scenic trail follows an extensive sidehill through rhododendron and hemlocks; it joins with the DHT after about .8 mile along Honey Run.

If Kettle Creek is fordable, cross it and turn right, proceeding upstream underneath hemlocks and fine scenery. After .6 mile, the trail ascends and bears left into Honey Run's scenic glen. Alice Trail joins from the right. Here you will find nice camping, rhododendron, and hemlocks. Continue the rocky climb up the side of the glen; the trail is often high above Honey Run. This ascent amounts to 800 vertical feet over .8 mile from Kettle Creek. Easier hiking resumes at the top of the plateau, and the DHT meets Crowley Road, on which it turns right. Follow the road for .5 mile, until the trail turns right on another forest road, which ends at an excellent vista of the surrounding plateau and Kettle Creek State Park. Behind the vista is an open field and a dry campsite that is accessible from the road.

The trail turns sharply to the left and follows the edge of the plateau until it recrosses Crowley Road. To the right along the road is another fine vista of Cooks Run. From the road, descend steeply 500 feet over .6 mile to Cooks Run. Turn left and proceed downstream along the run for about 1.3 miles. At the end of Cooks Run Road, the DHT bears right, descends to Cooks Run, crosses it, and proceeds upstream. Begin to bear left into a side glen. Gradually ascend the glen along a small stream for almost a mile. The trail follows an old forest road for .25 mile then turns right and gently ascends to the top of the plateau. For the next 1.3 miles, the trail is gentle until it gradually descends 300 feet over .5 mile into the headwaters of Cooks Run. Climb from the small stream via switchbacks until you reach the top of the plateau, then turn right onto an old forest road. The trail follows this old road for .5 mile, then turns left on Montour Road, and follows it for .8 mile. Leave the road to the right and level hiking ensues until you begin the long, steep descent into the glen of scenic Ellicott Run. This is a 1,200-foot descent over almost 2 miles. Follow the small stream closely. Leave Sproul State Forest and pass discreetly through private property, until you bear left on a road along the First Fork of the Sinnemahoning Creek. Follow the road through the small village of Jericho. The trail ends at PA 120.

17. Bucktail Path

Length: 34-mile linear trail

Duration: 2.5 to 4 days.

Difficulty: Moderate to difficult.

Terrain: Ascents and descents range from 400 to 1,000 feet. Trail climbs in and out of several glens and gorges; rocky and steep in sections.

Trail conditions: Trail is generally well blazed, though some sections are brushy and unestablished. Several stream crossings without bridges in the northern section of the trail. Stinging nettles an occasional problem along streams. There may be few established campsites.

Blazes: Orange.

Water: Generally plentiful, with many streams and springs; however, there is no reliable water source on the southern 10.7 miles of the trail.

Vegetation: Northern hardwoods predominate with oak, maple, and birch; thick underbrush of blueberry and ferns common on ridgetops; mountain laurel; spruce, pines, and hemlocks also can be found.

Highlights: Johnson Run Natural Area, views, scenic mountain streams, Rock Run, Sizerville State Park, isolation, wildlife, proposed Squaretimber Wild Area

Maintained by: Elk State Forest, Keystone Trails Association, volunteers.

Contact info:
Elk State Forest, 258 Sizerville Rd., Emporium, PA 15834;
 phone: 814-486-3353; e-mail: fd13@state.pa.us; website:
 www.dcnr.state.pa.us/forestry/stateforests/forests/elk/elk.htm,
 www.dcnr.state.pa.us/forestry/hiking/bucktail.htm, www.kta-hike.org.
Sizerville State Park, 199 E. Cowley Run Rd., Emporium, PA 15834-9608;
 phone: 814-486-5605; e-mail: sizervillesp@state.pa.us;
 website: www.dcnr.state.pa.us/stateparks/parks/sizerville.asp.

Maps and guides: Both maps and guides available for sale from the Keystone Trails Association.

Trailhead directions:
Sinnemahoning (southern trailhead): From Renovo, proceed west on PA 120 to the small town of Sinnemahoning. Turn right onto Grove Street, the last right before leaving town and the post office will be on your left. Follow Grove Street for .5 mile, past a piped spring to the right; a trail sign and small parking area will be to the right.
Sizerville State Park (northern trailhead): The state park is located 6 miles north of Emporium on PA 155. Turn right into the main entrance and follow the park road to the park office. Turn left onto East Cowley Run Road and follow it for .6 mile to a trail sign and small parking area on the right. The park is located 17 miles south of Port Allegany along PA 155.

The lonely Bucktail Path (BP) is one of the most isolated and least hiked trails in the state. Expect to have the trail to yourself, with plenty of opportunities to see wildlife. With such little use, the trail is unestablished and brushy in sections, so pay close attention to the blazes.

Hiking south to north, the trail begins in the small village of Sinnemahoning. This area represents an important junction of numerous trail systems. Only a mile east on PA 120 is Jericho, the western terminus of the Donut Hole Trail. Across the wide Sinnemahoning Creek from Jericho is Wyside, where you'll find the trailhead for the Old Sinnemahoning Trail, a spur that connects to the Quehanna Trail.

The BP begins at the end of Grove Street, descends to the left, and crosses Grove Run behind a hunting camp. The land is posted, but hiking is permitted. Get sufficient water, for there are no reliable springs for the next 10.7 miles. Pick up a dirt road and follow the Left Fork of Grove Run upstream. The run is well below the trail. This is a 2.1-mile ascent of 1,000 feet, with occasional steep sections. Along the way, you pass seasonal springs, streams, and a pipeline swath. At the top of the plateau, bear left on a grassy forest road. Enter Elk State Forest, turn right along the edge of the ridge, and enter Johnson Run Natural Area, containing old-growth hemlocks and hardwoods. The trail continues north along the ridge and plateau, with partial views in winter, and a nice view of Driftwood Fork.

For the next 1.5 miles, the BP follows old forest roads along the ridgetop. Bear right onto the National Fuel and Gas pipeline swath, and follow it for more than a mile through private property. Cross Ridge Road and bear left off the pipeline swath to avoid more private property. The BP passes through thick blueberries and offers views from a knob. Bear right and descend to Ridge Road, crossing it once again, and then pass Brooks Run Road. The trail follows the ridge and passes gated Brooks Run Fire Tower. Cross the pipeline swath again and bear right to descend to the Right Fork of Brooks Run. The trail descends along the small stream, the first reliable water source since Sinnemahoning. The scenic glen contains hemlocks and potential campsites. Bear left as the trail ascends along another small stream and passes another good campsite. Climb out of the glen along an old forest road and return to the ridge. Cross the pipeline and Ridge Road once again; follow the ridge, with rolling changes in elevation, for a mile before the trail bears left and traverses the ridge above Russell Hollow Run. Begin a 900-foot descent over .7 mile to Whitehead Run Road. As you near the road, pass a cabin, then cross the road and Whitehead Run. Follow the small run upstream, with several crossings. Bear left up Rock Run, with several more stream crossings. Here you'll find potential campsites; this stream also features cascades and small waterfalls in a scenic glen.

The BP ascends away from Rock Run as it climbs to the plateau; level hiking ensues for a mile before the trail bears left and descends along a small seasonal stream. This is a 600-foot descent over .8 mile. Pass several hunting camps. Turn right on Hunts Run Road, then turn

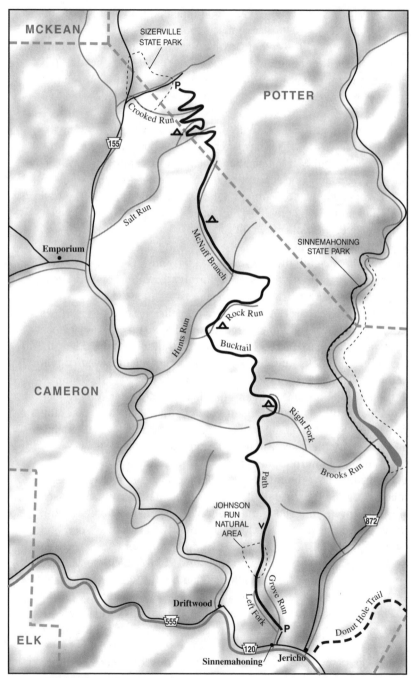

Hike 17: Bucktail Path

left, leaving the road and entering the forest. Descend to Hunts Run and turn upstream; the trail crosses the stream three times. Cross Hunts Run again on a bridge, make a sharp left, pass a cabin, and hike along an old railroad grade, following McNuff Branch upstream. For the next 4 miles, the BP follows McNuff Branch upstream into its gorge. The trail is level with gradual climbs; it is unestablished and brushy in sections, often very wet, and there is one ford of McNuff Branch. Pay close attention to the blazes after the ford. The BP ascends the slope above hemlocks and returns to the stream. McNuff Branch features old beaver dams, meadows, and hemlocks; there are several potential campsites along this scenic stream. The BP also crosses several small side streams.

As the BP nears the head of the gorge and the source of McNuff Branch, it crosses a pipeline swath and begins to climb away from the stream on old forest and logging roads. Turn left up a seasonal side stream and continue to climb along old forest roads and switchbacks. The trail becomes steeper for a short distance before reaching Steam Mill Road. The road is a 400-foot climb over .8 mile from McNuff Branch. Cross Steam Mill Road and descend along a gated, grassy forest road, which is also a snowmobile trail. The BP bears right and follows another snowmobile trail. Turn left onto Pine Camp Trail and descend to Salt Run, with nice campsites. The trail crosses the run, then turns right and begins a series of switchbacks along the side of a ridge above a tributary of Salt Run. Cross the head of the glen of the tributary and continue the climb to the ridge.

The BP follows the ridge for about a mile, with mild changes in elevation, until it crosses Crooked Run and reaches Crooked Run Road. Turn left on the road and follow it for .8 mile, then the trail makes a sharp right, passes a cabin, and ascends a hemlock-shaded glen of a seasonal side stream. The climb is steep and rocky but gradually becomes more moderate near the top. It's a 600-foot ascent over .8 mile. Bear left at the top of the ridge and begin a steep, rocky, and brushy descent of Buffalo Switch Hollow. The trail through here is unestablished in sections, especially at the beginning of the descent. The descent becomes more gradual as you near the bottom, and the trail becomes more defined. Cross a stream and powerline, and then pass a cabin. This is an 800-foot descent over 1.5 miles. The trail ends at a small parking area.

🥾 18. Elk Trail

Length: 16-mile linear trail.

Duration: 1.5 to 2 days.

Difficulty: Easy to moderate.

Terrain: Typically rolling, with gradual changes in elevation. Ascents and descents are generally moderate and range from 100 to 500 feet. Trail often follows logging and old forest roads, railroad grades, and pipeline swaths.

Trail conditions: Trail is well blazed, although brushy and unestablished in sections.

Blazes: Orange.

Water: Generally plentiful; trail passes several small streams and springs.

Vegetation: Northern hardwoods predominate, with oak, maple, and birch; thick understory of mountain laurel and ferns common; occasional pines and hemlocks found along streams; open glades and meadows.

Highlights: Wild elk, isolation, wildlife, scenic mountain streams, thickets of mountain laurel

Maintained by: Elk State Forest, volunteers.

Contact info:
Elk State Forest, 258 Sizerville Rd., Emporium, PA 15834; phone: 814-486-3353; e-mail: fd13@state.pa.us; websites: www.dcnr.state.pa.us/forestry/stateforests/forests/elk/elk.htm, www.dcnr.state.pa.us/forestry/hiking/elk.htm, www.kta-hike.org.

Maps and guides: Both available for free from Elk State Forest.

Trailhead directions:
Dents Run Road (eastern trailhead): Heading east on PA 555 from Benezette, Dents Run Road is on the left at 7.8 miles. Heading west on PA 555 from Driftwood, Dents Run Road is on the right at 8.8 miles. Follow Dents Run Road for 2.2 miles to a trail sign and small parking area on the left.
Benezette (western trailhead): From PA 555, turn onto Front Street and follow for .4 mile, where it becomes a dirt road and bears left; avoid the gated forest road straight ahead. You'll see a sign for Thunder Mountain Park. Continue .3 mile farther to a parking area and trail sign.

The Elk Trail (ET) is one of Pennsylvania's newest backpacking trails, especially routed to offer wilderness viewing of the elk herds that inhabit the region. Pennsylvania has one of the largest wild elk herds in the eastern United States, and the elk are a prime tourist attraction for the region. The animals that exist today were transplanted from the Rocky Mountains; the eastern elk that originally inhabited Pennsylvania were hunted to extinction.

Viewing the elk in the wild is an unforgettable experience. Prime times to hike this trail are in late June, when the mountain laurel are in bloom, and in October during the rut, when you'll hear the elk bugling. Elk are generally docile creatures, but always keep your distance, especially during the rut.

Hiking the trail east to west from Dents Run Road, ascend gradually into the hollow of Little Bear Run along an old forest road that traverses the side of the hollow. The ET levels off as it reaches the top of the plateau and bears left onto a logging road. Follow the level logging road across the top of the plateau for about .75 mile. Bear right off the logging road, pass through a clearing, and resume hiking along a trail for more than a mile through a regenerating hardwood forest. Pick up another logging road and bear right onto Shaffer Draft Road, a gated forest road. After a short distance, bear left onto another logging road.

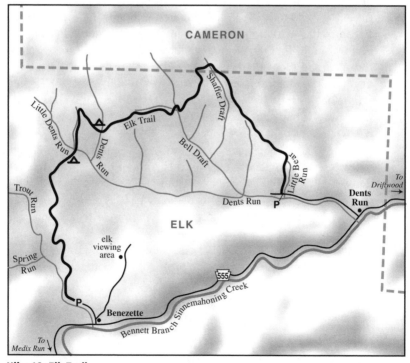

Hike 18: Elk Trail

You will pass an elk food plot and an open forest dominated by ferns and mountain laurel. The forest becomes more scenic, with hemlocks, birches, and other hardwoods, and boulders. To the left are springs that drain into Shaffer Draft. Turn left onto an old pipeline swath, which is being encroached by saplings.

Turn left and leave the swath. The trail picks up an old railroad grade and begins a gradual descent to Bell Draft Road. Off to your right is scenic Bell Draft, a high-quality native trout stream. Follow the road as it curves around Bell Draft and turns right onto another gated forest road. Cross a pipeline swath near a seasonal stream and ascend along a hollow with a small stream. At the top, bear left along an old forest road, and then turn right to begin a rocky, gradual descent to Dents Run Road. Turn left onto the road and follow it for a short distance before turning right, leaving the road, and crossing scenic Dents Run, which has no bridge. Nice camping can be found here, though it is close to the road. This is probably the best camping along the trail. Ascend gradually, reaching the top of the plateau, with mountain laurel, birches, and other hardwoods, and ferns. The trail turns left and gradually descends into the hollow of another small stream. The surrounding terrain is rocky. At the confluence of the hollow and Little Dents Run are cabins and an access road. Follow the road and cross the run via a bridge. Then leave the road and begin a gradual, rocky ascent back to the top of the plateau. The terrain becomes more level as the ET passes through thick mountain laurel and various hardwoods. The trail appears to follow the remnants of old logging or forest roads.

Pick up another logging road, following it for a few miles as it gradually descends to Benezette. A new section of trail leaves the road and descends to the right down to Trout Run. Descend the side of the gorge and reach this scenic, sizable stream. Pass a bridge and hike along a dirt road; there are cabins across the run. The trail ends at a parking area.

Although the ET does not offer outstanding natural features such as waterfalls or vistas, it does provide plenty of isolation, scenic streams, and a prime opportunity to view elk in the wild.

19. Quehanna Trail

Length: 73-mile loop; two connector trails are 9 and 9.6 miles; Cut Off Trail is 3.2 miles.

Duration: Main loop can take 5 to 8 days; shorter trips are possible using the connector trails.

Difficulty: Moderate to difficult.

Terrain: Significant portions of the trail are flat or rolling as it crosses the plateau. Southern half of the loop is more gentle than the northern half, which features greater changes in elevation, with deeper gorges and glens and steep, rocky climbs. Ascents and descents range from 200 to 800 feet. Trail often follows old grades or logging roads and passes pipeline or powerline swaths.

Trail conditions: Trail is generally well blazed and established. Several streams do not have bridges.

Blazes: Orange; connector trails and cross-country ski trails, blue.

Water: Generally plentiful; numerous streams and springs in close proximity to trail.

Vegetation: Northern hardwoods dominate, with understory of ferns; open fields and meadows; hemlocks, spruce, and pines more common along streams; mountain laurel and rhododendron; stand of white birch at Marion Brooks Natural Area.

Highlights: Quehanna Wild Area, Marion Brooks Natural Area, Parker Dam State Park, scenic mountain streams, vistas, Gifford Run, Wykoff Run, Sanders Draft, Red Run, good campsites, wildlife, isolation, logging history including old railroad and logging grades, remains of splash dams, boulders and rock outcrops, opportunities to view elk.

Maintained by: Quehanna Area Trails Club, Keystone Trails Association, volunteers.

Contact info:
Quehanna Area Trails Club, websites: www.kta-hike.org/Quehanna_Trail.htm, www.dcnr.state.pa.us/forestry/hiking/quehanna.htm, www.kta-hike.org.
Moshannon State Forest, 3372 State Park Rd., Penfield, PA 15849; phone: 814-765-0821; e-mail: fd09@state.pa.us; website: www.dcnr.state.pa. us/forestry/stateforests/forests/moshannon/moshannon.htm.
Elk State Forest, 258 Sizerville Rd., Emporium, PA 15834; phone: 814-486-3353; e-mail: fd13@state.pa.us; website: www.dcnr.state.pa.us/forestry/stateforests/forests/elk/elk.htm.
Parker Dam State Park, 28 Fairview Rd., Penfield, PA 15849-9799; phone: 814-765-0630; e-mail: parkerdamsp@state.pa.us; website: www.dcnr.state.pa.us/stateparks/parks/parkerdam.asp.

Maps and guides: Guide may be purchased; maps available for free from Moshannon and Elk State Forests.

Trailhead directions:

Parker Dam State Park: From I-80, take Exit 111 and proceed north on PA 153 for 5.5 miles. Turn right onto Mud Run Road and drive 2.5 miles into the park. Turn right onto a park road at the park office. Follow road across bridge over Laurel Run; it then turns left and reaches the trailhead parking with trail sign on the right.

Piper: From I-80, take Exit 147 at Snow Shoe. Turn left onto PA 144. Follow PA 144 to Moshannon, where the road turns right. Continue for 2 miles and turn left onto PA 879. Follow PA 879 to Karthaus, and about 1 mile after, turn right onto the Quehanna Highway (SR 1011). Follow for 5.2 miles. The trailhead is on the right, about .7 mile past the Quehanna Boot Camp.

Wykoff Run Road (Laurel Draft): Follow the same directions for the Piper trailhead to the juncture of PA 879 and Quehanna Highway, about 1 mile from Karthaus. Proceed 8.7 miles on the Quehanna Highway to the juncture with Wykoff Run Road. Turn right onto this road and follow for 5.3 miles to a small parking area on the right, at Laurel Draft. This trailhead is located 4.7 miles south of Sinnemahoning.

The Quehanna Trail (QT) represents a massive trail system that is beginning to attract more and more attention. Besides the main trail, there are the Cut Off Trail, two connector trails, 50 miles of cross-country ski trails, and the Old Sinnemahoning Trail. If you're looking for solitude, you'll find it here. This region epitomizes expansive isolation, with deep forests, wetlands, beautiful streams, open meadows, and scenic glens, yet it's an easy four- to five-hour drive for backpackers from New York, New Jersey, Ohio, or Maryland.

The QT offers something for all backpackers and is one of Pennsylvania's finest trails. One review of this trail compared it favorably to West Virginia's popular Dolly Sods, a prominent backpacking destination in the eastern United States. This is a backpacking wonderland, and the cross-country ski trail system offers even more route options, as well as great snowshoe trekking in winter. The trail system is maintained by the Quehanna Area Trails Club, led by Ralph Seeley, who is also the author of *Greate Buffaloe Swamp,* a guide to the QT, Allegheny Front Trail, and other area trails.

An additional feature of this trail is that the wild elk herds are expanding their range onto the Quehanna plateau. At present, you are most likely to see them along the north-central and northwest sections of the loop. A hike here in September and October may offer the experience of hearing the elk bugle, not to mention incredible fall foliage. Bears are also consistently seen along the trail.

The hike is described here heading counterclockwise from Parker Dam State Park.

Section One: Parker Dam State Park to Piper

Most backpackers begin at scenic Parker Dam State Park, at the western edge of the loop. This park features many dayhiking opportunities, a small lake, a campground with showers, and historical logging displays. If you plan to hike the entire loop, you may want to consider parking at Wykoff Run Road or Piper so that you can take a shower, rest, and have a food drop-off point at Parker Dam (fee required to take a shower). The Quehanna region is rich in logging history, and the state park features Woodhick Weekend on the Sunday of Labor Day weekend.

Begin by hiking the QT to the right from Parker Dam. In the park, the QT passes a log slide display as it follows the Log Slide Trail. Upon leaving the state park, the trail follows a railroad grade as it gently ascends along the edge of a shallow gorge carved by Little Laurel Run. Follow the trail as it bears left and enters a side glen, crossing a small stream. Continue to follow Little Laurel Run upstream and cross Laurel Run Road. Follow the run farther upstream until the QT bears left and leaves the run. Cross Laurel Run Road again, and soon thereafter, Tyler Road, with a large meadow. At 3.3 miles from Parker Dam, pass a juncture with the Cut Off Trail to your left. This easy 3.2-mile blue-blazed trail forms a 7-mile loop with the QT. It is mostly level but does make a gradual descent to Saunders Run, and crosses several pipeline swaths.

On the QT, level hiking ensues for the next mile. Reach the juncture of McGeorge and Wallace Mine Roads. Cross McGeorge Road and follow the trail to the left of Wallace Mine Road, which you will cross in .5 mile. At this crossing, the blue-blazed West Cross Connector (WCC) joins from the left. The WCC is 9 miles in length and forms an 18-mile loop with the QT from Parker Dam, offering a great weekend loop. The QT descends and crosses Alex Branch. Proceed downstream, cross a tributary, and cross Alex Branch again. The QT begins to climb away from Alex Branch and reaches the edge of the plateau, which you follow for about .5 mile, until you reach a side trail to a vista of Trout Run. Make a 100-foot descent over .25 mile to Trout Run. Cross the run and pick up the old Goodyear Logging railroad grade to your right.

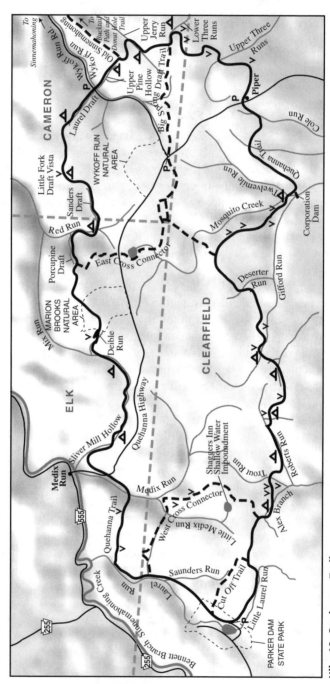

Hike 19: Quehanna Trail

Follow Roberts Run upstream for 1.4 miles, with possible camping. Pass near large rock outcrops and boulders and cross Roberts Run near a wetland. The QT circles to the left and crosses a small tributary with camping, then makes a short climb to a view of the wetlands of Roberts Run. Now the trail bears left and follows a small run upstream. Follow the trail up a 200-foot climb over .4 mile to the top of Chestnut Ridge, with a view and hemlocks. At 2,400 feet elevation, Chestnut Ridge is the highest point of the trail. Descend from the ridge and in another mile cross Knobs Road. Follow scenic Deer Creek, with hemlocks and white pines, downstream; you'll find camping along the creek.

After .6 mile, the QT leaves Deer Creek to the left, ascends the bank, and bears left where it climbs up the glen of a tributary. Cross the tributary and continue the mild ascent up the plateau, where you cross Caledonia Pike. The trail continues the easy ascent until it reaches the crest of the plateau and begins a 200-foot descent over .6 mile to Gifford Run, a beautiful mountain stream offering great camping. Cross the run via a bridge; just upstream are remains of splash dams, used by logging companies in the 1800s to float logs down streams. Turn right and follow the run downstream, passing a side trail to the left that leads to a nice vista from rock outcrops above Gifford Run. The trail begins to climb away from Gifford Run, bears left into the glen of a tributary, crosses the tributary to the right, and climbs the plateau to another vista. More than a half mile farther, the trail crosses Merrill Road, and in another .7 mile, the QT enters the shallow glen carved by Deserter Run. Here you enter the Quehanna Wild Area, one of the largest in the state. Climb away from Deserter Run, and after 1.3 miles of level hiking, cross Lost Run Road and the southern terminus of the East Cross Connector (ECC).

The QT leaves the road and reaches the edge of the 500-foot deep gorge carved by Mosquito Creek. For more than 2 miles, the trail passes along or near the edge of the gorge. Along the way are nice vistas, boulders, and rock ledges. You now begin a mile-long, 600-vertical-foot descent that features more vistas. The descent becomes steeper as you near beautiful Mosquito Creek, which you cross via a bridge. Turn right and cross scenic Twelvemile Run over a bridge. Here you will find nice camping. Proceed downstream and pass near the remains of Corporation Dam, a large splash dam used by the logging companies. The QT bears left and begins a 500-foot climb over .6 mile, the first real ascent of the trail. Mostly level hiking ensues for the next 4.5 miles, where the trail crosses two streams and follows Cole Run upstream for .6 mile before crossing the Quehanna Highway; just north along the highway is the Piper trailhead and parking area for the QT.

Section Two: Piper to Wykoff Run Road

Cross the Quehanna Highway, tunnel through maple and oak saplings, and passes a spring. The trail is rolling for a mile before gradually descending to a vista over Rider Draft. The QT turns left, proceeding north along a gradual .8-mile-long ascent. Turn left, and rolling terrain continues for a mile across the plateau before the trail descends 300 feet over .5 mile to Upper Three Runs. Follow the stream down to a small reservoir. Because it is used for drinking water, you should not camp along this stream. Climb 400 feet over .6 mile up Laurel Swamp Draft and reach a nice vista over the glens and gorges. The QT is level and rolling for another mile and passes the former site of a fire tower. Pass a vista to the south and east, and descend to Lower Three Runs. Hike upstream along this small run for .6 mile, until you reach the blue-blazed No. Fifteen Trail, where the QT bears right and gradually climbs to Three Runs Road.

Cross the road and descend gradually to beautiful Upper Jerry Run. Follow the run downstream for about a mile, with excellent scenery, including cascades and large boulders. Cross the run three times without bridges. At a pipeline, turn left and climb steeply out of the glen, passing massive boulders. This is a 400-foot climb over .6 mile. At the top, turn right onto a grassy forest road and follow for .3 mile.

The QT makes a sharp left and begins to descend into Upper Pine Hollow; watch carefully for this turn. The Old Sinnemahoning Trail continues straight ahead; it is a 5-mile spur trail that ends at the small village of Wyside and enables a backpacker to continue on to the southern trailhead of the Bucktail Path, in Sinnemahoning, or the western trailhead of the Donut Hole Trail, in Jericho. No water is available along the Old Sinnemahoning Trail until it is near Wyside.

The nature of the trail now changes as you begin to hike the northern half of the QT loop. Descents and ascents are steeper, longer, and more rugged; there also isn't as much level hiking across the plateau. The QT begins its descent into Upper Pine Hollow, a rugged, scenic glen with cascades, hemlocks, and a small stream. A potential campsite can be found about halfway down, where Upper Pine Draft joins. This is a 700-foot descent over a mile. At the bottom, cross beautiful Wykoff Run, a trout stream with hemlocks and rhododendron.

Section Three: Wykoff Run Road to Parker Dam State Park

Cross Wykoff Run Road, with a small parking area, and begin an 800-foot ascent over 1.5 miles up beautiful Laurel Draft, a glen similar to Upper Pine Hollow. Near the top of the plateau, you pass through a meadow, campsites, and a couple pipeline swaths. Gentle hiking with a gradual ascent follows for a mile, and the QT crosses Hoover Road and a junction with the Foley cross-country ski trail.

After another mile of level hiking, the QT passes an excellent vista of Little Fork Draft, one of the finest along the trail. Soon thereafter, the trail crosses a small stream that features Arch Spring about 100 feet to the left. The trail bears left along an old forest road with potential campsites. The trail begins a mild descent and passes a junction with the blue-blazed Sanders Trail, a cross-country ski trail, to the left. The QT now turns right and descends into Sanders Draft, a scenic glen with a small stream, hemlocks, white pines, and nice campsites. The trail crosses the stream several times. The descent into the draft is 600 feet over approximately 1.7 miles. This is one of the most scenic places along the QT, with hemlocks, rhododendron, boulders, cascades, and waterfalls. At the bottom is another campsite, and the QT crosses beautiful Red Run via a bridge and climbs to Red Run Road, on which it turns right.

Red Run has carved a beautiful gorge almost 900 feet deep. Follow the road for about .6 mile, past massive boulders to your left. Then the trail leaves the road to the left to begin the climb up Porcupine Hollow or Draft. At first the trail follows an old grade, but it becomes steeper as it climbs into the scenic glen with cascades. This is a 900-foot climb over 1.6 miles. At the top of the plateau, the QT meets the junction with the East Cross Connector (ECC) to the left. Descend into Mud Lick Hollow, with boulders and water; there are no water sources for the next 3 miles. Climb out of the hollow and into the Marion Brooks Natural Area, featuring stands of white, gray, and paper birch trees. Leave the natural area and gradually descend toward Deible Run. The trail steepens before reaching a vista. The steep descent continues from the vista, a 250-foot drop over .25 mile. Reach Deible Run and proceed downstream to scenic Mix Run, with campsites.

The QT turns left and proceeds upstream along Mix Run, often following an old railroad grade. The QT crosses the stream three times via bridges. Proceed up this beautiful valley known for its wildflowers and isolation. Mix Run is a wilderness trout stream with stable populations of native brook trout, offering great opportunities for backcountry fly fishing. Gradually climb out of Mix Run's valley and reach the plateau, crossing pipeline swaths and Grant Road. Level hiking follows for almost 1.5 miles, then the QT descends into Sliver Mill Hollow along an old forest road and a small stream. Bear left off the old road and follow the trail on a sidehill around the base of Haystack Mountain, leaving the hollow. Cross the Quehanna Highway and Sullivan Run thereafter; the trail once again follows a sidehill. Descend to and cross Medix Grade Road and cross scenic Medix Run via a bridge. The trail now begins its ascent up Bear Run's glen, a 600-foot climb over .7 mile. Upon reaching the plateau, there is camping. A mile of level hiking ensues where the QT crosses over the plateau, passing the Caledonia Pike along the way.

Reach a vista over Laurel Run and a side glen, and begin a 400-foot descent over .8 mile along a small stream. At the bottom, the trail bears left and follows an old forest road above scenic Laurel Run, a sizable mountain stream. After about 2 miles, the trail follows Saunders Road, and the blue-blazed West Cross Connector joins from the right. Follow the road for more than a mile as it enters Saunders Run's gorge. The QT bears right, leaves the road and crosses Little Saunders Run. Proceed upstream along scenic Saunders Run along an old forest road and cross the run via a bridge. A steep 300-foot climb over .3 mile follows as the trail reascends the plateau and enters the salvage cut of the May 31, 1985, tornado zone. Follow logging roads along a gradual descent and enter Parker Dam State Park. The blue-blazed Cut Off Trail joins from the left, and the QT returns you to the trailhead.

19a. West Cross Connector

Length: 9-mile linear trail forming a 18-mile loop with the western section of the Quehanna Trail from Parker Dam State Park. The West Cross Connector also creates a 51-mile middle loop with the East Cross Connector and the Quehanna Trail.

Duration: The 18-mile loop can be hiked in 2 days.

Difficulty: Easy to moderate.

Terrain: Very similar to Quehanna Trail.

Trail conditions: Trail is sufficiently blazed but brushy in sections. There are small stream crossings without bridges.

Blazes: Blue; Quehanna Trail, orange.

Water: Generally plentiful.

Vegetation: Open hardwoods with understory of ferns; meadows; mountain laurel; hemlocks and pines generally near streams.

Highlights: Views, isolation, Medix Run, Shaggers Inn Shallow Water Impoundment.

Maintained by: Quehanna Area Trails Club, volunteers.

Contact info:
Quehanna Area Trails Club, websites: www.kta-hike.org/Quehanna_Trail.htm, www.dcnr.state.pa.us/forestry/hiking/quehanna.htm, www.kta-hike.org. Moshannon State Forest, 3372 State Park Rd., Penfield, PA 15849; phone: 814-765-0821; e-mail: fd09@state.pa.us; website: www.dcnr.state.pa.us/ forestry/stateforests/forests/moshannon/moshannon.htm. Elk State Forest, 258 Sizerville Rd., Emporium, PA 15834; phone: 814-486-3353; e-mail: fd13@state.pa.us; website: www.dcnr.state.pa.us/forestry/stateforests/forests/elk/elk.htm.

Maps and guides: Maps available for free from Moshannon and Elk State Forests.

Trailhead directions: Trail used in conjunction with Quehanna Trail.

Hiking the loop from south to north counterclockwise from Parker Dam State Park, the West Cross Connector (WCC) begins at mile 4.8 and ends at mile 68.8 of the Quehanna Trail (QT). This creates an enjoyable weekend loop that gives you a taste of the Quehanna.

This trail is level or rolling for approximately the first 5.5 miles. From mile 4.8, the WCC follows Wallace Mine Road for .7 mile before turning left. Level hiking ensues for a mile. The trail crosses Caledonia Pike and passes behind the Shaggers Inn Shallow Water Impoundment, a large, shallow pond created for wildlife habitat. After another mile of level hiking, the WCC crosses Shagger Inn Road and begins a short descent to an old forest road. Follow the old road to the left as it traverses the edge of Medix Run's gorge.

The trail passes vistas of the gorge and plateau at pipeline swaths, as well as the May 31, 1985, tornado zone. It begins the first substantial change in elevation on its descent to Medix Run, passing another vista. This 700-foot descent over .7 mile becomes increasingly steeper as you near the bottom. Turn left, following Little Medix Road, and then bear right, leaving the road and crossing Little Medix Run. The trail now begins an ascent up a hollow carved by a small stream. This is a 500-foot climb over almost .7 mile. Upon reaching the plateau, cross Caledonia Pike and a pipeline swath. The WCC crosses the headwaters of a small stream and begins a mile-long gentle descent. Turn left and the descent becomes much steeper, a drop of 200 feet over .3 mile. Turn right and proceed down a scenic stream in a hollow. At the bottom, the WCC joins with the QT at mile 68.8.

19b. East Cross Connector

Length: 9.6-mile linear trail creating a 40-mile eastern loop with the Quehanna Trail. The East Cross Connector also creates a 51-mile middle loop with the West Cross Connector and the Quehanna Trail.

Duration: The eastern loop generally take 3 to 4 days to complete, the middle loop 4 to 5 days.

Difficulty: Easy to moderate.

Terrain: Trail is mostly flat or rolling, with several stream crossings, wetlands, and wet meadows. The southern section of the trail, near Mosquito Creek, is the most difficult.

Trail conditions: Trail is sufficiently blazed but often brushy and boggy in sections.

Blazes: Blue; intersecting cross-country ski trails also blue; Quehanna Trail, orange.

Water: Generally plentiful.

Vegetation: Open hardwoods with an understory of ferns; open meadows; mountain laurel; wild blueberries; occasional hemlocks and pines.

Highlights: Mosquito Creek, scenic mountain streams, isolation, Beaver Run Shallow Water Impoundment, nice campsites.

Maintained by: Quehanna Area Trails Club, volunteers.

Contact info:
Quehanna Area Trails Club, websites: www.kta-hike.org/Quehanna_Trail.htm, www.dcnr.state.pa.us/forestry/hiking/quehanna.htm, www.kta-hike.org.
Moshannon State Forest, 3372 State Park Rd., Penfield, PA 15849; phone: 814-765-0821; e-mail: fd09@state.pa.us; website: www.dcnr.state.pa.us/forestry/stateforests/forests/moshannon/moshannon.htm.
Elk State Forest, 258 Sizerville Rd., Emporium, PA 15834; phone: 814-486-3353; e-mail: fd13@state.pa.us; website: www.dcnr.state.pa.us/forestry/stateforests/forests/elk/elk.htm.

Maps and guides: Shown on the Quehanna Trail map; available for free from Moshannon and Elk State Forests.

Trailhead directions: Trail used in conjunction with Quehanna Trail.

Heading south to north, the East Cross Connector (ECC) leaves the southern section of the Quehanna Trail's (QT) loop at mile 19.2 (from Parker Dam) and rejoins the QT on the northern section at mile 50.8. With the eastern section of the QT, the ECC forms a 40-mile loop.

From the southern section of the QT, the ECC proceeds along Lost Run Road and descends into a glen with a small stream. The trail makes a 300-foot descent over .3 mile down this glen, until it bears left above scenic Mosquito Creek. Follow the trail as it heads upstream and begins a gradual descent until it meets Lost Run Road and crosses the creek over a bridge. Follow the road for approximately .6 mile and begin a mild ascent through the May 31, 1985, tornado zone.

About .5 mile east of here is the former site of a nuclear reactor facility. In the 1950s, the Pennsylvania state government worked with private military contractors to develop this facility and others with hopes of bringing economic development to this isolated region. The costly project failed, and there is residual contamination and pollution at certain sites, although not at levels harmful to humans. The region is now protected as the Quehanna Wild Area.

The ECC leaves the road to the left and descends to Meeker Run, a scenic glen containing boulders and hemlocks. Follow the run upstream along an old grade for about .7 mile. You pass junctures with cross-country ski trails, and the ECC turns left upon reaching the top of the plateau. The remainder of the trail is mostly flat or rolling, with several potential campsites in open meadows or along small streams. In 1.4 miles, the trail crosses Beaver Run, with expansive meadows of blueberry bushes. Cross a grassy meadow and pipeline swaths. In .5 mile, the ECC wraps around the Beaver Run Shallow Water Impoundment, a large, shallow pond with wetlands and meadows. The treeless and marshy characteristics of the plateau are a result of past logging practices. The original forest of pines and hemlocks was eradicated. Hemlocks transpire a lot of water, and after they were cut, the water table rose significantly in the poorly drained soil. The resulting changes in the soil made it difficult for trees to take root as they did before, but they are slowly regenerating and the forest will ultimately heal. Trail blazes are inconsistent through this section.

The trail passes through a boggy red and white pine plantation before crossing the Quehanna Highway. Proceed north and cross Paige Run, with camping, and in another .6 mile, cross another small stream, Roaring Run. The trail bears left onto an old forest road, which it follows for almost a mile before turning onto Losey Road, a forest road. Follow Losey Road for .5 mile before reaching the northern section of the QT at mile 50.8.

19c. Wykoff Loop

Length: 32-mile loop.

Duration: 1.5 to 2.5 days.

Difficulty: Easy to difficult.

Terrain: Western and southern portions of the loop are flat or rolling. Eastern and northern sections are more difficult, climbing in and out of several glens, with ascents and descents ranging from 200 to 1,000 feet.

Trail conditions: Trails are generally well blazed but sometimes brushy. Sections of trail are often wet and boggy.

Blazes: Quehanna Trail, orange; East Cross Connector and cross-country ski trails, blue.

Water: Plentiful.

Vegetation: Hardwoods dominate the plateau, with mountain laurel and ferns; expansive meadows of lowbush blueberries, ferns, and grass; hemlocks, rhododendron, and pines often found in the glens along streams.

Highlights: Big Spring Draft, Upper Jerry Run, Wykoff Run, Laurel Draft, Little Fork Draft Vista, Sanders Draft, Red Run, Beaver Run Shallow Water Impoundment, scenic streams, cascades, wetlands, expansive meadows.

Maintained by: Quehanna Area Trails Club, volunteers.

Contact info:
Quehanna Area Trails Club, websites: www.kta-hike.org/Quehanna_Trail.htm, www.dcnr.state.pa.us/forestry/hiking/quehanna.htm, www.kta-hike.org.
Moshannon State Forest, 3372 State Park Rd., Penfield, PA 15849; phone: 814-765-0821; e-mail: fd09@state.pa.us; website: www.dcnr.state.pa.us/forestry/stateforests/forests/moshannon/moshannon.htm.
Elk State Forest, 258 Sizerville Rd., Emporium, PA 15834; phone: 814-486-3353; e-mail: fd13@state.pa.us; website: www.dcnr.state.pa.us/forestry/stateforests/forests/elk/elk.htm.

Maps and guides: Maps available for free from Elk and Moshannon State
Forests; guides may be purchased.

Trailhead directions:
Wykoff Run Natural Area: From the east, proceed west on I-80 to Exit 147 at
Snow Shoe. Bear right off the exit and turn left onto PA 144. Follow PA 144
to Moshannon, where the road turns right. Continue for 2 miles and turn
left onto PA 879. Follow PA 879 to Karthaus, and about 1 mile after, turn
right onto the Quehanna Highway (SR 1011) and proceed 8.7 miles to the
juncture with Wykoff Run Road, where there is a small parking area. The dirt
road to the left also offers parking. From the west, take Exit 120 off I-80 and
follow PA 879 east to Shawville and onto Karthaus. Where PA 879 turns
right to Karthaus, at the One Stop Gift Shoppe, continue straight onto the
Quehanna Highway. Continue 8.7 miles farther to the parking area.

Despite its great beauty and numerous trails, the Quehanna Trail
(QT) and its cross connector trails do not offer many weekend
loops. The loops that are created by these trails are either too short or
too long. In the northeast corner of the QT's loop, however, an extensive system of cross-country ski trails can be used to create an excellent weekend loop.

To hike this loop counterclockwise, hike south on the Quehanna
Highway from the trailhead for a short distance, then turn left onto the
blue-blazed Wykoff Trail. Descend gently into a shallow glen with a
small stream, wet meadows, and potential campsites, though none are
established. Cross another small stream and bear right onto the Big
Spring Draft Trail, also blazed blue. Follow this trail across rolling terrain for 1.5 miles before descending into the glen of Big Spring Draft, a
very scenic stream with cascades, boulders, thickets of rhododendron,
and groves of hemlock. Hike along the stream for .7 mile, until you
reach Big Spring, an excellent water source. Soon thereafter, turn left
onto Three Springs Road. Follow this road for .3 mile, until you reach
the blue-blazed No. Fifteen Trail to your right. You can hike this trail
for .7 mile as it descends to the QT, turn left onto the QT, and hike out
of the glen to cross Three Springs Road, or you can continue on Three
Springs Road for almost a mile and turn left onto the QT.

Descend gradually to beautiful Upper Jerry Run and follow it downstream for about a mile, with excellent scenery, including cascades
and large boulders. Cross the run three times without bridges. At a
pipeline, turn left and climb steeply out of the glen, passing massive
boulders. This is a 400-foot climb over .6 mile. At the top, turn right

onto a grassy forest road and follow it for .3 mile. Turn left off the grassy road. The orange-blazed Old Sinnemahoning Trail continues straight, so watch carefully for the QT. After a period of level hiking, descend 700 feet over 1.6 miles into Upper Pine Hollow. The descent is rocky and steep. Possible camping can be found in the fork halfway down the hollow. Cross scenic Wykoff Run over a bridge and bear right onto Wykoff Run Road, passing a parking area. Cross the road and turn left up Laurel Draft. Over the next 2 miles, the trail ascends 700 feet along scenic cascades. At the top, pass a campsite and meadow. Climb up a hill and cross pipeline swaths. Descend and cross a small stream in a meadow. Level hiking ensues for almost a mile as the trail crosses Hoover Road. A mile farther, the trail traverses the edge of the plateau and reaches Little Fork Draft Vista as it overlooks a deep gorge. Pass Arch Spring and turn left onto an old grassy road past meadows and campsites. Descend to a stream and juncture with Sanders Trail.

For the next 2 miles, descend along Sanders Draft with cascades, boulders, rhododendron, and hemlocks. The scenery becomes more spectacular at the bottom, with an impressive boulder cascade and pool. The forest is deep and verdant. Small campsites may be found in this area. Cross Red Run, with more excellent scenery; this is one of the most scenic areas along the QT. Bear right onto Red Run Road and

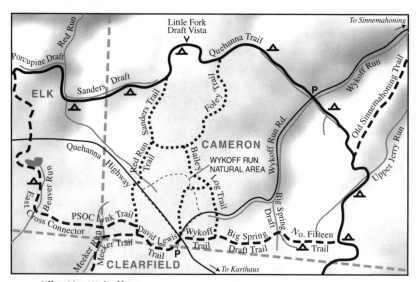

Hike 19c: Wykoff Loop

follow for .7 mile. Turn left along an old grade up Porcupine Hollow to begin a 900-foot climb over 1.6 miles. There are numerous stream crossings, many cascades and boulders, and a steep climb near the top. Turn left onto Losey Road; the QT leaves to the right. Follow the blue-blazed East Cross Connector (ECC) for .5 mile along the road. The trail leaves the road to the left and over the next 2 miles is level or rolling, crossing two stream and scenic meadows, until it crosses the Quehanna Highway.

Enter a scenic pine plantation where the trail is often boggy. Hike through a series of expansive meadows and forests around the scenic Beaver Run Shallow Water Impoundment, nothing more than a shallow pond. Through here, blazes may be far apart, and the trail isn't really established. The trail is level and rolling for the remainder of the trip, as it crosses pipeline and powerline swaths and more meadows. Descend to a series of ponds, wetlands, and meadows along Beaver Run, which the trail crosses over a footbridge. Pass the Bridge Trail to the right, and a mile farther, pass another blue-blazed trail to the right. Follow the ECC to Meeker Run, where you can either turn left and follow the PSOC Link Trail or continue on the ECC for .2 mile farther and turn left onto the Meeker Trail. The PSOC Link Trail features scenic boulders and outcrops, as well as a small stream, and joins with the Red Run Trail; turn right here and continue for .1 mile to the Meeker Trail. Bear left and continue .5 mile to Reactor Road and a small parking area. Bear left onto the broad, level David Lewis Trail, which ends at the trailhead along the Quehanna Highway.

19d. Piper Loop

Length: 26-mile loop.

Duration: 1.5 to 2.5 days.

Difficulty: Easy to moderate.

Terrain: Trails are mostly level or rolling. Ascents and descents range from 100 to 500 feet and can be steep in sections.

Trail conditions: Trails are generally well blazed but brushy in sections.

Blazes: Quehanna Trail, orange; East Cross Connector and cross-country ski trails, blue.

Water: Plentiful.

Vegetation: Hardwoods predominate, with large, open meadows of low-bush blueberries, ferns, and grass; mountain laurel; wetlands and bogs; hemlocks and rhododendron often found along streams.

Highlights: Vistas, Mosquito Creek Gorge, Big Spring Draft, isolation, scenic streams, open meadows, boulders, Corporation Dam.

Maintained by: Quehanna Area Trails Club, volunteers.

Contact info:

Quehanna Area Trails Club, websites: www.kta-hike.org/Quehanna_Trail.htm, www.dcnr.state.pa.us/forestry/hiking/quehanna.htm, www.kta-hike.org.

Moshannon State Forest, 3372 State Park Rd., Penfield, PA 15849; phone: 814-765-0821; e-mail: fd09@state.pa.us; website: www.dcnr.state.pa.us/forestry/stateforests/forests/moshannon/moshannon.htm.

Elk State Forest, 258 Sizerville Rd., Emporium, PA 15834; phone: 814-486-3353; e-mail: fd13@state.pa.us; website: www.dcnr.state.pa.us/forestry/stateforests/forests/elk/elk.htm.

Maps and guides: Map available for free from Moshannon State Forest; guides may be purchased.

Trailhead directions:

Wykoff Run Natural Area: From the east, proceed west on I-80 to Exit 147 at Snow Shoe. Bear right off the exit and turn left onto PA 144. Follow PA 144 to Moshannon, where the road turns right. Continue for 2 miles and turn left onto PA 879. Follow PA 879 to Karthaus, and about 1 mile after, turn right onto the Quehanna Highway (SR 1011) and proceed 8.7 miles to the juncture with Wykoff Run Road, where there is a small parking area. The dirt road to the left also offers parking. From the west, take Exit 120 off I-80 and follow PA 879 to Shawville and onto Karthaus. Where PA 879 turns right to Karthaus, continue straight onto the Quehanna Highway. Continue 8.7 miles to the parking area.

Piper trailhead: Follow the same directions as above to the juncture of PA 879 and the Quehanna Highway, near Karthaus. Follow the Quehanna Highway for 5.2 miles, and the trailhead is on the right, about .7 mile past the Quehanna Boot Camp.

Like the Wykoff Loop, the Piper Loop is formed by the Quehanna Trail (QT), East Cross Connector (ECC), and several cross-country ski trails. This is a great weekend loop for beginners or those looking for a fairly easy trail.

To hike this loop counterclockwise from Piper, follow the Quehanna Highway south from the trailhead, and turn left onto the QT. The trail is level for a mile as it enters the headwaters of Rider Draft and reaches a vista. Turn left, and rolling terrain continues for a mile across the plateau before the trail descends 300 feet over .5 mile to Upper Three Runs. Follow the stream down to a small reservoir. Because it is used for drinking water, you should not camp along this stream. Climb 400 feet over .6 mile up Laurel Swamp Draft and reach a nice vista over the glens and gorges. The QT is level and rolling for another mile and passes the former site of a fire tower. Pass a vista to the south and east, and descend to Lower Three Runs. Hike upstream along this small run for .6 mile, until the QT reaches the blue-blazed No. Fifteen Trail, where you leave the QT and bear straight onto the No. Fifteen Trail. Gradually climb for .7 mile, and then bear left onto Three Runs Road. Follow the road for .2 mile and turn right onto the blue-blazed Big Spring Draft Trail.

Pass Big Spring, an excellent water source, and descend gradually along a small stream through meadows, hemlocks, pines, and mountain laurel. Descend into Big Spring Draft's glen, a truly scenic area with more hemlocks, and mountain laurel, as well as tunnels of rhododendron. The stream has cascades and small waterfalls. Climb gradually out of the glen, and for the next 1.5 miles, the trail is rolling, crossing small streams. At a juncture with the Bailey Log and Wykoff Trails, turn left onto the Wykoff Trail. Descend gradually, crossing

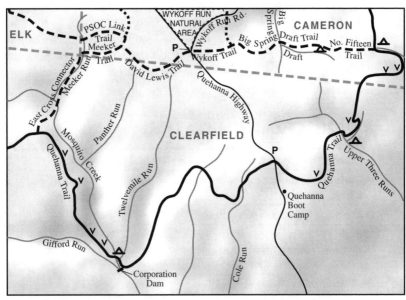

Hike 19d: Piper Loop

small streams and wet meadows, before crossing the Quehanna Highway, with parking to your right.

Follow a dirt road for a short distance, with parking, and pick up the blue-blazed David Lewis Trail to the right. Follow this grassy, rolling trail for 1.5 miles to paved Reactor Road. Cross the road and follow a blue-blazed trail for .5 mile. Turn left onto Meeker Trail and follow it for a mile as it descends along a small stream, crosses Meeker Run, and meets the ECC. Turn left onto the ECC and descend along Meeker Run, with boulders. Cross the run and climb the bank to Lost Run Road, on which you turn right. Descend to scenic Mosquito Creek. Cross the creek over a bridge, bear left off the trail, and follow the creek downstream. The ECC turns right and begins a steep climb up a side glen, a 300-foot climb over .4 mile. Turn left onto Lost Run Road and reach the QT.

Turn left onto the QT for the return hike back to Piper. For the next 3 miles, the trail follows along or in close proximity to the rim of the Mosquito Creek Gorge, with occasional views. Begin a 400-foot descent over .8 mile along a ridge that steepens near the bottom. Cross beautiful and sizable Mosquito Creek via a bridge, and soon thereafter cross Twelvemile Run. Great campsites are in this vicinity. The QT proceeds downstream for a short distance before bearing left to begin a 500-foot climb over .6 mile to the top of the plateau. The remaining 5 miles back to the Quehanna Highway are level and rolling, as the trail crosses small streams, passes boulders, and explores the hardwood forests with open meadows, ferns, and lowbush blueberries. Upon reaching the highway, turn left to the parking area.

🥾 20. Chuck Keiper Trail

Length: 50-mile loop; East Branch Trail is a 2.5-mile connector trail.

Duration: East Loop; 2 to 3 days; West Loop; 2 to 4 days; entire trail; 4 to 6 days.

Difficulty: Moderate to very difficult.

Terrain: Northern sections of both loops have several steep ascents and descents, ranging from 200 to 1,000 feet, often without switchbacks. Sidehill hiking in gorges along streams. Isolated hiking.

Trail conditions: Trail is sufficiently blazed but often brushy on top of plateau. Several small stream crossings without bridges.

Blazes: Orange.

Water: Generally plentiful.

Vegetation: A few sections of the plateau have been clear-cut and are open; occasional meadows and fields; plateau often brushy, with blueberry bushes and mountain laurel; plateau forest dominated by hardwoods; hemlocks and rhododendron occasionally found in gorges; stinging nettles common in the gorges along streams; trail passes near swamps and wetlands with diverse vegetation.

Highlights: Views, scenic streams, rock outcrops and boulders, East Branch Natural Area, Cranberry Swamp Natural Area, Yost Run, cascades and waterfalls, Fish Dam and Burns Run Wild Areas.

Maintained by: Keystone Trails Association, volunteers.

Contact info:
Sproul State Forest, HCR 62, Box 90, Renovo, PA 17764; phone: 570-923-6011; e-mail: fd10@state.pa.us; websites: www.dcnr.state.pa.us/forestry/stateforests/forests/sproul/sproul.htm, www.dcnr.state.pa.us/forestry/hiking/keiper.htm, www.kta-hike.org.

Maps and guides: Free maps available from Sproul State Forest; no guides available.

Trailhead directions: The main trailhead is located 10.1 miles south of Renovo on PA 144, or 20.4 miles north on PA 144 from its juncture with PA 879 near Moshannon. The trailhead is located at the impressive Dennison Run Vista.

The Chuck Keiper Trail (CKT) is a 50-mile loop. The 2.5-mile-long East Branch Trail serves as a connector trail that essentially divides the CKT into two loops: the 33-mile West Loop, and the 22-mile East Loop. Either of these loops is an ideal weekend trip. The CKT is known for its isolation, wildlife, and scenery. It is also one of Pennsylvania's more difficult trails. The southern sections of both loops traverse the plateau and have moderate terrain. The northern sections are much more difficult, as the trail climbs in and out of numerous gorges and glens of streams that have carved deep into the plateau. Some roadwalking has been eliminated by recent trail relocations.

At the trailhead, you are treated to an excellent view of the Fish Dam Wild Area, with its deep gorges. The end of the loop comes in from the right. Hike down to PA 144. The trail to the left that follows PA 144 is the East Branch Trail, the CKT's connector trail. This trail fol-

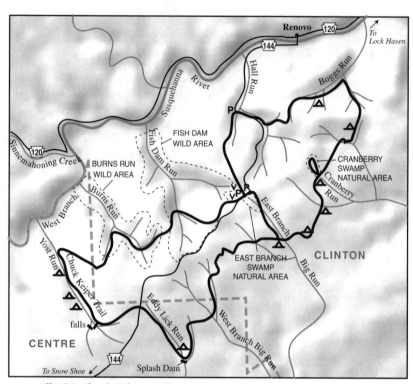

Hike 20: Chuck Keiper Trail

lows PA 144 for almost .5 mile, turns right, and winds through pine trees, following old forest roads and passing a pipeline swath. The terrain is level as the trail traverses the edge of the East Branch Swamp Natural Area. Blueberry bushes are common. Turn right onto Beech Road, follow it for a short distance, and turn left, leaving the road. The trail follows the remnants of an old grade through a hardwood forest, passing occasional campsites. The small stream nearby is the East Branch of Big Run. The East Branch Trail rejoins with the CKT.

The two loops are described separately below, hiking counterclockwise.

Section One: West Loop

To hike the West Loop, follow the trail right along PA 144, with more views. After .5 mile, the CKT leaves PA 144 through pines and begins a 300-foot ascent over .3 mile. The trail levels off after the ascent and begins a gradual descent that steepens as the trail approaches Fish

Dam Run, a small stream. Follow the run downstream for about a mile as you descend deeper into the surrounding gorge. The trail turns left to begin a steep ascent up a side hollow. Now begins a steep, rocky 800-foot ascent over .5 mile with little help from switchbacks. At the top, level hiking ensues. Cross Jews Run Road, turn right onto the JU Branch Trail, and begin a descent into the Burns Run Wild Area, with a nice view from the top. The CKT descends into the hollow carved by the JU Branch, a small seasonal stream. At the bottom of the gorge at Burns Run, the CKT follows the run closely, with an extensive sidehill that takes the trail above the stream. After .75 mile, descend to Burns Run and cross Packer Fork with potential campsites. Cross Burns Run. Begin to bear left up Owl Hollow, with potential campsites near Burns Run. Begin a long 900-foot climb over .75 mile up Owl Hollow and its small seasonal stream.

In typical fashion, level hiking follows upon reaching the plateau. Cross Fisher Fire Road and turn left onto Plantation Trail, with campsites. A gradual descent begins as the trail nears Second Fork. Turn right and descend along this small stream. The descent steepens, and the CKT follows a sidehill above the stream before turning left and dropping to Yost Run and its beautiful gorge, one of the CKT's highlights. The trail follows the bottom of the gorge for more than 2 miles.

This deep, narrow gorge harbors hemlocks, pines, cascading side streams, rhododendron, and Yost Run, a crystal-clear mountain stream. The CKT initially followed this scenic stream closely, with numerous crossings. This proved to be difficult in high water, and the trail now follows a sidehill above the stream and occasionally dips down close to Yost Run, with campsites. The former trail along Yost Run has been blazed blue and is the more scenic route; I suggest you hike it. Many backpackers feel the construction of the sidehill to avoid stream crossings, thus keeping the trail away from the stream, has compromised the beauty of the CKT. With fine scenery and reliable water, the gorge is an ideal place to camp. Continue to head upstream, passing ledges and boulders, and reach a scenic spot where Kyler Run drops over a 15-foot waterfall into Yost Run. Beneath the waterfall is a small, beautiful campsite. Just upstream along Yost Run is a similar waterfall. The trail continues upstream, passes a cabin, and bears left, ascending Bloom Draft along a forest road. Pass a piped spring and another cabin. At the top of the plateau, turn right on another forest road and cross PA 144.

The terrain south of PA 144 is much more moderate, with mild inclines and descents as the CKT traverses the plateau. Turn left onto a forest road and descend into Eddy Lick Run's valley. At first the trail is above the stream on the bank, but then it begins to descend to the stream, crossing it five times. The trail follows a railroad grade along Eddy Lick Run and passes the remains of a stone splash dam, with camping. Continue downstream, then turn left, away from the run, along the state forest boundary. Follow a forest road, and then join another railroad grade. After about .75 mile, turn right off the grade, passing a spring to your right, and climb to DeHaas Road along an old forest road. Level hiking ensues for about a mile before an increasingly steep 200-foot descent to the West Branch of Big Run. Head upstream and bear right, following Panther Branch for more than a mile. Along the way, you cross the stream four times, with potential campsites.

Bear right and begin a gentle climb away from Panther Branch. Cross Hicks Road and begin a gentle descent for almost a mile, until you cross a small stream. Turn right onto Penrose Road near a hunting cabin. Follow the road for .3 mile and turn left near Camp Rockspar. The CKT begins a gentle climb over the saddle between two knobs and descends gently to Swamp Branch, with campsites. Cross Coon Run Road near another hunting cabin and begin another moderate climb before descending to the East Branch Trail and the beginning of the East Loop along the East Branch of Big Run. A campsite is to the right.

Section Two: East Loop

Begin hiking the East Loop by gradually ascending along the state forest boundary along a field reverting to forest. Cross Beech Creek Road and follow a forest road behind a cabin. Here the trail also passes a seasonal spring. The trail follows the road out of the forest and into an expansive clear-cut. Cross this clear-cut and descend along the edge of another to Rock Run. Here you'll find a campsite near a cabin. Climb away from Rock Run through thick laurel and blueberry bushes underneath a hardwood forest. Cross Shoemaker Ridge Road and pass through another clear-cut before a steep 200-foot descent to Clendenin Branch; small campsites can be found downstream to your right. A long, gradual ascent for more than a mile follows, before another steep 350-foot descent to Cranberry Run. There are potential campsites along this scenic stream. To the left is a side trail that wraps around the Cranberry Swamp Natural Area, which contains a 144-acre mountain bog. A 400-foot climb over .5 mile follows, then a similar descent, part of which is along a forest road, to Benjamin Run. Turn right at the road along Benjamin Run and follow it for .25 mile, then turn left and pass behind a cabin with a pipe spring.

Now begin the ascent of Sled Road Hollow. Cross the small stream several times, with possible campsites. The ascent steepens and passes through a glade with a dry campsite. The climb continues to steepen as the trail follows an old forest road. Upon reaching the top of the ridge, cross Mill Run Road and begin a steep, rocky descent into Boggs Run Gorge. There are no switchbacks along this descent. For the next mile, the CKT follows a small stream, however, the trail traverses a sidehill high above the stream. The trail turns left high above Boggs Run and begins a gradual descent to the stream. Cross a small tributary and bear right on the trail. Here the terrain is fairly level and offers nice campsites near Boggs Run under hemlocks. I camped here alone one summer night, encompassed by the isolation of the gorge. It was odd waking up at night to absolute darkness, with no light from towns or even the moon. A powerful thunderstorm rumbled through early the next morning. It was awesome seeing the lightning and hearing the storm echo and bounce off the sides of the gorge. It is safer camping down in the gorges, because powerful thunderstorms sweep across the plateau tops in summer and tornados have occurred.

Continue upstream and cross another side stream. Descend to Boggs Run and cross it at a campsite. The trail climbs above Boggs Run along an extensive sidehill. After almost a mile, the trail bears left underneath impressive hardwoods and rhododendron and passes a spring. Stinging nettles are a problem along Boggs Run but are particularly bad here. Pick up an old railroad grade and continue to head upstream, almost to the Boggs Run source, passing a few nice campsites. It was here I once saw a ten-point buck, the most impressive I've ever seen in the wild. Bear right and climb along a seasonal stream. The ascent steepens until the trail levels off before crossing a powerline swath. Turn left onto Pete's Run Road, and then turn right onto a forest road and pass a dry campsite. The trail bears right off the road and begins a long, rocky, and steep descent down Diamond Rock Hollow, with no switchbacks. This is a difficult 900-foot descent over the course of less than .75 mile. Along the way, there is a campsite where the two branches of the hollow meet, but camping is not allowed because the hollow is part of a public watershed. The trail follows the small stream closely, and at times precariously, until it reaches Hall Run and PA 144.

Turn right onto PA 144 and follow it for .75 mile then turn left into Drake Hollow, a scenic place with hemlocks and rhododendron. Hardwoods take over as the trail makes a gradual 1.3-mile ascent up the hollow along an old forest road. Near the top, a side stream features a seasonal waterfall. Reach the top of the plateau along rocky terrain and bear right onto a jeep road. Turn left onto Dry Run Road and bear left on Barney's Ridge Road. Follow the road for .5 mile, until you come to a road to your left that leads to Big Rocks. This short side trip takes you to impressive boulders, ledges, and formations. Continue to follow Barney's Ridge Road for about .6 mile farther, then bear right off the road and follow an old jeep road or powerline swath with thick brush. Ascend gradually over Barney's Ridge, with broken views to the south, and descend to the parking area and trailhead.

21. Allegheny Front Trail

Length: 40-mile loop.

Duration: 2.5 to 4 days.

Difficulty: Moderate.

Terrain: Generally flat or rolling, with gradual descents and ascents. A few climbs can be steep and rocky, but are typically short. Significant amount of sidehills along Sixmile Run, Allegheny Front, and Moshannon Creek.

Trail conditions: Trail is generally well blazed and maintained, although brushy in sections.

Blazes: Orange; Shingle Mill Trail, blue.

Water: Generally plentiful.

Vegetation: Open hardwoods with thick understory of ferns and mountain laurel on plateau; rhododendron and hemlocks common along streams; blueberries; red and white pine plantations; tamaracks; bogs and wetlands; a few open meadows.

Highlights: Vistas of Moshannon Creek, vistas from Allegheny Front, Sixmile Run, Benner Run, wetlands, Moshannon Creek, Black Moshannon Creek, Black Moshannon State Park, Wolf Rocks, scenic mountain streams, wildlife.

Maintained by: Volunteers.

Contact info:
Moshannon State Forest, 3372 State Park Rd., Penfield, PA 15849; phone:
814-765-0821; e-mail: fd09@state.pa.us; websites: www.dcnr.state.pa.
us/forestry/stateforests/forests/moshannon/moshannon.htm,
www.aft.altoona-pa.com.
Black Moshannon State Park, 4216 Beaver Rd., Philipsburg, PA 16866-9519;
phone: 814-342-5960; e-mail: blackmoshannonsp@state.pa.us; website:
www.dcnr.state.pa.us/stateparks/parks/blackmoshannon.asp.

Maps and guides: Free map from Moshannon State Forest and Black
Moshannon State Park; a guide may be purchased.

Trailhead directions:
Main trailhead: From the east, take I-80 west to Exit 158. Proceed south on
Alt. US 220 for 6.7 miles to Unionville. Turn right onto PA 504 and drive 7.1
miles to the parking area, on the right. From the west, take I-80 east to Exit
133. Proceed south on PA 53 to Philipsburg and turn left onto US 322 east.
Drive through Philipsburg, following US 322. Turn left onto PA 504 and
drive 13.2 miles to the parking area, on the left.
Black Moshannon State Park: Follow same directions as above to PA 504. The
park is 11.5 miles from Unionville and 9 miles from Philipsburg.
Western trailhead: Follow same directions as above to PA 504. The trail crosses
PA 504 along the western side of its loop, 14.1 miles from Unionville and
6.2 miles from Philipsburg. There is some parking along the road, but there
isn't a sign.

The Allegheny Front Trail (AFT) is a scenic loop that is quickly gaining popularity among both dayhikers and backpackers. This trail
offers a lot of great scenery, nice campsites, vistas, and scenic streams.
It is conveniently located in the center of the state and is close to I-80,
making the trail a reasonable drive for backpackers from Ohio, New
York, New Jersey, or Maryland.

The trail was founded by Ralph Seeley. Through his determination,
and with help from the Keystone Trails Association, Penn State Outing
Club, and the Quehanna Area Trails Club, a great trail has been created. Seeley has also been a driving force behind the Quehanna Trail.

Completed in 1998, the AFT is one of Pennsylvania's newest backpacking trails. The trail is entirely within Moshannon State Forest, with
a short section of trail within Black Moshannon State Park. The loop
can be divided in half by using the 4-mile Shingle Mill Trail, which follows beautiful Black Moshannon Creek and connects the northern section of the AFT to the dam and swimming area at the state park. From

there you can hike south along Julian Pike or the Moss Hanne Trail to the southern section of the AFT's loop. A roadwalk along Julian Pike is more direct and takes you past the state park office.

Hiking clockwise from the main trailhead at PA 504, cross the road and proceed south. The trail makes a moderate descent along an old forest road, which steepens as the trail begins to drop from the plateau. Pay special attention to the blazes here, as the trail discreetly turns right off this old road, which continues downhill. Many backpackers miss this turn and have to retrace their steps uphill. The AFT quickly reascends the plateau and passes through thick mountain laurel across level terrain. Reach the Allegheny Front at Whetstone Run Vista and a small campsite. The trail descends into the glen carved by a branch of Whetstone Run, a seasonal stream. Bear right, and level hiking ensues along a sidehill; the trail is below the rim of the Allegheny Front and passes rock outcrops and boulders. The terrain is rocky. Climb back to the plateau along the other branch of Whetstone Run and pass a series of vistas overlooking Bald Eagle Mountain and the ridges and valleys to the south. One of the finest vistas is Ralph's Majestic Vista, named after the man who helped create this trail. From here the trail leaves the Allegheny Front, ascends through flaking rock outcrops, and crosses the plateau, passing Underwood Road and a pipeline swath near the headwaters of Smays Run. Begin a gradual descent and cross Smays Trail at a small stream with camping.

In another .6 mile, the AFT crosses Julian Pike and enters Black Moshannon State Park; backcountry camping is not permitted within the park. Here the AFT also follows the circuitous Moss Hanne Trail. The terrain is level but is often wet and boggy. Cross boggy Shirks Run under a pine plantation. The trail follows near the wetlands of the Black Moshannon Bog Natural Area and crosses another small stream. In about .3 mile, reach Shirks Road and cross Black Moshannon Creek. Turn left and leave the road, staying close to the boggy creek. Follow the small creek upstream, turn right, and cross Clay Mine Road. The trail begins a slight descent, crosses a small stream with potential camping, and .25 mile thereafter, reaches gated Wolf Rock Road. Turn left on the road, following it for about .25 mile, then turn right, leaving the road along a pipeline swath. Cross another small creek and bear right. After about a mile, the trail winds through Wolf Rocks, a series of interesting ledges and outcroppings. Descend to Horse Hollow Road and Sixmile Run.

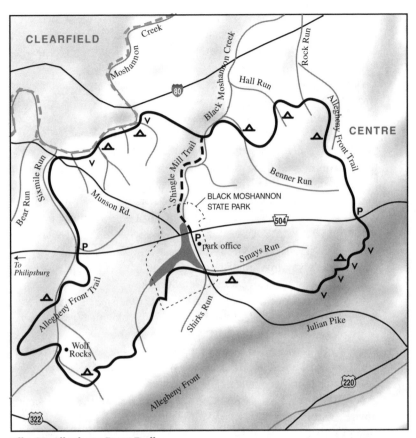

Hike 21: Allegheny Front Trail

The next segment of the loop is within the Sixmile Run watershed, forming the western boundary of the loop. Sixmile Run is a beautiful trout stream with hemlocks and rhododendron. The trail may also be boggy in this section.

Cross the run and proceed downstream, passing a small, scenic pond. After .7 mile, the AFT turns left, leaves Sixmile Run, and begins a gradual ascent up Slide Hollow, a 250-foot climb over about a mile. The trail turns right, crosses two small streams, and returns to Sixmile Run after 1.7 miles. Cross the run via a road bridge and continue along this beautiful stream for almost a mile. Then the AFT turns right and makes an initially steep 350-foot climb over .7 mile to the top of the plateau. The trail bears left and descends steeply into a side glen carved by a small stream back to Sixmile Run. This is a 400-foot descent over about .6 mile. Return to Sixmile Run and hike downstream to Hufton Run and PA 504.

Cross PA 504 and again follow Sixmile Run downstream, which has carved a gorge almost 500 feet deep. Over the next 3 miles, the AFT follows Sixmile Run closely, ascending away from the stream only for short distances if the run flows against a steep embankment. This section is one of the highlights of the AFT, with thick hemlocks and rhododendron next to a clear stream. At times the trail is very close to the run, so it could possibly be flooded during periods of high water. You also pass rock ledges alongside the run. This section of trail is mostly a sidehill. There are potential campsites along the run where the terrain permits. Sixmile Run is heavily fished for trout when the season opens. Before Sixmile Run passes under Munson Road, the AFT climbs away from the run to the right. Cross Munson Road and follow an old grade above Moshannon Creek.

Moshannon Creek is a large stream, almost the size of a small river. It would be a creek of great beauty if it weren't polluted by acid mine drainage, which gives the creek a red-orange hue. As a result, the creek is often called Red Moshannon Creek. Many streams in central and western Pennsylvania are lifeless from acid mine drainage, a heavy price to pay for man's careless extraction of coal.

For about the next 4 miles, the trail follows Moshannon Creek downstream. The trail is usually above the creek as it traverses the side of its gorge. There are a few ascents and descents, as well as a nice vista. This section of trail is another highlight of the AFT, with views, rhododendron, and nice campsites along side streams. The trail crosses five small tributaries that have carved their own glens into the plateau: Panther Hollow, Sawdust Hollow, Tark Hill Run, Dry Hollow, and Potter Run. The last vista of this section is that of the I-80 bridge and a railroad bridge. Now begin a steep 400-foot ascent over .7 mile, which levels off as the trail ascends the plateau.

A slight ascent continues for more than a mile before the trail crosses a forest road and descends to Black Moshannon Creek. Here the AFT meets the Shingle Mill Trail. The trail turns left and follows this beautiful creek downstream. After .7 mile, cross the creek via a bridge and follow Benner Run upstream. This is another scenic trout stream with rhododendron and camping. Follow Benner Run for about 1.2 miles, then turn left and gradually ascend along a small sidestream. The trail levels off and descends gradually to Hall Run, where the AFT turns right and follows the stream for about .7 mile. Camping exists along the run. The trail turns left, leaves the run, and in .5 mile cross Tram Road, a forest road. Descend to the headwaters of a small stream; Rock Run Trail joins from the left. Bear right and reach Rock Run in about .7 mile. Follow a grade to the right above the run, with campsites, and pass a side trail to the left that leads to the Rock Run Trail.

The AFT leaves Rock Run and passes several small streams that form the headwaters of Benner Run. Here you'll find more scenic campsites. Begin a slight ascent along an old logging road through a clear-cut planted with Norway spruce. The trail passes a pipeline swath with a view of Benner Run's drainage. The AFT ends where you started, at PA 504.

Southwestern Pennsylvania and the Laurel Highlands Region

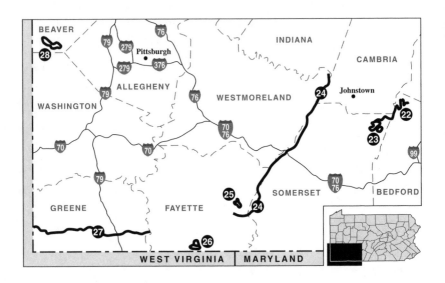

The popular Laurel Highlands and Southern Alleghenies have long been prime destinations for hikers and backpackers. This region features the highest elevations in the state and plenty of incredible scenery. Spectacular Ohiopyle State Park serves as the southern trailhead of the Laurel Highlands Trail, the region's premier trail. The park is not to be missed, with its whitewater rapids, beautiful gorge, vistas, waterfalls, and natural waterslides.

Beyond the well-known Laurel Highlands Trail, this region offers many more backpacking opportunities. Bear Run Nature

Reserve, Raccoon Creek State Park, and Quebec Run Wild Area each feature trail systems affording excellent weekend excursions with great scenery. The Warrior Trail wanders through the hilly pastoral countryside of Greene County. Lost Turkey Trail and John P. Saylor Trail are located farther to the east, along the Allegheny Front, and both provide fine weekend getaways. The trails here will not disappoint and are within easy driving distance of backpackers from Pittsburgh, Ohio, West Virginia, and Maryland.

22. Lost Turkey Trail

Length: 26.28-mile (42.3-kilometer) linear trail.

Duration: 1.5 to 2.5 days.

Difficulty: Moderate to difficult.

Terrain: The first half of the trail is the most difficult, with the greatest changes of elevation and ascents and descents ranging from 400 to 1,000 feet. Steep and rocky in sections. The second half is level and rolling across the plateau; the greatest ascent and descent is 300 feet. Trail often follows old forest roads and railroad grades.

Trail conditions: Trail is generally well blazed and maintained. A few stream crossings.

Blazes: Red with posts every kilometer.

Water: Generally plentiful.

Vegetation: Northern hardwoods predominate, with hemlocks, pines, mountain laurel, aspen, and apple trees; pine plantations; open meadows and wetlands.

Highlights: Blue Knob State Park, Lost Cox Children Monument, Bobs Creek, vistas, scenic streams, isolation, Allegheny Front.

Maintained by: Gallitzin State Forest, volunteers.

Contact info:
Gallitzin State Forest, P.O. Box 506, Ebensburg, PA 15931;
   phone: 814-472-1862; e-mail: fd06@state.pa.us; websites:
   www.dcnr.state.pa.us/forestry/stateforests/forests/gallitzin/gallitzin.htm,
   www.dcnr.state.pa.us/forestry/hiking/turkey.htm.
Blue Knob State Park, 124 Park Rd., Imler, PA 16655-9207;
   phone: 814-276-3576; e-mail: blueknobsp@state.pa.us;
   website: www.dcnr.state.pa.us/stateparks/parks/blueknob.asp.

Maps and guides: Free map and guide available from Gallitzin State Forest

Trailhead directions:
Herman Point (Blue Knob State Park): From the north, head south on US 99. Get off at Exit 23 and turn right onto PA 164. Follow this west for 7.7 miles. Turn left onto SR 3003 (Blue Knob Road), and proceed 5 miles to Blue Knob State Park. At the park sign, bear left and follow the road for .5 mile. Turn left on a gated, paved road with a white trail post. Parking is limited. From the south, head north on US 99. Get off at Exit 7 and follow PA 869 west 9.5 miles to Pavia. Turn right onto Pavia Road, at a sign for the state park. Follow the road 3.8 miles through the state park; the incline is steep. Before leaving the park, make a sharp right and follow the road for .5 mile to a gated, paved road to your left. Parking is limited.

Burnt House Picnic Area: From Exit 7 along US 99, this trailhead is located 11.5 miles along PA 869 west. Parking area on left just after picnic area; there is a white trail post.

PA 56 (Western Trailhead): From Exit 3 along US 99, follow PA 56 west for 18.9 miles, where there is a large parking area to the right. This trailhead is located 8 miles along PA 56, east of US 219, on the left.

The Lost Turkey Trail (LTT) was constructed in 1976 and traverses the highest point of any backpacking trail in Pennsylvania: 3,034 feet at the summit of Herman Point in Blue Knob State Park. Because of its high elevation, the LTT often receives heavy snowfalls, providing great opportunities for snowshoeing and cross-country skiing; a few sections of the trail are also open to snowmobiles. The length of the trail is marked with kilometer posts.

Unfortunately, because of camping restrictions on state park and game lands, it is difficult to backpack the trail in its entirety. For the first 17 miles, the trail crosses private, state park, and game lands where backcountry camping is not permitted. This section also features the most strenuous terrain and is very difficult for most backpackers to hike in one day.

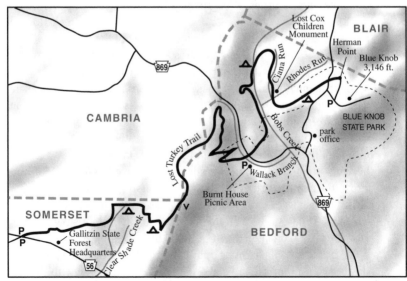

Hike 22: Lost Turkey Trail

From Herman Point, the trail descends 400 feet over .4 mile to SR 4035. The descent continues beyond the road, then the trail levels off for a mile and passes behind the state park's camping area. Enter private land and descend gradually along Conrad Ridge. Bear right and begin a steep 500-foot descent over .6 mile off the ridge. At the bottom, cross Monument Road and Rhodes Run; proceed upstream along Ciana Run and pass the Lost Cox Children Monument, where the bodies of George and Joseph Cox were discovered in April 1856. Follow an old grade along Ciana Run as you gradually ascend upstream. Climb over the top of Hog Back Ridge and descend 500 feet over .4 mile to scenic Bobs Creek. Cross the creek via a bridge; this is a nice area for camping. Follow the LTT downstream, then bear right and ascend into the glen carved by Ickes Run. Climb 500 feet over a mile and traverse the crest of Fork Ridge. Pass a nice vista to the east of Bobs Creek and Blue Knob. The LTT continues to follow the ridge for about a mile across level terrain before descending to Wallack Branch. Here the trail drops almost 500 feet over .5 mile and becomes steeper at the bottom. Cross the stream and PA 863, with parking. To the left is the Burnt House Picnic Area, with restrooms, parking, and drinking water.

You now begin the last, long climb of the trail as the LTT ascends the Allegheny Front. Although long, this climb is gradual as it follows old railroad grades and crosses several small streams. The trail ascends 1,000 feet over 3 miles. It begins its circuitous ascent up scenic Big Break Hollow, switchbacks, and crosses over to Little Break Hollow; then it makes a sharp left and reaches the crest of the Allegheny Front. Parts of this trail are also open to cross-country skiing. It's amazing to realize all the effort it must have taken to construct this grade.

The remaining 13 miles of the trail are easy as it crosses the Allegheny Plateau with level and rolling terrain. You pass several streams, open fields and meadows, and wetlands. After the first 2 miles, the trail passes active beaver dams and descends slightly into the headwaters of the South Fork of the Conemaugh River. On May 31, 1889, one of the worst tragedies in America's history occurred, when a dam built across the South Fork several miles downstream burst after heavy rains. The negligently maintained dam was owned by an exclusive private club. The ensuing flash flood descended upon Johnstown, devastated the city, and claimed almost 3,000 lives.

The trail gradually ascends and in 1.6 miles reaches the crest of the Allegheny Front for the last time, with an exceptional view to the east provided by a pipeline swath. The view overlooks the ridges, valleys, and farmlands of Bedford County. Descend gradually and enter the Gallitzin State Forest, where backcountry camping is permitted. The LTT crosses a road and follows extensive grades and old forest roads for its remainder; this section of trail is also open to snowmobiles in winter. Gradually descend to a small stream, bear right, and gradually ascend until the trail reaches the state forest boundary, which it follows. Descend and cross another small stream, followed by another easy ascent along the boundary. The LTT descends gradually again to another small stream, leaves the boundary, and begins a 300-foot climb over .6 mile to the crest of Pot Ridge. The trail passes through open fields created by poor lumbering in the past when the forest was clear-cut, exposing the underlying soil to erosion and fires; as a result, trees have not been able to regenerate, and in many places the lack of trees caused the water table to rise, creating marshes and wetlands.

Cross another road and follow the trail for 3 miles across easy, rolling terrain to the western trailhead, located at the Babcock Picnic Area, which is also the trailhead for the John P. Saylor Trail.

23. John P. Saylor Trail

Length: 17.5-mile double loop.

Duration: 1.5 to 2 days.

Difficulty: Easy.

Terrain: Mostly level or rolling, with ascents and descents ranging from 100 to 200 vertical feet. Often rocky. Trail often follows old forest roads or railroad grades.

Trail conditions: Trail is generally well blazed and maintained. Often wet and boggy in sections along Clear Shade Creek. Small stream crossings.

Blazes: Orange, with mileage posts.

Water: Generally sufficient.

Vegetation: Hardwoods dominate, with hemlocks and pines often found near streams; meadows along Clear Shade Creek.

Highlights: Wolf Rocks, Clear Shade Creek, Clear Shade Wild Area.

Maintained by: Gallitzin State Forest, volunteers.

Contact info:
Gallitzin State Forest, P.O. Box 506, Ebensburg, PA 15931;
  phone: 814-472-1862; e-mail: fd06@state.pa.us; websites:
  www.dcnr.state.pa.us/forestry/stateforests/forests/gallitzin/gallitzin.htm,
  www.dcnr.state.pa.us/forestry/hiking/saylor.htm.

Maps and guides: Free map from Gallitzin State Forest; no guide available.

Trailhead directions:
Babcock Picnic Area: From Exit 3 along US 99, follow PA 56 west for 19 miles.
  Turn left into the Babcock Picnic Area. Bear right at a Y and enter the picnic
  area. The trailhead is .1 mile from PA 56. This picnic area is located 7.9
  miles east of US 219 along PA 56, on the right.

This trail is named after Congressman John P. Saylor, who represented Pennsylvania from 1949 to 1973. He was a conservationist with a deep concern for the environment. While in Congress, Saylor sponsored the National Scenic Trails Act and supported national wilderness preservation.

With easy terrain and scenic natural features, the John P. Saylor Trail (JST) is an excellent trail for beginning backpackers.

The trail begins at the Babcock Picnic Area, with sufficient parking, restrooms, and water. To hike the trail counterclockwise, begin the loop to the right. The trail makes a slight descent for .15 mile, crosses a small stream, and follows it for a short distance. Bear left, leaving the stream, and cross Verla Road. For the next mile to Wolf Rocks, the JST makes a slight ascent across increasingly rocky terrain. The trail follows a small stream to the left that offers some camping. As you near Wolf Rocks, you pass rock outcrops and boulders and begin a short ascent. The section of trail between the Babcock Picnic Area and Wolf Rocks is heavily used by dayhikers.

Wolf Rocks is a grouping of massive rock outcrops and boulders that are deeply fractured with crevices and small caves. Unfortunately, the rocks have extensive graffiti, which compromises the beauty of this natural feature. The JST leaves Wolf Rocks and passes the yellow-blazed Bog and Boulder Trail to the left. This 3.3-mile-long trail serves as a cross connector to the main loop of the JST and features boulders, outcrops, and a loop around a large bog with wildlife viewing. It's a trail worth hiking if you have the time.

For the next mile, the trail makes an easy ascent, bears right, and begins an equally easy descent. Then it reaches a meadow. From here the JST bears right; the unblazed trail that proceeds straight leads to

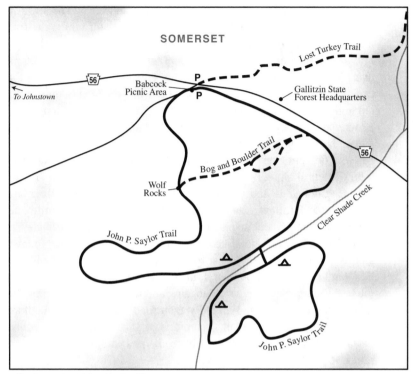

Hike 23: John P. Saylor Trail

Shade Road. For the next 1.5 miles, the trail makes a slight descent and joins a small stream off to the right. Cross Crum Road and descend along a small stream. Then the trail bears left, leaves the stream, and joins an old railroad grade. Cross another small stream and follow it upstream for a mile, until the trail crosses Crum Road once again and enters the Clear Shade Wild Area.

The JST is mostly level for the next mile, until it begins a mild descent to scenic Clear Shade Creek, a sizable mountain stream that has escaped the ravages of acid mine drainage, which has afflicted many streams in this region. Clear Shade Creek features good trout fishing, nice camping, and Class III whitewater rapids a few miles downstream. Follow the creek upstream for about .5 mile, passing through meadows and boggy areas. Several sections of this trail are often wet.

A suspension bridge crossing Clear Shade Creek connects the JST's 12-mile main loop to the trail's 5-mile smaller loop. Turn right and cross the bridge, then turn right to begin the smaller loop, hiking downstream along Clear Shade Creek. For the next mile, the trail often follows a level railroad grade across meadows and boggy areas. Off to your right is Clear Shade Creek. Watch the blazes for where the trail makes a sharp left and ascends away from the creek; an obvious unblazed trail continues straight. The JST makes a mild 160-foot climb over .6 mile, crosses a small stream, and enters a meadow. Follow the trail as it bears right and follows level terrain for .5 mile, then turns left and begins a slight ascent for another .5 mile. The trail then makes a moderate descent and crosses a small stream. It traverses the side of a glen, becoming more level, climbs over a ridge, and makes a steeper 180-foot descent over .4 mile back to Clear Shade Creek. Bear left and follow the trail along the creek, which soon returns you to the bridge.

Cross the bridge and turn right to hike the remainder of the main loop. The JST follows Clear Shade Creek upstream for .7 mile and passes the remnants of a splash dam. Bear left and ascend the glen of a small stream, a 100-foot ascent over .4 mile. A gradual ascent follows as the trail picks up old forest roads and bears left, crossing Shade Road and the Bog and Boulder Trail soon thereafter. The remainder of the trail is easy, as it follows old logging and forest roads, including the former route of PA 56 and an old wagon road that connected Bedford to Johnstown. Cross a small stream and in another mile cross paved Verla Road. Continue the slight descent, pass a small stream, and return to the Babcock Picnic Area.

24. Laurel Highlands Trail

Length: 70-mile linear trail.

Duration: 5 to 9 days.

Difficulty: Moderate.

Terrain: Greatest changes in elevation occur at the northern and southern ends of the trail. There is a 1,400-foot ascent and descent in Ohiopyle and Conemaugh River Gorge. Trail is most rugged through Ohiopyle State Park. In between, the terrain is rolling, with ascents and descents of 100 to 400 feet. The trail crosses several roads.

Trail conditions: Trail is well blazed and maintained.

Blazes: Yellow; side trails to shelter and camping areas, blue.

Water: Generally plentiful; all shelters and campsites have potable water. The trail crosses a few small seasonal streams.

Vegetation: Hardwoods dominated by oaks; understory of ferns, mountain laurel, and brush; meadows, occasional pines, hemlocks, and rhododendron.

Highlights: Ohiopyle State Park, Youghiogheny River Gorge, scenic vistas, Laurel Ridge State Park, shelters and scenic camping, Beam Rocks, rock outcrops and boulders, Conemaugh River Gorge.

Maintained by: Park employees, volunteers.

Contact info:

Laurel Ridge State Park, R.R. 3 Box 246, Rockwood, PA 15557; phone: 724-455-3744, 1-888-PA-PARKS; e-mail: laurelridgesp@state.pa.us; websites: www.dcnr.state.pa.us/stateparks/parks/laurelridge.asp, www.dcnr.state.pa.us/forestry/hiking/laurel.htm.

Forbes State Forest, Rte. 30 East, P.O. Box 519, Laughlintown, PA 15655; phone: 724-238-1200; e-mail: fd04@state.pa.us; website: www.dcnr.state.pa.us/forestry/stateforests/forests/forbes/forbes.htm.

Ohiopyle State Park, P.O. Box 105, Ohiopyle, PA 15470-0105; phone: 724-329-8591; e-mail: ohiopylesp@state.pa.us; website: www.dcnr.state.pa.us/stateparks/parks/ohiopyle.asp.

Maps and guides: Both available for sale; free map also available from Laurel Ridge State Park.

Trailhead directions:

Northern trailhead (Conemaugh River Gorge): From the juncture of PA 56 and PA 403, proceed west onto PA 56 for 6.5 miles toward Seward. At a sign for Laurel Ridge State Park, turn left and follow this road for .5 mile to a parking area. This road is a mile east of Seward, along PA 56.

PA 271: From Johnstown, proceed on PA 271 south for 9.7 miles to an access road and parking area on the left. From Ligonier, proceed on PA 711 north for 2.7 miles to PA 271, then follow PA 271 north for 8.5 miles.

US 30: From Ligonier, follow US 30 east for 8.1 miles to an access road and parking area on the right. From US 219, follow US 30 west 6.5 miles.

PA 31: From Bakersville, follow PA 31 west for 4 miles. Turn left onto Tower Road, with a sign for Roaring Run Natural Area. Follow this road for .6 mile to access road and parking area on the left. From the PA 381/PA 711 juncture at Jones Mills, follow PA 31 east for 4.6 miles.

PA 653: From the juncture of PA 381 and PA 653 at Normalville, follow PA 653 east for 5.6 miles. The parking area will be on the right.

Southern trailhead (Ohiopyle State Park): There are two trailheads in the state park. From the town of Ohiopyle, follow PA 381 north across the bridge. A large parking area on the left is the main trailhead. To reach the trail from here, cross PA 381 and follow Garrett Street to the gate, where the trail begins. If the main parking area is filled, follow PA 381 north from Ohiopyle for .3 mile. Turn right onto a road and follow for .7 mile to another trailhead on the right. This trailhead may be very difficult to reach in winter. From US 40, Ohiopyle is located 6.2 miles north along PA 381. From the PA Turnpike, take the Donegal exit. Turn left on PA 31 east, proceed 2 miles, and turn right onto PA 381/PA 711. Drive 10 miles to Normalville. Follow PA 381 south for 11 miles to Ohiopyle.

he Laurel Highlands Trail (LHT) is the premier trail in this corner of
the state and is also one of Pennsylvania's most popular trails. It is
part of the Potomac Heritage Trail and is designated as one of the state's
three National Scenic Trails. Camping is limited to the shelter/camping
areas, which are reached by side trails every 8 to 10 miles along the
LHT. Each area contains five Adirondack-style shelters with fireplaces,
pit toilets, potable water, and spaces for about thirty tents. Because of
the shelters, the LHT is an excellent trail for winter backpacking or
snowshoeing; the Laurel Highlands typically receive heavy snowfall.

The LHT consistently traverses the highest elevations of any trail in
the state, but other than at the northern and southern ends of the trail,

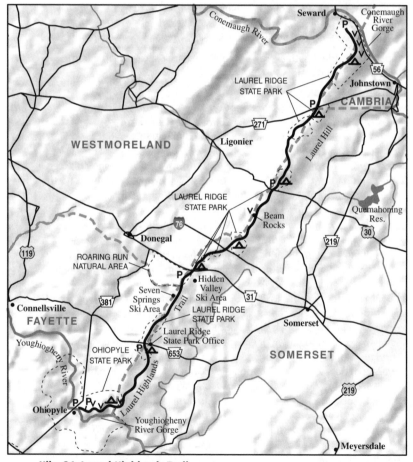

Hike 24: Laurel Highlands Trail

there are relatively few vistas. The trail is ideal for beginners, particularly between Ohiopyle and the Conemaugh River Gorge. The trailheads are well maintained and are often marked by signs for Laurel Ridge State Park. Overnight use of this trail requires a fee and reservations; contact Laurel Ridge State Park.

The descriptions below follow the trail from Ohiopyle State Park to Conemaugh River Gorge.

Section One: Ohiopyle State Park to PA 31

Many people consider the 9-mile section from Ohiopyle to the top of Laurel Hill the most scenic and rugged of the entire trail. Any trail within Ohiopyle State Park is bound to be beautiful, and the LHT is no exception, as it explores the isolated northern section of this popular park. From the trailhead in Ohiopyle, cross PA 381 and follow Garrett Street to a gate; follow this gated road. A blue-blazed side trail descends from the left; this side trail leads to the second trailhead in the state park.

The LHT is level as it follows close to railroad tracks along the Youghiogheny River. Begin a steep 800-foot climb over 1.4 miles to an excellent vista over Rock Spring Run and the Youghiogheny River Gorge. Descend steeply to Rock Spring Run and begin another climb to a ridge with a view. Descend once again until the trail levels off and crosses Lick Run, where you'll find the first camping/shelter area. The LHT begins a 1,400-foot climb over 2 miles to the top of Laurel Hill, passing two views over Ohiopyle State Park near the top. Descend gradually for more than a mile and cross Little Glade Run; soon thereafter, cross Maple Summit Road, with a parking area.

Descend gradually for 1.3 miles and cross scenic Cranberry Glade Run. For the next 6 miles, the LHT traverses rolling terrain, occasionally crossing small streams, before reaching the shelter/camping area near PA 653. A short distance farther, the trail reaches the parking area along PA 653. The Laurel Ridge State Park office is a short distance down the road to the right. Cross PA 653 and continue along level and rolling terrain for 2 miles until you reach a vista to the left, overlooking Middle Fork. Rolling terrain continues for 3 miles, until the LHT passes a side trail to the Grindle Ridge shelter/camping area. Descend to Blue Hole Creek and cross it, then climb gradually to the summit of Seven Springs, with an elevation of 2,950 feet, the highest point along the trail. The trail subsequently descends and crosses a local road. The terrain becomes more hilly as the trail passes Kooser Tower and a parking area before crossing PA 31.

Section Two: PA 31 to Conemaugh River Gorge

From PA 31, descend gradually and pass another shelter/camping area. Rolling and hilly terrain ensues for more than 4 miles to where the LHT crosses over the PA Turnpike. Gradually ascend for 1.5 miles, crossing small streams, and reach another shelter/camping area. The trail is level for 1.5 miles and crosses a road. A mile farther, massive boulders and ledges appear along the trail as it passes beneath Beam Rocks, a 90-foot cliff, offering an excellent view from the top to the southeast. This cliff is popular with climbers. The jumbled boulders and ledges make this section of trail particularly scenic. Cross the headwaters of Beam Run, and 1.8 miles farther, cross Spruce Run. Three miles farther, cross PA 30, with a parking area nearby.

Ascend gradually and pass another shelter/camping area. Descend to Pickings Run, cross the stream, climb over a low ridge, and descend to and cross Machine Run. The subsequent 9 miles feature rolling and level terrain along the crest of Laurel Hill, then the LHT passes a side trail to the right that leads to another shelter/camping area. Cross PA 271 soon thereafter, with a parking area. The trail traverses rolling terrain for the next 8 miles, until it reaches another side trail leading to the final shelter/camping area. Proceed 2 miles farther to the edge of the Conemaugh River Gorge, thought by many to be the deepest gorge east of the Mississippi River. The trail descends 4 miles over the last 1,400 feet, passing scenic views of the gorge. The LHT ends at a parking area along PA 56.

25. Bear Run Nature Reserve

Length: 23-mile interconnecting system of 16 individual trails.

Duration: 1 to 2 days.

Difficulty: Easy to moderate.

Terrain: Several ascents and descents are long and gradual, but a few are steep and short. Trails often follow old grades and forest roads. Rock outcrops and boulders along the trail, which is sometimes rocky.

Trail conditions: Trails are established, well blazed, and maintained, but some are brushy. Rocky and wet in sections. Several stream crossings.

Blazes: White, yellow, or orange circles or rectangles.

Water: Generally plentiful.

Vegetation: Hardwoods predominate, with understory of brush, ferns, and saplings, occasional groves and plantations of pines and hemlocks; mountain laurel; thickets of rhododendron along streams; fields and meadows dot the reserve.

Highlights: Scenic streams, Bear Run, Laurel Run, scenic campsites, rhododendron and mountain laurel, Youghiogheny River Gorge, Ohiopyle State Park, vistas, Fallingwater, Bear Run Interpretive Center, old-growth hemlocks, boulders and outcrops.

Maintained by: Western Pennsylvania Conservancy, volunteers.

Contact info: Western Pennsylvania Conservancy, 209 Fourth Ave., Pittsburgh, PA 15222-2075; phone: 412-288-2777; website: www.wpconline.org.

Maps and guides: Free pamphlet with map and brief descriptions available at trailhead.

Trailhead directions: From Ohiopyle, follow PA 381 north for 4 miles to a sign and parking area on the right.

The 5,000 acre Bear Run Nature Reserve is owned and operated by the Western Pennsylvania Conservancy (WPC). The renowned WPC has done an incredible job of preserving the ecology, habitat, and culture of countless sites throughout this part of the state. It was instrumental in the creation of Ohiopyle State Park, which adjoins the reserve. Frank Lloyd Wright's architectural masterpiece, Fallingwater, is located within the reserve but is not accessed by the trails. You must pay a fee to tour this famous home.

For the backpacker, the reserve permits overnight backcountry camping at six campsites and a group camping area. The campsites typically are located near water and provide enough space for two tents; the group camping area can accommodate groups of ten with several tents. You must fill out a reservation form at the trailhead for the campsite you plan to use; there is no fee. Pets are not permitted. With moderate terrain, great scenery, camping, accessibility, and a well-maintained trail system, this is an excellent place for the beginning backpacker.

The reserve's trail system is made up of sixteen individual, interconnecting trails offering countless trip options. These individual trails vary from .3 to 2.5 miles in length. Most junctures are marked with signs and blazes. Some trails within the system are very popular with dayhikers; others offer more isolation. The description below follows a loop within the reserve that passes its most scenic areas and a majority of campsites. You can take a longer or shorter hike by using the reserve's numerous other trails.

From the trailhead, hike down to PA 381. Cross the road and follow the white-blazed Peninsula Trail along an access road. This trail passes through a pine plantation and fields along an old forest road. Descend

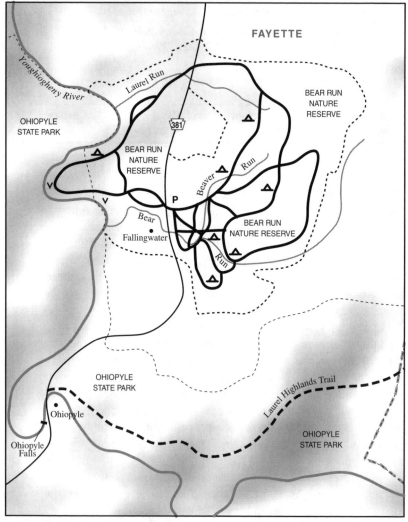

Hike 25: Bear Run Nature Reserve

and reach the edge of the Youghiogheny River Gorge, where the trail becomes rocky, with steep but short ascents and descents as it follows along the side of the gorge. To the left is Paradise Overlook, offering a scenic view of the gorge from a rock outcrop. Continue to follow the contour of the gorge across rocky, rugged terrain to another excellent vista of the gorge. The whitewater rapids can be clearly heard. The Peninsula Trail continues to follow the contour of the gorge, passing some evidence of quarrying, and picks up an old grade. Pass a campsite perched on the edge of the gorge. This trail ends at the juncture of Saddle and Laurel Run Trails.

Proceed straight onto white-blazed Laurel Run Trail. This is a level or rolling trail that often follows old grades, crossing rivulets, boulders, and outcrops. After .3 mile on this trail, you pass a juncture with the short but beautiful Laurel Glen Trail to your left. This is a worthwhile side trip, descending to scenic Laurel Run, with its cascades, large boulders, and thick rhododendron; this trail is not shown on the maps available at the trailhead. After .3 mile, the Laurel Glen Trail ascends and rejoins Laurel Run Trail. Proceed on Laurel Run Trail as it crosses Laurel Run and PA 381. Begin a gradual ascent over rocky terrain and outcrops. Cross a seasonal stream and reach the juncture of Snow Bunny Trail and Tulip Tree Trail, where Laurel Run Trail ends.

You are now in the eastern section of the reserve, which is also its most isolated. Hardwoods dominate the forest. Turn right onto orange-blazed Snow Bunny Trail, a wide, easy, and level trail that is more than a mile long. Pass Campsite No. 3 along a seasonal stream. The larger group campsite is .6 mile farther along Beaver Run. Cross scenic Beaver Run and turn left onto Rhododendron Trail. This trail ascends gradually, crossing seasonal streams, and traverses rocky terrain. Rock outcrops can be seen along the trail through a hardwood forest. Reach the end of Rhododendron Trail at the four-way intersection with Tulip Tree Trail, Ridge Trail, and Bear Run Trail. Proceed straight onto orange-blazed Bear Run Trail, which continues a gradual ascent to one of the highest elevations in the reserve. The surrounding terrain is rocky with outcrops. Bear right and begin a long, gradual descent of 450 feet over 1.4 miles to the glen carved by Bear Run. Follow the scenic run downstream, passing large boulders and hemlocks, and reach the end of the trail at scenic Campsite No. 1 and a juncture with white-blazed Hemlock Trail.

Turn left onto Hemlock Trail and cross Bear Run. Begin a steep ascent, bear right, and descend into a scenic ravine with large hemlocks and boulders. Ascend and pass the Warbler Trail to your left, then descend gradually and pass Wintergreen Trail to your left. Descend to Bear Run and cross the stream, passing Campsite No. 5, and reach the yellow-blazed Ridge Trail. You are now entering the section of the reserve that is popular with dayhikers.

Turn left onto Ridge Trail for a short distance, then turn left onto popular and beautiful white-blazed Arbutus Trail. This trail features several crossings of Bear Run, a state scenic stream, through impressive tunnels of rhododendron, which blooms in late June or early July. This trail is level or rolling but is wet and rocky in sections. The trail leaves the run, enters a hardwood forest, and passes junctures with Ridge Trail, Poetry Trail, and Wagon Trail along an old forest road. Enter a pine plantation and reach the trailhead.

26. Quebec Run Wild Area

Length: 26-mile interconnecting system of 11 individual trails.

Duration: 1 to 2 days.

Difficulty: Easy to moderate.

Terrain: Mostly rolling, with short, steep sections. Trails often follow streams with wet or boggy terrain

Trail conditions: Trails are well blazed and maintained. Most junctures have signs.

Blazes: All trails blazed blue.

Water: Plentiful.

Vegetation: Hardwoods, mountain laurel, and ferns predominate along higher slopes and ridges; hemlocks, pines, meadows, and impressive rhododendron thickets often found along streams.

Highlights: Scenic streams, Mill Run, Quebec Run, nice camping, rhododendron, hemlocks.

Maintained by: Forbes State Forest, volunteers.

Contact info: Forbes State Forest, Rte. 30 East, P.O. Box 519, Laughlintown, PA 15655; phone: 724-238-1200; e-mail: fd04@state.pa.us; website: www.dcnr.state.pa.us/forestry/stateforests/forests/forbes/forbes.htm.

Maps and guides: Free pamphlet with map and short description, as well as state forest map, available from Forbes State Forest.

Trailhead directions: From the juncture of US 40 and PA 381 near Farmington, follow PA 381 south for more than 5 miles. Keep an eye out for where PA 381 makes a very sharp left near the village of Elliotsville; turn right onto Wharton Furnace Road. Make the next immediate left onto Quebec Road (SR 2004). Follow this road 2.5 miles to a parking area and sign on left.

The 7,441-acre Quebec Run Wild Area is a beautiful place to visit, featuring some of the most scenic backpacking in this corner of the state, and is growing in popularity. With its mild terrain and fine scenery, Quebec Run is ideal for beginning backpackers. Its numerous scenic streams also provide backcountry fly-fishing opportunities and beautiful campsites.

The wild area has an interconnecting network of short trails and forest roads that can be combined for a great weekend backpacking trip. Here you'll find many possible routes that allow you to lengthen or shorten your hike. The Miller, Hess, and Brocker Trails, as well as Quebec, Tebolt, and West Roads, explore the drier, higher elevations

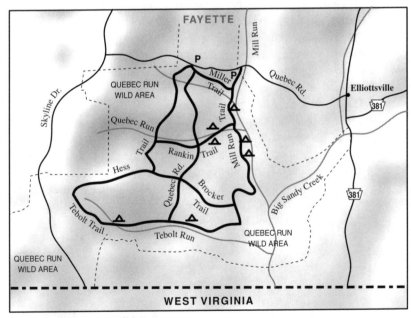

Hike 26: Quebec Run Wild Area

and ridges of the wild area, with open hardwood forests, mountain laurel, and ferns. These trails follow the rolling plateau and ridges, but they are steep in sections where they descend and climb in and out of gorges and glens carved by streams.

There are three exceptional trails you should incorporate into your backpacking trip: Mill Run, Rankin, and Tebolt Trails. The 2.5-mile-long Mill Run Trail follows the narrow, meandering valley of Mill Run, a beautiful, clear trout stream, and connects Quebec Road to Tebolt Trail and West Road. This trail traverses the valley bottom but also climbs along the banks above Mill Run as it passes through hemlock and rhododendron tunnels and around boulders. Many excellent campsites are located near the creek. Mill Run is particularly scenic at the bridge accessing the Grist Mill Trail, where you'll find rapids, deep pools, and boulders. At its southern end, the Mill Run Trail climbs the side of the valley along a steep, old forest road and ends at the juncture of West Road and Tebolt Trail.

The 4-mile-long Tebolt Trail explores the narrow gorge of Tebolt Run and connects Skyline Drive and Hess Trail to Mill Run Trail and West Road. In the upper section of the gorge, near the headwaters of Tebolt Run, this trail follows the stream closely, with incredible thickets of rhododendron, groves of hemlocks, and small campsites. The stream cascades along boulders and ledges through incredible greenery. As the trail explores the eastern section of the gorge, it stays primarily above the stream, along the north side of the bank, then climbs to a ridge to a juncture with the Brocker Trail, and soon thereafter, with West Road and Mill Run Trail.

The 1.2-mile-long Rankin Trail follows scenic Quebec Run through a shallow gorge. The trail connects Mill Run Trail to Hess Trail and crosses Quebec Road halfway in between. Like the other streamside trails in the wild area, there are incredible tunnels of rhododendron, hemlocks, boulders, rock outcrops, and a verdant forest. The trail generally stays close to Quebec Run but does occasionally climb up the bank. East of Quebec Road, there are two stream crossings with bridges and nice potential campsites.

27. Warrior Trail

Length: 45-mile linear trail (Pennsylvania's section).

Duration: 3 to 4 days.

Difficulty: Easy to moderate.

Terrain: Rolling and hilly forestlands and farms. A few short, steep ascents and descents. Trail often follows country roads.

Trail conditions: Trail often follows roads, but some sections are brushy, and briers and wild rose bushes often occur along the trail. Blazes may be inconsistent or faded.

Blazes: Yellow.

Water: The trail follows hills and ridges between watersheds; as a result, there are no streams and few springs directly along the trail. Expect a lot of sun exposure, and carry extra containers.

Vegetation: Farmlands, fields, meadows, and hardwood forests.

Highlights: Excellent pastoral views, rock outcrops, scenic countryside, wildflowers, historic path used by Indians to trade flint.

Maintained by: Warrior Trail Association, volunteers.

Contact info: Warrior Trail Association, P.O. Box 103, Waynesburg, PA 15370-0103; website: www.greenepa.net/community/WarriorTrail/.

Maps and guides: Both available for sale from the Warrior Trail Association.

Trailhead directions: The trail crosses and follows many roads; there are no established trailheads. The eastern terminus is located just north of the town of Greensboro. From the juncture of PA 88 and PA 21, follow PA 88 south for 5 miles to a blinking light near a bank. Turn left onto SR 2016 and proceed 1.2 miles. Pass through the small village of Glassworks and reach the Ice Plant Bar and Restaurant on your right, where the trail begins. There should be a trail sign here. Parking may be found at Mon-View Park, just down the road, on the left.

The five thousand-year-old Warrior Trail (WT) is possibly the oldest footpath in the nation. American Indians used this route to acquire flint and conduct commerce. The current WT follows close to the original route, and in some places, the same worn footpath used by the Indians can still be seen. The WT is a unique trail that explores Greene County's hilly terrain with several beautiful pastoral views. Not a wilderness trail, the WT resembles the countryside paths found in Europe. Although it is located primarily on private land, this trail has

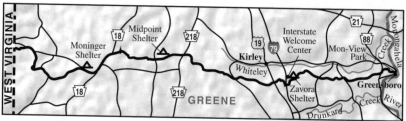

Hike 27: Warrior Trail

been able to survive and even has three shelters. Unfortunately, in 2003, it was listed as an Endangered Hiking Trail, primarily because of the loss of permission from private landowners, which has forced large sections of the trail onto roads. As always, respect private property, hike across fields and fences with care, and use stiles over fences when available.

The WT continues into West Virginia and ends at the Ohio River, south of Moundsville, with a total length of 68 miles. The description below is abbreviated.

Hiking from east to west, begin at the WT's eastern trailhead, located just north of Greensboro, along SR 2033, north of Mon-View Park. Hike across a field and follow a powerline around a reclaimed strip mine. Enter the woods along an old forest road and emerge to cross a road. Enter another field. The blazes have disappeared; simply head to a barn, with a sign that says "Kendralla & Sons," to the southwest. Meet PA 88, on which you turn left and proceed for several hundred yards. Continue to follow roads until the trail bears left to follow a coal conveyor for 1.5 miles. Turn right onto SR 2011 and follow for .6 mile, then the trail turns left off the road. For the next 6 miles, the WT traverses hilly terrain across fields, meadows, and dirt roads, with several nice views. Portions of this trail also pass through State Game Lands 223. Reach scenic Zavora Shelter, a total of 11.5 miles from the eastern trailhead.

Hike along fields and follow a road across I-79. Follow the road for a short distance, then the WT enters the woods and fields, with hilly terrain for almost 2 miles. The trail crosses busy US 19 at a curve, so be careful. Continue along the hilly ridgeline, with great pastoral scenery and some of the steepest sections of trail. Similar scenery prevails, with sections following roads, for about 8 miles to Midpoint Shelter, which sits on a hill with a great view a little farther down the trail. Nearby is a home; please ask permission there before using the shelter, which is a short distance from the road. The next 11 miles to Moninger Shelter primarily follow or are near roads, some of which are paved state roads and others dirt township roads.

The remainder of the trail to the West Virginia border largely follows roads, with short sections off the road along hillsides or across fields.

28. Raccoon Creek State Park

Length: 19.5-mile loop.

Duration: 1.5 to 2 days.

Difficulty: Easy to moderate.

Terrain: Rolling and hilly forestlands; hills and ridges are interspersed with the valleys and glens of small streams. Most ascents and descents are gradual and range between 100 to 300 vertical feet, but there are a few steep sections.

Trail conditions: Trails are generally well maintained and blazed.

Blazes: The backpacking loop is blazed green. The three trails that form the loop also have their own blazes: Heritage Trail, blue; Forest Trail, white; and Appaloosa Trail, yellow.

Water: Generally plentiful.

Vegetation: Hardwoods dominate, with pines, hemlocks, and several pine plantations.

Highlights: Raccoon Creek State Park, Raccoon Lake, Frankfort Mineral Springs with small waterfalls, Wildflower Reserve, small streams, fall foliage.

Maintained by: Raccoon Creek State Park, Keystone Trails Association, volunteers.

Contact info: Raccoon Creek State Park, 3000 State Route 18, Hookstown, PA 15050-9416; phone: 724-899-2200; e-mail: raccooncreeksp@state.pa.us; website: www.dcnr.state.pa.us/stateparks/parks/raccooncreek.asp.

Maps and guides: Maps and guide pamphlet available for free from the state park.

Trailhead directions: The trail crosses many roads and parking areas within the park. From the juncture of US 22 and PA 18, follow PA 18 north for 5.7 miles to the Frankfort Mineral Springs trailhead, on the left. The park office is .4 mile farther, on the left. From where US 30 and US 22 split near Imperial, follow US 30 west for 9.6 miles to the park. Turn left onto the park road and follow for .7 mile to a parking area on the left.

On May 10, 2003, the Raccoon Loop Backpacking Trail was formally opened, making Raccoon Creek the third state park in Pennsylvania to offer backpacking trails. The backpacking loop is composed of three of the park's trails—Heritage, Forest, and Appaloosa Trails—and a short segment of the Lakeside Lodge Road. Backcountry camping is permitted in two locations, Sioux and Pioneer, where trail shelters are being built. Before backpacking this loop, contact the state park to make reservations and pay a permit fee.

This loop is ideal for the beginner, as it is relatively easy and is always fairly close to a road. The state park features an extensive trail system for hiking, cross-country skiing, and horseback riding; these trails intersect the backpacking loop at numerous junctures. This trail is ideal for a quick weekend trip and is only about 30 miles from Pittsburgh. The Pittsburgh International Airport is only 7 miles away, so expect air traffic. With extensive deciduous forests, this trail is great to hike in fall to enjoy the colorful foliage.

To hike the loop clockwise, start from the Heritage Trail parking area along the park road, below the dam and just west of Traverse Creek. Climb a series of hills that are steep in sections. Descend to a

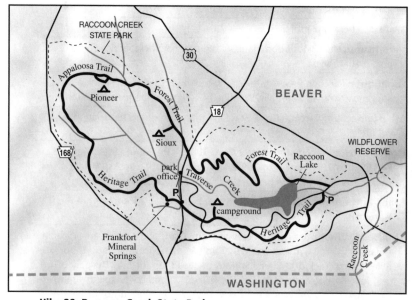

Hike 28: Raccoon Creek State Park

stream, cross over a bridge, and hike alongside the water. The trail then climbs away from the stream and levels across the hilltop. Pass a cross-country ski trail and hike through a pine plantation. Pass two more junctures with the ski trail. Descend to a small stream, climb away from it, and cross the park road. Descend to another small stream and climb gradually back to the park road, which the trail crosses. Descend gradually to PA 18, a distance of 4.4 miles from where you began.

Cross PA 18 and pass the parking area for the Frankfort Mineral Springs. Climb along a service road. I recommend a side trip down the trail to the left to the Frankfort Mineral Springs and a scenic glen with small waterfalls. Back on the loop, cross the Mineral Springs Loop Trail again and continue to hike along the service road. The trail leaves the road to the right and for the next 2 miles traverses several hills divided by small streams and drainages. Cross the park road and continue to hike through hilly terrain before descending into a stream valley. Turn left and proceed up this valley for .6 mile, with several stream crossings. Climb gradually out of the valley, cross Nichol Road, and continue the easy ascent to the hilltop. Descend to the juncture with the Appaloosa Trail, where the Heritage Trail ends. Turn right onto the Appaloosa Trail. You have hiked 5.1 miles from PA 18.

The 3-mile Appaloosa Trail is also open to horseback riders and mountain bikers. This is an easy trail with gradual changes in elevation as it explores some of the highest elevations in the park. Pass a side trail to Pioneer Camp, and in another mile, the Appaloosa Trail ends at Nichol Road. Bear left onto the road and turn right onto the 6.2-mile-long Forest Trail. This trail explores gentle, hilly terrain and crosses Nichol Road twice and the Palomino Trail. Pass a side trail to the Sioux camping area. Descend to Little Service Run, cross the stream, and climb the other bank to PA 18, a distance of 2.5 miles from the beginning of the Forest Trail.

The remaining 3.7 miles of the Forest Trail are a little more rugged, with short, steep sections as the trail climbs in and out of valleys and drainages of four small streams and over the hills that separate them. From PA 18, gradually ascend the hill and begin a steep descent to a small stream. Cross the stream, climb over a broad hilltop, and descend via switchbacks to another small stream. Gradually ascend, meet the Lake Trail, climb the contour of the ridge, and descend steeply to another stream. Cross the stream and climb more gradually over the final hill. Descend to a small stream and the parking area along Lakeside Lodge Road, where the Forest Trail ends. Turn left on this road and follow it .7 mile to the park road. Turn right onto the park road, cross over Traverse Creek, and reach the parking area where you began your hike on the left. There aren't any blazes along the roads.

While at Raccoon Creek, I suggest you visit the Wildflower Reserve, only .5 mile from the eastern trailhead, along US 30. The reserve has more than five hundred species of plants and a 5-mile trail system along Raccoon Creek that explores a wide variety of wildflowers, some of them rare in Pennsylvania. Spring and summer are ideal times to visit the reserve.

Northwestern Pennsylvania and the Allegheny National Forest

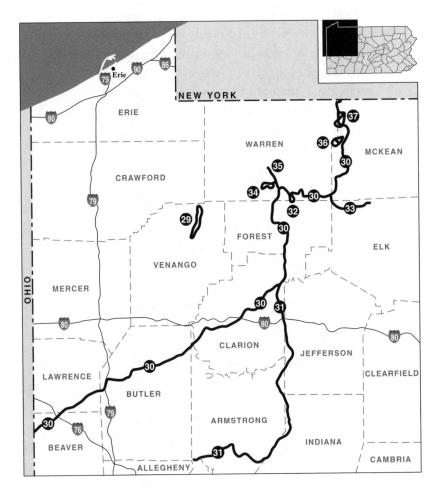

The Allegheny National Forest is the outdoor recreation epicenter of northwestern Pennsylvania, western New York, and northeastern Ohio. The national forest covers more than 500,000 acres and is visited by 3 million people a year. There is something for everyone: extensive public land for hunting; hundreds of miles of streams and rivers to fish and canoe; fishing and boating on the scenic Allegheny Reservoir; biking, bridle, and ATV trails; and numerous campgrounds. For the backpacker, the Allegheny National Forest features the North Country National Scenic Trail and several other trails.

Among my favorite features of the national forest are its impressive caprock cliffs, massive boulders, and other rock formations. There also are numerous beautiful streams and rivers, including two National Scenic Rivers, the Allegheny and Clarion. Like much of Pennsylvania, the national forest is dominated by plateaus, which reach 2,400 feet in elevation and are dissected by numerous streams and rivers that have carved scenic glens and gorges. But the terrain here is more mild than that found along other plateau trails, such as the Quehanna, Chuck Keiper, Donut Hole, Black Forest, or northern Mid State.

Unfortunately, the incredible beauty and wilderness of the Allegheny National Forest have been compromised. The forest is laced with hundreds of miles of logging roads, and countless oil and gas wells, and their attendant machinery, dot the forest. Few other national forests are so heavily logged and drilled for oil and natural gas. Wilderness areas cover only 2 percent of the forest, one of the lowest percentages of any national forest. Ironically, the author of the Wilderness Act of 1964, Howard Zahniser, was from Tionesta. Two organizations are working hard to protect and conserve the beauty of the Allegheny National Forest: the Allegheny Defense Project (P.O. Box 245, Clarion, PA 16214, 814-223-4996, info@alleghenydefense.org, www.alleghenydefense.org); and the Allegheny Group Sierra Club (P.O. Box 8241, Pittsburgh, PA 15217, www.alleghenysc.org/ag.htm.)

For a heavily visited national forest of this size, there are few hiking trails. Currently there are less than 200 miles of hiking trails. In comparison, the White Mountain National Forest in New Hampshire has 1,000 miles of trails, and the Monongahela National Forest in West Virginia has 500 miles of trails. As a result, existing trails, such as Minister Creek, Morrison, and Hickory Creek, are being overused. There is a definite need for more trails and wilderness areas. Nevertheless, the scenic trails of the Allegheny National Forest should be on any backpacker's list, especially those living near Buffalo, Cleveland, or Pittsburgh.

The Allegheny National Forest isn't all that northwestern Pennsylvania has to offer backpackers. Oil Creek State Park features the scenic Gerard Hiking Trail; beautiful segments of the North Country Trail pass through Morraine and McConnell's Mill State Parks; and the Baker Trail offers a pleasant woodland and pastoral trek.

🚶🚶 29. Gerard Hiking Trail

Length: 36-mile loop.

Duration: 2 to 3 days.

Difficulty: Easy to moderate.

Terrain: Tends to be rolling with relatively short ascents and descents, which can be steep in sections. Most ascents and descents range from 100 to 300 feet. Circuitous trail occasionally traverses very steep banks along Oil Creek Gorge and side glens carved by small streams.

Trail conditions: Trail is well maintained and blazed.

Blazes: Yellow; connector trails, white.

Water: Generally plentiful; trail crosses numerous small seasonal streams, and Oil Creek flows year-round. Water seasonally available at shelter areas.

Vegetation: Northern hardwoods predominate, with hemlocks.

Highlights: Oil Creek Gorge, Oil Creek State Park, scenic side glens, small waterfalls and cascades, Drake Well Museum and oil history, boulders, rock outcrops, historic sites, shelters, views.

Maintained by: Oil Creek State Park staff, volunteers.

Contact info: Oil Creek State Park, 305 State Park Rd., Oil City, PA 16301-9733; phone: 814-676-5915; e-mail: oilcreeksp@state.pa.us; website: www.dcnr.state.pa.us/stateparks/parks/oilcreek.asp .

Maps and guides: Oil Creek State Park provides free maps and pamphlet guide.

Trailhead directions:

Southern trailhead (Rynd Farm): From Oil City, take PA 8 north for 4.4 miles and turn right onto State Park Road. The parking area is .2 mile farther, on the right.

Park Office (Petroleum Centre): From Oil City, take PA 8 north for 4.4 miles and turn right onto State Park Road. Follow the road for 3.2 miles, until it crosses the bridge and reaches the park office, on the left.

Northern trailhead (Drake Well Museum): From the PA 8 and PA 27 juncture in Titusville, take PA 8 south for .3 mile. Turn left onto Bloss Street and proceed for a mile. A parking area is on the right before crossing the bridge.

The Gerard Hiking Trail (GHT) was named in honor of Ray Gerard, a park volunteer who developed the trail and maintained it for sixteen years before he died in 1997. The GHT is a long, narrow, circuitous loop that explores the length of the state park; four connector trails can be used to shorten your trip. Backpackers enjoy this trail,

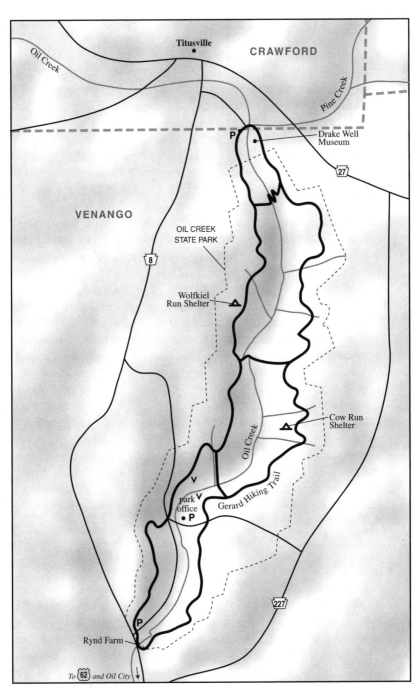

Hike 29: Gerard Hiking Trail

with its moderate terrain, scenic shelters, several small waterfalls and side glens, and views of the Oil Creek Gorge. The trail is also very historic. It was here in 1859 that Col. Edwin Drake's well first struck oil. The historic trail system passes old oil machinery; the sites of abandoned farms, homesteads, towns; and the Drake Well Museum.

The state park is one of Pennsylvania's finest, with a bike trail, cross-country ski trails, historic sites, and fishing and canoeing on beautiful Oil Creek. Before beginning your hike, you must first contact the park office to make reservations and pay a fee to camp overnight. Camping is limited to the Wolfkiel Run and Cow Run Shelter areas, both of which are a short hike from a road and parking. Each area has six Adirondack-style shelters with fireplaces, tent sites, and restrooms. Water is provided seasonally; firewood is usually provided. With these amenities, the GHT is a great trail for winter backpacking and snowshoeing.

Hiking the trail counterclockwise from the park office area, follow the white-blazed trail behind the office, or follow SR 1004 to the left for .25 mile. Turn left onto the GHT to begin the loop. An initially steep climb soon levels off as the trail reaches the top of the gorge. The GHT gradually descends and, 2 miles from the park office, crosses T-599, a local road. Descend to Hemlock Run, cross the stream, and pass a juncture with a connector trail. Hike along the side of the gorge as the trail winds through the scenic side glen of Bull Run. Reach the Cow Run Shelter, 2.67 miles from T-599. The trail curves through Gregg Run's glen, traverses the side of the gorge, and reaches Plum Dungeon Run, with cascades and small waterfalls. Descend gradually to T-635 and a parking area; the road to the left can be used as connector. Over the next 3.5 miles, hike across hilly and rolling terrain as the trail winds through the side glens of Jones and Toy Runs. Reach scenic Boughton Run, with cascades and small waterfalls. A mile farther, pass the Boughton Trail connector, which switchbacks down the side of the gorge and connects to the other side of the loop. Descend gradually for 1.5 miles to the Drake Well Museum and parking area. Cross railroad tracks and a bridge over Oil Creek; begin to hike the western side of the loop.

Gradually ascend along the side of the gorge for 2 miles, to the juncture with the Boughton Trail connector along Spring Run. Follow the contour of the gorge, climb over the ridge, and descend to Miller Run with cascades. A climb ensues and the trail crosses Miller Farm Road, T-635. Hike .6 mile farther and reach the Wolfkiel Run Shelter. Descend via switchbacks to Wolfkiel Run, cross the run, and climb along steep switchbacks up the side of the gorge. The trail levels off to the left and passes a nice vista of Oil Creek. Follow the contour of the gorge for almost 4 miles, then cross T-621. Enter the glen of Pioneer Run and pass a waterfall. Descend to SR 1009, and soon thereafter, T-617, which can be followed to the left across Oil Creek and to the park office. Follow T-617 for a short distance, until GHT bears left off the road and ascends to the top of the gorge. Descend gradually for 3 miles back to the bottom of the gorge, along Oil Creek, and reach the Rynd Farm Bridge, the southern end of the loop.

Cross the bridge and bear left as the trail gradually ascends along the side of the gorge and passes through several side glens of small streams. After 4 miles, reach SR 1004 near the state park office; this road also serves as a connector across Oil Creek and to the other side of the loop.

30. North Country Trail

Length: A linear trail that will be 3,200 miles in length when completed; Pennsylvania's section will be approximately 200 miles in length when completed, and is presently over halfway completed. This description follows the 90-mile segment through the Allegheny National Forest.

Duration: 7 to 12 days (Allegheny National Forest segment).

Difficulty: Moderate to difficult.

Terrain: Rolling terrain on the plateau and through numerous glens and hollows carved by streams. Ascents and descents range from 200 to 700 feet, typically gradual but steep in sections. Trail often follows old grades and forest roads. Section along Allegheny Reservoir follows a narrow sidehill along steep banks.

Trail conditions: Trail is generally well blazed and maintained, but may be brushy in sections. Several stream crossings, many without bridges.

Blazes: Blue.

Water: Generally plentiful; the trail passes many streams and springs.

Vegetation: Northern hardwood forests, typically open with ferns, but sometimes have understory of saplings, mountain laurel, lowbush blueberries, and brush; hemlocks and pines generally found along streams; areas of old-growth forest.

Highlights: Allegheny Reservoir, Allegheny National Forest, Allegheny National Recreation Area, scenic streams and campsites, Nelse Run, old-growth forest, Tionesta Scenic Area, rock outcrops, boulders and cliffs, Minister Creek, and Tionesta Creek.

Maintained by: Local chapters of North Country Trail Association, volunteers.

Contact info:

North Country Trail Association, 229 E. Main St., Lowell, MI 49331; phone: 888-454-6282; e-mail: HQ@northcountrytrail.org; websites: www.northcountrytrail.org/explore/ex_pa/pa.htm, www.dcnr.state.pa.us/forestry/hiking/north.htm.

Cook Forest State Park, P.O. Box 120, Cooksburg, PA 16217-0120; phone: 814-744-8407; e-mail: cookforestsp@state.pa.us; website: www.dcnr.state.pa.us/stateparks/parks/cookforest.asp.

Moraine State Park, 225 Pleasant Valley Rd., Portersville, PA 16051-9650; phone: 724-768-8811; e-mail: morainesp@state.pa.us; website: www.dcnr.state.pa.us/stateparks/parks/moraine.asp.

McConnell's Mill State Park, R.R. 2 Box 16, Portersville, PA 16051-9401; phone: 724-368-9401; e-mail: morainesp@state.pa.us; website: www.dcnr.state.pa.us/stateparks/parks/mcconnellsmill.asp.

Allegheny National Forest, P.O. Box 847, Warren, PA 16365; phone: 814-723-5150; websites: www.fs.fed.us/r9/forests/allegheny, www.allegheny-online.com/hikingtrails.html.

Maps and guides: Free overview map with general description from Allegheny National Forest; more detailed maps may be purchased from North Country Trail Association.

Trailhead directions:

Schoolhouse Hollow (PA 346): Trailhead and small parking area are located on the right, along PA 346, .9 mile west of the juncture with PA 321.

PA 59: Trailhead is located along PA 59, almost 25 miles west of Smethport and 15.5 miles east of the PA 59 juncture with US 6, near Warren. Turn onto dirt forest road on the south side of PA 59 and follow to a parking area.

PA 321: From the juncture of PA 59 and PA 321, at the Bradford Ranger Station, take PA 321 south 4.6 miles to a small parking area (14 miles north of Kane).

Red Bridge: From the juncture of PA 59 and PA 321, at the Bradford Ranger Station, take PA 321 south 9.5 miles to a parking area on the right before the bridge (9 miles north of Kane).

Longhouse trailhead: From the juncture of PA 59 and PA 321, at the Bradford Ranger Station, take PA 321 south 11 miles to a large parking area on the left (8 miles north of Kane). To reach the trail, cross PA 321 and hike up FR 262 until juncture with trail.

US 6 (Ludlow): There is a small parking area, with a sign, on the south side of US 6, 1.7 miles east of Ludlow and 21 miles east of Warren (7.3 miles west of Kane).

PA 948: From the juncture of PA 948 and PA 66 near Chaffee, take PA 948 north for 5.4 miles and turn right on FR 148. Follow FR 148 for .3 mile to a parking area on the left. FR 148 is 3 miles south of Barnes along PA 948, and about 5 miles south of Sheffield.

PA 666: From the juncture of PA 666 and PA 948 at Barnes, take PA 666 west for 3.8 miles to Henrys Mills. After crossing the bridge, there is a parking area to the left.

Dunham Siding: From Warren along US 6, get off at the Mohawk Avenue exit (there is a sign for Hearts Content Scenic Area), and proceed south. Bear right along Pleasant Drive (SR 3005), and follow for 11.5 miles. Bear left onto SR 2002, and follow for 3.7 miles to Hearts Content, on your left. From Tidioute, follow SR 3005 for 12 miles to SR 2002, and turn right. Heading south from Hearts Content and Hickory Creek Wilderness trailhead along SR 2002, proceed 2.1 miles farther, until you reach FR 116 to your right. Follow this dirt forest road for .4 mile, until you reach a sign for the Tanbark and North Country Trails. There is parking along the road for two cars; a larger parking area for about five cars is just a short distance farther, on the right.

Kellettville: The best parking is at Kellettville Campground. From East Hickory, take PA 666 east for 10 miles to Kellettville, turn right, and cross the bridge to the campground. Park on the left side of the road. From Sheffield, take PA 666 west for 23.5 miles to Kellettville.

Amsler Springs: This is the southern trailhead in the Allegheny National Forest. From Kellettville Campground, follow FR 127 for a mile and turn right onto FR 145. Follow this road for 7.3 miles, until you reach a small parking area. A shelter and large camping area are nearby. From Marienville, take PA 66 south for 1.6 miles. Turn right onto Muzette Road and follow for 1.7 miles. Turn right onto FR 145 and follow for 1.2 miles to the trailhead.

The North Country Trail (NCT) is one of three national scenic trails in Pennsylvania, the others being the venerable Appalachian Trail and Laurel Highlands Trail. Just as the Appalachian Trail slices diagonally across southeastern Pennsylvania, the NCT does the same in the northwestern part of the state. The NCT is poised to become this region's equivalent to the Appalachian Trail. These two trails, however, could not be more different: The Appalachian Trail in Pennsylvania is primarily a dry, rocky, ridgetop trail with numerous vistas; the NCT in the Allegheny National Forest offers a deep woods experience with old-growth forests, scenic mountain streams, meadows, massive boulders, rock outcrops, the Allegheny Reservoir, and relatively few vistas. The NCT has a lot of potential, and the Pennsylvania chapters of the North Country Trail Association are working hard to complete the trail in the state.

Hike 30: North Country Trail

The NCT is envisioned as a 3,200-mile-long trail stretching from North Dakota to New York. When completed, it will be the longest trail in the nation. Pennsylvania's section of the NCT will be about 200 miles long, and more than half of that length is currently completed. Because of camping restrictions along large portions of the NCT, there is really only one section of the trail that is amenable to backpacking: the 90-mile segment in the Allegheny National Forest. This segment represents some of the most scenic, and best established, trail along the entire NCT, with great campsites. The NCT is the backbone of the Allegheny National Forest's trail system. Virtually every one of the forest's other trails connect with or are close to the NCT.

With a new shelter under way in Moraine State Park, the sections of the NCT in Moraine and McConnell's Mill State Parks will become more suitable for backpackers as well. I recommend hiking the NCT through McConnell's Mill State Park, one of western Pennsylvania's most scenic areas, with a beautiful gorge carved by Slippery Rock Creek, boulders and rock outcrops, waterfalls, and whitewater rapids. Just south of the Allegheny National Forest, the NCT passes through Cook Forest State Park, where you'll find old-growth forest, views, and the Clarion River. With so many features, the NCT will become one of Pennsylvania's premier trails when completed.

The description below follows the trail from east to west.

Section One: New York border to PA 59

The NCT crosses into Pennsylvania from New York's Allegany State Park and makes a 300-foot descent over .4 mile into Schoolhouse Hollow. Follow the small run downstream, with potential campsites. As you near PA 346, a side trail to the right leads to a parking area along the road. Cross the run and reach PA 346, following it to the left. Cross Willow Creek over the road bridge and turn right, reentering the forest. Turn right and cross a small seasonal stream; begin a gradual 1.3-mile ascent climbing 300 feet. Along the way, the NCT passes behind the Willow Bay Recreation Area. The trail passes through a saddle above the reservoir and begins a slight 1-mile descent to small Williams Brook. The trail crosses the brook and levels as it follows the contour of the plateau above the reservoir. Begin another gradual descent to the reservoir. Cross North Branch and Tracy Run, beautiful streams with fine camping near the reservoir. Hike through hemlocks above the reservoir. The Tracy Ridge Trail joins from the left.

For the next 2.4 miles, the trail traverses the steep bank of the reservoir, often along a narrow sidehill. The NCT gradually moves farther from the reservoir and crosses seasonal streams, including Whiskey Run. Descend gradually through a pine plantation with campsites and reach the Johnnycake Trail, which joins from the left. Cross scenic Johnnycake Run, which has no bridge. This area around the reservoir contains several nice campsites. Continue to follow the contour of the plateau and gradually climb above the reservoir. Enter a scenic hemlock-shaded glen; a side trail to the left descends to Handsome Lake campground, a hike-in or boat-in campground with vault toilets, grassy campsites with picnic tables and fire rings, water, and nice views of the reservoir. Use of this facility requires self-registration and an $8 daily fee.

The NCT continues up this scenic glen, crosses a small stream, and climbs 200 feet over .3 mile to the crest of the plateau. At the top, the NCT turns left and follows the level top of the plateau, while the Tracy Ridge Trail descends 400 feet over a mile to scenic Hopewell campground, offering the same amenities and registration requirements as Handsome Lake. Follow the level top of the plateau for .7 mile, where the Tracy Ridge Trail crosses the NCT. Level hiking follows for a short distance, then the trail begins a descent into the beautiful glen of a hemlock-shaded stream. This descent is long and gradual as it follows an old forest road into the glen; overall the trail drops 500 feet over 1.3 miles. The trail is often high above the stream, but there are great potential campsites along the stream. The NCT reaches the bottom of the glen and crosses scenic Nelse Run over a bridge. This section of trail is very scenic and should not be missed.

Climb the bank on the other side of Nelse Run and pass a side trail to the left leading to a small parking area along PA 321. Pass a plaque and descend to the reservoir. Follow the shoreline, with views over Sugar Bay. The trail joins PA 321 and follows the road for .25 mile. Descend to Sugar Run and follow it upstream. Cross a bridge, proceed upstream along the run, where the trail is often boggy, and begin a short climb up the side of the plateau. The NCT turns left and follows the level contour of the plateau into the scenic glen of Hammond Run. Ascend upstream for about 1.5 miles, with great scenery and fine campsites. Leave the run and gradually climb out of the glen back to the top of the plateau. Upon reaching the top, level and rolling hiking ensues for 1.3 miles, until the NCT reaches and crosses PA 59.

Section Two: PA 59 to PA 666

Level terrain follows for about a mile, with open meadows and ferns, then the trail begins a gentle descent into the glen carved by Hemlock Run. For the next 3 miles, the NCT gradually descends along this scenic run, with several small campsites. Upon reaching Chappel Bay, turn left and hike along the shoreline. Hike a mile up Chappel Fork's valley, turn right, and cross the stream and PA 321. The trail gradually climbs 550 feet over 1.6 miles into the glen, with a small seasonal stream. Reach the top of the plateau, with level hiking, and cross a forestry road; thereafter, the NCT gradually descends 520 feet over 1.5 miles into the scenic glen of Root Run. Turn right and leave the run, gradually climbing along the flank of the plateau. Gradually descend to PA 321, on which you'll turn left and cross the bridge over Kinzua Bay. Leave the road to the right and begin the most difficult climb of the NCT thus far, a 700-foot climb over .8 mile. At the crest of the plateau, pass a view to the north and east.

The trial follows the edge of the plateau for almost a mile, then descends into a glen and crosses a small seasonal stream. Ascend gradually and cross Gibbs Hill Road, a paved road, and continue the ascent to the top of the plateau. For about the next 2 miles, the NCT traverses near the eastern edge of the plateau, descending into gentle glens with small seasonal streams. The trail then turns west, gently crosses over the level top of the plateau, and gradually descends to US 6. Cross the highway, Twomile Run, and a railroad. Begin to ascend and cross Wetmore Road. The trail bears to the right and levels off at the top of the plateau for almost a mile. Descend gradually into another glen and cross FR 133. Continue the gradual descent along a small stream for .6 mile, until the trail rejoins the forest road and crosses the East Branch of Tionesta Creek. Turn left and proceed upstream along the creek until the trail turns right and makes a quick ascent up the side of the plateau. This beautiful creek features cascades, fine fishing, and hemlock-shaded banks.

The trail soon levels and gradually descends into the valley of a tributary stream. Follow this small stream 1.5 miles to its source, until the NCT bears right and leaves the hollow. Rolling hiking follows. The trail crosses FR 469 and soon enters the Tionesta Scenic Area, a tract of old-growth hemlock and beech that was damaged by tornadoes in 1985; a short interpretive trail explores the area. Join a pipeline swath to the left and descend to the headwaters of Cherry Run. Climb 200 feet over .4 mile away from the run, bear right, and cross FR 148. Soon thereafter, pass a juncture with the Twin Lakes Trail to the left. Once again the NCT crosses FR 148 and makes a gradual 350-foot descent over .7 mile into the glen of Cherry Run, a scenic stream with potential camping. At the bottom of the glen, the trail joins with FR 148 and crosses the South Branch of Tionesta Creek; here you'll find more potential campsites and fine fishing. Leave the road to the right and climb gently to PA 948.

Cross the road and ascend gradually into another glen with a small stream; this is a 350-foot climb over a mile. The trail levels off at the top, crosses FR 413 and a pipeline swath, and begins a 400-foot descent over .8 mile to PA 666 and Henrys Mills. Bear left onto PA 666 and cross beautiful Tionesta Creek.

Section Three: PA 666 to FR 116 and
Tanbark Trail (Dunham Siding)

This section is one of the most scenic along the NCT. Follow PA 666 for a few hundred feet until you reach Messenger Run. The NCT turns right and makes a 200-vertical-foot climb via switchbacks, then levels off, and enters the glen of Messenger Run along a grade above the stream. The trail climbs gradually, and as it nears the top of the glen, it follows the stream more closely. Reach the top of the plateau, where the terrain is level or rolling for 1.5 miles. The trail briefly meets with the headwaters of Pell Run. Turn left and leave the run; level and rolling terrain continues for 1.6 miles, until the trail descends along a side stream to scenic Upper Sheriff Run. Cross the run, with camping, and follow it upstream for about a mile along an old railroad grade. Turn left and gradually climb from the stream; cross FR 179 at the top. After a short period of level hiking, the NCT descends 300 feet over .5 mile to scenic Lower Sheriff Run. Cross the run and immediately begin climbing out of the glen.

At the top, the trail crosses FR 255, then gradually descends into the shallow glen of Fools Creek. In typical fashion, it climbs out of the glen, and at the top, crosses SR 2001 (Minister Hill Road). The NCT now enters one of the most beautiful places in the Allegheny National Forest: Minister Creek has carved a shallow gorge in the plateau and features scenic streams, excellent campsites, and massive boulders, cliffs, crevasses, and rock outcrops. This is a popular place, so expect company.

Descend along a small side stream and meet Minister Creek Trail, a loop that explores the rock outcrops along the sides of the gorge. The NCT bear right and gradually descends, passing massive boulders.

Reach scenic Triple Fork Camp, a primitive camping area where the forks of Minister Creek meet. I suggest you camp here and dayhike the Minister Creek Trail about 2 miles along the western side of its loop to a beautiful overlook and some of the most impressive cliffs and rock outcrops in this part of the state.

At Triple Fork Camp, the NCT leaves the Minister Creek Trail to the right and gradually proceeds upstream for a mile along the creek, with more potential campsites. Climb out of the glen and meet FR 419 at the top. The trail follows the road for a short distance, then leaves it to the left, descending slightly. The next 1.8 miles to FR 116 and Tanbark Trail are rolling and level. Meet the southern terminus of the Tanbark Trail and cross FR 116, with a small parking area nearby.

Section Four: FR 116 and Tanbark Trail (Dunham Siding) to Baker Trail (near Muzette Road)

Begin a gradual descent along an old grade into the shallow valley of Queen Creek; the descent becomes more gentle as you near the bottom. The trail never actually meets Queen Creek but bears left, leaves the grade, and gradually ascends along a small side stream. Cross over the top of the plateau and descend to Coalbed Run. Follow this small run downstream for about a mile, with potential campsites. Leave the run and climb to the left, ascending 250 feet over .4 mile. Level and rolling terrain ensues for a mile as the trail crosses old forest roads. Begin a gradual descent along a side stream to Beaver Run. Bear left and hike upstream along the run, and then cross it. Cross an old forest road and begin an easy climb. Cross FR 449 at the top and descend to East Fork; pass a good spring at the bottom of the descent, near the stream. Proceed downstream above the fork until the trail climbs to the right to avoid private property. After a short period of rolling hiking, descend to East Fork and cross the stream. Hike downstream to the confluence with Middle Fork, where the stream becomes Fork Run. For the next 2.5 miles, the NCT follows Fork Run downstream through its shallow gorge. The trail follows the stream closely at times but periodically climbs the bank above the stream. Stay to the left of the stream until the trail crosses it and climbs to PA 666. Turn left onto the road and follow it for .6 mile to Kellettville, where PA 666 turns left. Follow the road for another .5 mile, turn right onto FR 127, cross Tionesta Creek, and pass a campground with parking. Hike this road for more than a mile, until the trail bears right and gradually ascends the side of the plateau; this is a 400-foot ascent over 1.2 miles.

After you reach the top of the plateau, there is a short period of level hiking, then you descend gradually to Fourmile Run. Proceed downstream, often along an old forest road, for 1.3 miles, with fine scenery and nice camping. The NCT turns right and climbs away from the run along moderately steep terrain. The trail levels and follows the contour of the plateau. Descend into a glen with a small stream, climb out to the plateau with a view, and descend once again into the glen of a small side stream to Guiton Run. Cross the run and turn right, following it downstream for a short distance. Gradually climb out of the glen along the side of the plateau and descend to Little Salmon Creek. Hike upstream and cross the creek to begin a short, steep climb via switchbacks. The NCT levels and begins a gradual ascent along another small stream. Reach the crest of the plateau, with level or rolling terrain for .8 mile, and pass large rock outcrops. Here the trail tunnels through saplings and brush. The NCT then descends 400 feet over .6 mile to scenic Salmon Creek. Join a road and cross a bridge over the creek. Turn right off the road, pass a shelter and camping area, and proceed up a small stream.

Climb back to the top of the plateau and cross Muzette Road. Begin another gradual descent along a stream for more than a mile, turn left, leave the stream and glen, and descend to Coon Creek. Cross the creek and gently climb again, crossing the national forest boundary. Enter State Game Lands No. 24, and descend to a small side stream. Cross the stream, then gently climb back to the plateau and meet the Baker Trail. From here the NCT and Baker Trail proceed south to Cook Forest State Park.

🚶🚶 31. Baker Trail

Length: 141-mile linear trail.

Duration: 9 to 14 days.

Difficulty: Easy to moderate.

Terrain: Rolling terrain with mild ascents and descents ranging from 100 to 300 feet, although there are short steep sections. The trail often follows and crosses many roads.

Trail conditions: Blazes may be inconsistent in places, and sections may be brushy. Side trails to shelters not blazed or signed; must use trail guide to locate shelters.

Blazes: Yellow.

Water: Generally plentiful, but expect a lot of sun exposure; carry extra containers.

Vegetation: Farmlands, meadows, fields, Christmas tree farms, and hardwoods.

Highlights: Allegheny River, Crooked Creek Lake, Amish culture, Mahoning Creek Lake, Cook Forest State Park, Redbank Creek, Mill Creek, Clarion River, scenic streams, farmlands, shelters, North Country Trail, Allegheny National Forest.

Maintained by: Volunteers.

Contact info:
Harmony Trails Council: P.O. Box 243, Ingomar, PA 18127; websites: www.harmonytrails.com, www.rachelcarsontrail.com, www.kta-hike.org.
Crooked Creek Lake: R.D. 3 Box 323A, Ford City, PA 16226; phone: 724-763-3161; website: www.recreation.gov.
Mahoning Creek Lake: R.R. 1 Box 229, New Bethlehem, PA 16242-9603; phone: 814-257-8811; e-mail: mahoning@usace.army.mil; websites: www.lrp.usace.army.mil/rec/lakes/mahoning.htm, www.recreation.gov.
Cook Forest State Park, P.O. Box 120, Cooksburg, PA 16217-0120; phone: 814-744-8407; e-mail: cookforestsp@state.pa.us; website: www.dcnr.state.pa.us/stateparks/parks/cookforest.asp.

Maps and guides: Available soon through Harmony Trails Alliance.

Trailhead directions: The trail crosses and follows many roads.
Garvers Ferry: The trail begins in the village of Garvers Ferry. From Freeport, follow PA 356 south across the river and continue for about .3 mile. There is a trail sign on the left, but parking is not available.
Crooked Creek Lake: From Leechburg, follow PA 66 north for 8.8 miles and turn right onto Crooked Creek Dam Road (SR 2019). Follow this road 1.2 miles across the dam and reach the Spillway Recreation Area on the left, where there is parking. From Kittanning, follow PA 66 south for 8 miles and turn left onto Crooked Creek Dam Road (SR 2019), then follow the above directions. Call ahead if you plan to leave your car overnight.
Mahoning Creek Lake: From New Bethlehem, follow PA 839 south for about 10 miles to the Milton Loop Campground.
Cook Forest State Park: From the west, take Exit 60 off I-80. Take PA 66 north to Leepers and turn right on PA 36. Drive 7 miles to the state park. From the east, take Exit 78 off I-80 and follow PA 36 north to the park. In the park, the trail crosses SR 1015 about .3 mile north of the park office.

The Baker Trail (BT) is one of western Pennsylvania's best-known trails. Most of the trail crosses private property, and it often follows roads and pipeline and powerline swaths. Surprisingly, there are ten shelters along the trail. To prevent partying and misuse, however, the shelters can be reached only by unmarked side trails identified in the trail guide, which should be republished in the future. The shelters are often on private property, so be respectful, acquire permission, and register where required. The BT was recently listed as an Endangered Hiking Trail because of landowner problems that threaten to sever the trail.

The BT explores the rolling hills of western Pennsylvania; fields, farms, towns, developed areas, and powerline and pipeline swaths are common experiences along the trail. When hiking this trail, expect a lot of roadwalking, limited wilderness, and many developed areas. A trail guide is essential to help locate the shelters. The Pittsburgh Council of American Youth Hostels established the trail in 1960, but unfortunately, the council has had financial difficulty, resulting in reorganization to avoid bankruptcy. In 2004, the council divested itself of the Baker Trail, and Harmony Trails Council assumed stewardship. The trail is often rerouted; always follow the blazes. It crosses some posted property in sections; if there are blazes, hikers are permitted to cross discreetly. The description that follows is abbreviated.

Hiking the BT south to north from PA 356 in Garvers Ferry, proceed northeast above the Allegheny River. From here to Crooked Creek Lake, the trail explores hilly farmlands and forests, often following country roads. There are two shelters along this section. Cross PA 66, proceed upstream along scenic Crooked Creek, and pass the dam. Enter the park area with restrooms, water, camping for a fee, fishing, swimming, picnic facilities, and boating. Cross the spillway and descend to Elbow Run. Hike along roads, fields, and woodlands for about 8 miles along the northeast sections of Crooked Creek Lake project to Cochrans Mills Shelter.

The BT continues to the southeast but then turns northward to Mahoning Creek Lake, another Army Corps of Engineers project. This 40-mile segment passes three shelters along similar scenery. Amish farms are common along this section. Descend to scenic Little Mahoning Creek and follow it downstream, with potential camping. Reach PA 839 and cross Mahoning Creek, passing the boat launch area and Milton Loop Campground. Follow roads north of the lake.

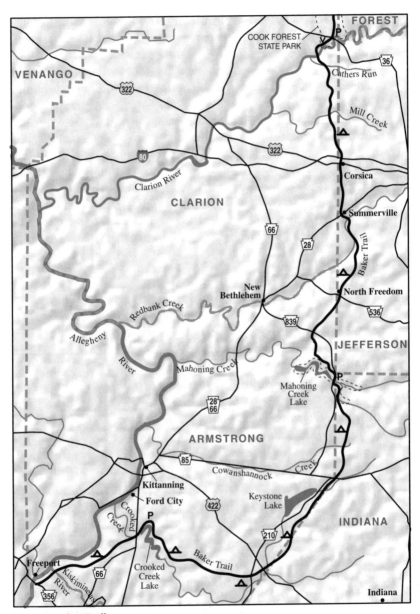

Hike 31: Baker Trail

Continue northward to Redbank Creek, Heathville, and Summerville. Cross PA 28 and proceed north to Corsica, where the trail crosses I-80. From here to Cook Forest State Park, the BT is more isolated, with fine scenery and beautiful streams, including Mill Creek. The terrain is rolling, and there are two shelters north of I-80. Cross the beautiful Clarion River over a bridge and enter Cook Forest State Park, where the North Country Trail (NCT) joins; both trails follow the same route. Follow the river upstream and climb up to Seneca Point Vista, offering a nice view of the river and its gorge from rock outcrops. The BT is level for 1.5 mile, crosses PA 36, and descends to Toms Run. Cross the run and explore the famous Forest Cathedral, with massive hemlocks and pines. The trail follows Toms Run and Browns Run northward through the state park, then it follows the NCT north through state game lands and private land, along roads, and into the Allegheny National Forest, where the BT ends.

32. Minister Creek Trail

Length: 7.3-mile loop.

Duration: Can be completed in 3 to 5 hours; also makes an excellent one-night trip.

Difficulty: Easy to moderate.

Terrain: Cliffs, outcrops, and massive boulders are prevalent along sections of the trail, which is often rocky. The steepest ascent and descent are from Minister Creek Vista to the beginning of the loop, an elevation change of about 300 feet.

Trail conditions: Trail is well maintained and blazed. Crosses small streams without bridges.

Blazes: White/gray.

Water: Generally plentiful; Minister Creek usually flows year round.

Vegetation: Forest is dominated by hardwoods with an understory of ferns and mountain laurel, there are hemlocks and pines, typically near streams.

Highlights: Minister Creek Vista, Minister Creek, massive cliffs, outcrops, boulders and crevasses, scenic campsites.

Maintained by: Allegheny National Forest, volunteers.

Contact info: Allegheny National Forest, P.O. Box 847, Warren, PA 16365; phone: 814-723-5150; websites: www.fs.fed.us/r9/forests/allegheny, www.allegheny-online.com/hikingtrails.html.

Maps and guides: Maps and pamphlet guide free from Allegheny National Forest.

Trailhead directions: From Sheffield, drive almost 15 miles west along PA 666 to a large parking area on the south side of the road. From East Hickory, drive 19 miles east along PA 666.

At a mere 7.3 miles in length, Minister Creek Trail (MCT) is really a dayhike. It is included in this guide because it is also a popular one-night loop, with two scenic backcountry campsites. It features a scenic mountain stream and a valley ringed with caprock cliffs, massive boulders, and rock formations. This trail is excellent for first-time backpackers. Another option is to set up a base camp and explore the numerous cliffs, boulders, and crevasses off the trail. Minister Creek is one of the most beautiful places in the Allegheny National Forest and should not be missed. This trail is very popular and can be crowded on weekends. The northern section of the trail links with the North Country Trail.

From the trailhead and primitive campground, follow the trail north along the west side of the valley. Gradually ascend along an old forest road. After almost .5 mile, the loop begins. To hike the loop counterclockwise, turn right and descend to Minister Creek. The trail bears left, following the creek upstream, and begin a gradual climb up the valley's east side. The trail bears right and large rocks begin to appear. A side trail to the left descends to Deerlick Camp, one of the backcountry sites, along a seasonal stream. The trail is primarily level but begins a gradual rocky descent along the contour of the valley. More massive boulders loom off to your right. The trail crosses more seasonal streams and springs.

The MCT meets the North Country Trail and turns left, passing jumbled boulders and square monoliths. Gradually descend to scenic Triple Fork Camp, the other backcountry site, and cross two of Minister Creek's branches. The North Country Trail leaves to the right and the MCT bears left, heading downstream along Minister Creek, with more boulders and formations to your right. Cross a seasonal stream and begin a gradual ascent to the plateau, with massive caprock cliffs and boulders. The trail climbs to the edge of the plateau, above the

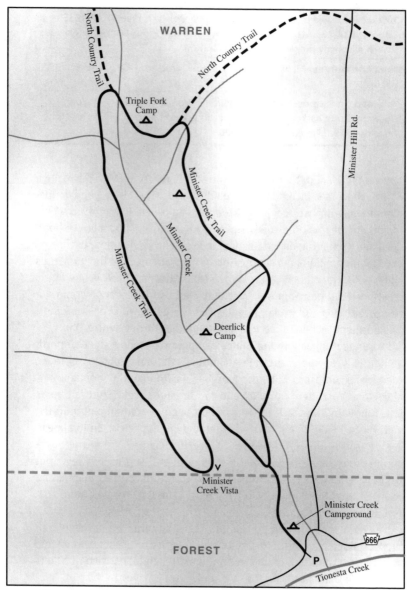

Hike 32: Minister Creek Trail

cliffs and rock formations, and reaches Minister Creek Vista, which offers a beautiful sylvan view of the valley and plateau. Descend from the vista, with more formations and rock overhangs, and switchback to the beginning of the loop. Return the way you came.

33. Twin Lakes Trail

Length: 15.8-mile linear trail.

Duration: 1.5 to 2 days.

Difficulty: Easy to moderate.

Terrain: Mostly level or rolling, with gradual changes in elevation. Trail often follows old railroad grades.

Trail conditions: Trail is generally well blazed, though some sections may be brushy and unestablished. Wet and boggy in numerous sections. Some stream crossings may not have bridges.

Blazes: White/gray.

Water: Generally plentiful.

Vegetation: Northern hardwoods predominate, with thick understory of ferns; hemlocks and pines common along streams; open meadows and wetlands.

Highlights: Scenic streams and woodlands, good camping, wildlife, beaver dams.

Maintained by: Allegheny National Forest, volunteers.

Contact info: Allegheny National Forest, P.O. Box 847, Warren, PA 16365; phone: 814-723-5150; websites: www.fs.fed.us/r9/forests/allegheny, www.allegheny-online.com/hikingtrails.html.

Maps and guides: Maps and pamphlet guide free from Allegheny National Forest.

Trailhead directions:

Twin Lakes Campground: From Kane, drive 6.1 miles south on PA 321. Turn right and proceed 2 miles to the campground area. The trail begins a few hundred feet along a gated road, straight ahead from the entrance road. From Wilcox, proceed north for 3 miles along PA 321, and turn left to the campground area.

PA 66: From Kane, follow PA 66 south for 4.6 miles, where the trail crosses with a sign. Some parking is available along a forest road that joins from the left, before where the trail crosses PA 66. From the juncture of PA 948 and PA 66, proceed north on PA 66 toward Kane for almost 3 miles until where the trail crosses.

FR 443: The western end of the trail does not have an established trailhead; it is best reached by FR 443. From the juncture of PA 948 and PA 66 near Chaffee, proceed north on PA 948 for 3.7 miles to Brookston. Turn right onto Fork Run Road. Bear straight onto Beanfarm Road and proceed 1.5 miles as the road ascends and enters the national forest, where it becomes FR 443. The road passes the trail, marked by an Overlook sign. Continue a short distance farther until the road makes a sharp left; you'll find a place to park on the right. This road can be gated and may be impassable in winter. Brookston is located 7 miles south of Sheffield, along PA 948.

The Twin Lakes Trail (TLT) is a linear connector trail from the Twin Lakes Recreation Area west to the North Country Trail in the Tionesta Scenic Area. The recreation area is a modern campground with electrical hookups, showers, restrooms, and picnic area; you can camp here for a fee.

To reach the beginning of the TLT from the recreation area, you must first hike a .7-mile section along the Black Cherry Interpretive Trail. The TLT leaves from the far end of this trail's half loop. Gradually ascend until the trail levels off at the top of the plateau. The trail follows an old forest road and crosses FR 331 at a telephone swath. In another .3 mile, cross FR 331 again. After a slight descent, the trail levels and crosses FR 138, with some parking. You then pass a juncture with the Mill Creek Trail to your left. After more level hiking for almost .6 mile, cross SR 4009 and begin a gradual descent into the upper valley of Wolf Run. The trail gradually descends to the stream over the course of a mile, often following an old railroad grade across boggy terrain. Follow the run downstream to your left, until you cross it over a footbridge, and gradually ascend the side of the plateau.

Begin a mild descent to PA 66 and cross a small stream. The TLT once again traverses the side of the plateau and enters a small glen. It mildly ascends the plateau, then makes a long, gradual descent to Coon Run. The trail follows the run along an old grade for almost a mile across boggy terrain with beaver dams and hemlocks. Here you'll find potential camping. The TLT then climbs gradually away from

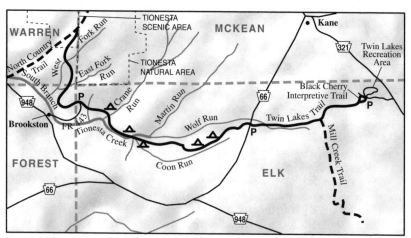

Hike 33: Twin Lakes Trail

Coon Run, crosses FR 152 and a small parking area, and descends 200 feet over .5 mile to Wolf Run. Bear left near the run and proceed downstream; the trail is rarely in sight of the run and stays on the side of the bank. After 1.4 miles, the trail mildly descends and crosses Coon Run. Nice camping is available in this area.

Follow Tionesta Creek downstream for roughly a mile, across wet terrain and past more beaver activity. Cross the run over a footbridge and ascend gradually away from the run. The TLT levels off, wraps around the side of the plateau, and drops gradually to Crane Run. Scenic Crane Run has hemlocks, pines, and potential campsites. This is now the western end of the trail, where there are greater variations in elevation. This terrain presents more of a challenge, although it still can be handled easily by the beginning backpacker. Cross Crane Run and make a long, gradual ascent, until the trail crosses a small stream.

You now begin a steeper climb to the plateau, covering 200 feet over .3 mile. Cross FR 443. At the top, maintain your elevation along the edge of the plateau until you begin a long, gradual descent around its flank. The trail crosses East Fork Run and in typical fashion begins another moderate climb, this one covering almost 300 feet over .5 mile. Then it makes a 180-foot descent over .4 mile to West Fork Run. Cross the run and begin the longest and most difficult ascent of the trail, climbing almost 300 feet over .5 mile. You'll notice more logging roads and oil wells along this section. At the top, the ascent tapers off and the trail becomes level as it enters the Tionesta Scenic Area. The TLT ends at its juncture with the North Country Trail.

🥾 34. Hickory Creek Trail

Length: 12-mile loop.

Duration: 1 to 2 days.

Difficulty: Easy.

Terrain: Mostly level or rolling terrain, with gradual changes in elevation ranging from 100 to 200 feet. Trail often follows old railroad grades.

Trail conditions: Trail is well established and maintained.

Blazes: Yellow, but most are faded and not maintained.

Water: Generally plentiful.

Vegetation: Northern hardwood forests predominate, with occasional hemlocks and white pines; some trees are sizable; glades and meadows; understory dominated by ferns.

Highlights: Hickory Creek Wilderness (a designated wilderness area), scenic streams, Hearts Content Scenic Area with old-growth forest, woodlands, meadows and glades, nice campsites, wildlife.

Maintained by: Allegheny National Forest, volunteers.

Contact info: Allegheny National Forest, P.O. Box 847, Warren, PA 16365; phone: 814-723-5150; websites: www.fs.fed.us/r9/forests/allegheny, www.allegheny-online.com/hikingtrails.html.

Maps and guides: Maps and pamphlet guide free from Allegheny National Forest.

Trailhead directions:

Hearts Content Scenic Area and Hickory Creek Wilderness trailhead: From Warren along US 6, get off at the Mohawk Avenue exit (there is a sign for Hearts Content Scenic Area), and proceed south. Bear right onto Pleasant Drive (SR 3005) and follow for 11.5 miles. Bear left onto SR 2002 and follow for 3.7 miles to Hearts Content, on your left. From Tidioute, follow SR 3005 for 12 miles to SR 2002 and turn right.

The Hickory Creek Trail (HCT) traverses the Hickory Creek Wilderness, one of two such wilderness areas in the national forest; the other is the Allegheny Islands Wilderness Area. These special areas are free from the forest roads, logging, oil wells, ATV and snowmobile trails, and gas lines that intrude on much of the Allegheny National Forest. The serenity of Hickory Creek is something to cherish, as are its scenic woodlands, which will only grow more beautiful as the trees mature. The HCT is an easy and popular trail that can be dayhiked. This is a great trail for younger or beginning backpackers.

The trail leaves the Hearts Content Scenic Area through a symmetrical plantation of red pine. Bear left, cross SR 2002, and pass under utility lines. The HCT passes a register and reaches the beginning of the loop, which is about .5 mile from Hearts Content. To hike the trail clockwise, turn left and gradually descend along a grade through hardwoods and some hemlocks. Cross a small stream and continue a mild descent along the side of the plateau. Here you'll find some nice campsites. The HCT gradually ascends near the rim of the plateau, then makes a right turn, continuing to follow the contour of the plateau. Begin a mild descent into Coon Run's valley and bear left. Cross headwaters and tributaries of Coon Run as the gentle descent

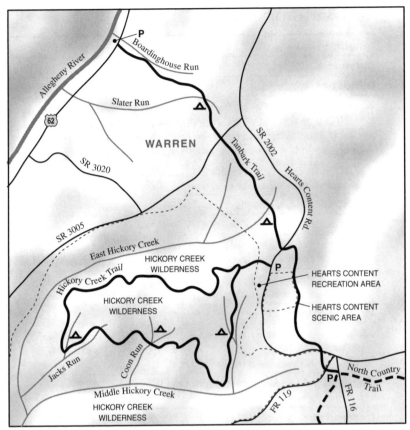

Hike 34: Hickory Creek Trail
Hike 35: Tanbark Trail

continues. The trail then crosses Coon Run, with nice campsites in meadows and under hemlocks.

Gradually climb out of Coon Run's valley and follow the contour of the plateau. The trail passes through a saddle and gradually descends for about .5 mile to the headwaters of Jacks Run. Follow this small tributary downstream for about .5 mile, then cross the main branch of Jacks Run among more scenic campsites. Climb out of Jacks Run's valley, ascending about 150 feet over .5 mile. Follow the rim of the plateau for about .6 mile, passing boulders through an open hardwood forest. The remaining 3 miles of the loop are across rolling, easy terrain on top of the plateau. Upon completing the loop, retrace your steps to Hearts Content. I recommend also hiking the short loop within Hearts Content Scenic Area to view the old-growth forest.

35. Tanbark Trail

Length: 9-mile linear trail.

Duration: 1 to 2 days.

Difficulty: Easy to moderate.

Terrain: Rolling or level along the top of the plateau. Ascents and descents reach 200 vertical feet where the trail crosses stream valleys and glens. Most difficult terrain is found at the northern end, where the trail climbs or drops 800 feet over 2 miles, with the section closest to US 62 being particularly steep.

Trail conditions: Trail is well blazed and established.

Blazes: White/gray diamonds.

Water: Generally plentiful.

Vegetation: Northern hardwood forest, with thick understory of ferns and mountain laurel; groves of hemlock and pine; open meadows and glades.

Highlights: Impressive boulders, rock outcrops, and other rock formations; scenic streams with cascades; Allegheny National Recreation Area.

Maintained by: Allegheny National Forest, volunteers.

Contact info: Allegheny National Forest, P.O. Box 847, Warren, PA 16365; phone: 814-723-5150; websites: www.fs.fed.us/r9/forests/allegheny, www.allegheny-online.com/hikingtrails.html.

Maps and guides: Maps and pamphlet guide free from Allegheny National Forest.

Trailhead directions:

Southern trailhead (FR 116): Heading south from Hearts Content and Hickory Creek Wilderness trailhead along SR 2002, proceed 2.1 miles farther, until you reach FR 116 to your right. Follow this dirt forest road for .4 mile, until you reach a sign for the Tanbark and North Country Trail. There is parking along the road for two cars; a larger parking area for about five cars is just a short distance farther, on the right.

Hearts Content Scenic Area and Hickory Creek Wilderness trailhead: The Tanbark Trail can also be conveniently accessed from this trailhead. From Warren along US 6, get off at the Mohawk Avenue exit (there is a sign for Hearts Content Scenic Area), and proceed south. Bear right onto Pleasant Drive (SR 3005) and follow for 11.5 miles. Bear left onto SR 2002 and follow for 3.7 miles to Hearts Content, on your left. From Tidioute, follow SR 3005 for 12 miles to SR 2002 and turn right.

Northern trailhead (US 62): From the Warren area, proceed south on US 62 from US 6 for 7.2 miles. There is a small trailhead sign and parking along the road. This trailhead is also located 9 miles north of Tidioute along US 62.

The Tanbark Trail (TT) is a short linear trail that can be dayhiked (if you shuttle cars) or backpacked for a pleasant two-day, one-night trip. It also can be used as part of an extended trip accessing Hickory Creek Wilderness, the North Country Trail, or Minister Creek. The TT's southern end is at its juncture with the North Country Trail; the TT passes near the Hearts Content Scenic Area and proceeds northwest to US 62, where the northern trailhead can be found. This trail's finest features are massive boulders and rock outcrops that it passes by in its northern section. Another highlight is the scenic glen carved by Boardinghouse Run, with its moss-covered boulders, cascades, and hemlocks.

Hiking the trail south to north, depart from the TT's southern end at its juncture with the North Country Trail and FR 116. From here the TT proceeds west and then turns north, crossing Middle Hickory Creek. Cross SR 2002 (Hearts Content Road) and bear left, passing a juncture with the Ironwood Trail to your right. Begin a slight ascent, until the trail bears right and becomes level; rolling terrain follows for about .5 mile. Begin a gradual descent and cross a small stream among hemlocks and pines. A side trail to the left leads to Hearts Content Scenic Area, famous for its virgin forest. Pass a juncture with Tom Run Loop Trail to your right. The TT climbs gradually away from the stream and descends more steeply to Tom Run and the other juncture with the Tom Run Loop Trail. Turn left, pass a juncture with a side trail that leads to Hearts Content and Hickory Creek, and cross the small stream. Turn right and cross SR 2002 (Hearts Content Road). Level hiking ensues for about .2 mile, then the TT descends steeply to East Hickory Creek; this is a 220-foot descent over about .25 mile. During the descent, you pass through a crevasse between rock outcrops and hike near massive boulders. Cross the creek, with scenic camping and more impressive rock outcrops nearby.

The TT begins a 200-foot climb over .25 mile and reaches the plateau again, with mountain laurel and more large rocks. Level hiking follows for less than a mile, then the trail slightly descends and crosses a small stream. Ascend slightly and in another .4 mile pass near Sandstone Spring and cross US 337, with parking. The trail turns left and begins a gradual descent to Slater Run, with nice campsites. Slater Run Trail proceeds downstream, but the TT heads north and ascends the plateau, with a 200-foot climb over .3 mile. Upon reaching the top of the plateau, bear left and begin an 800-foot descent over 2 miles. At first the descent is gradual, but it becomes increasingly steeper as the trail nears US 62. Along the way, the trail follows Boardinghouse Run down its scenic glen, with hemlocks, boulders, rock outcrops, and cascades. The trail's northern trailhead is at US 62.

36. Morrison Trail

Length: 12.3-mile loop with connector trail.

Duration: 1 to 2 days.

Difficulty: Easy to moderate.

Terrain: Trail follows level top of plateau. Steepest section is a 500-foot ascent and descent over .7 mile along Campbell Run.

Trail conditions: Trail is well blazed, maintained, and established. Several stream crossings without bridges. Often near streams and can be wet.

Blazes: White/gray, fading blue.

Water: Plentiful.

Vegetation: Oaks and hardwoods dominate plateau; hemlocks found along streams; abundant mountain laurel; open meadows and glades.

Highlights: Rock outcrops and massive boulders, scenic mountain streams with cascades, Allegheny Reservoir, beautiful campsites.

Maintained by: Allegheny National Forest, volunteers.

Contact info: Allegheny National Forest, P.O. Box 847, Warren, PA 16365; phone: 814-723-5150; websites: www.fs.fed.us/r9/forests/allegheny, www.allegheny-online.com/hikingtrails.html.

Maps and guides: Maps and pamphlet guide free from Allegheny National Forest.

Trailhead directions: The trailhead, with plenty of parking and a pit toilet, is located along PA 59, almost 27 miles west of Smethport and 13.5 miles east of the PA 59 juncture with US 6, near Warren.

The Morrison Trail (MT) is a small, popular loop that is ideal for beginning backpackers or hikers looking for a quick one-night trip. At about 12.3 miles in length, the MT can also be dayhiked by a fit hiker. But you'll want to take your time, because this trail offers fine scenery and nice camping. The MT is one of the most scenic and popular trails in the Allegheny National Forest.

From the trailhead along PA 59, proceed south on the .5-mile-long spur trail that connects to the main loop. This spur trail descends, crosses a small seasonal stream, and meets the main loop. To hike the loop clockwise, turn right and descend again to the small stream, the West Branch of Morrison Run, where you encounter a 1.3-mile-long connector trail that follows the run downstream. This is an incredibly scenic segment that is worth hiking, with massive boulders the size of houses crowding the stream, creating cascades. This connector trail crosses the West Branch three times and features several good campsites, ending where it joins the main loop at the juncture of the branches of Morrison Run. This is the most beautiful section along the MT.

To continue the hike on the main loop, climb away from the West Branch of Morrison Run to reach the top of the plateau. For about the next 2 miles, the trail is flat as it crosses the plateau underneath oaks and through mountain laurel. The MT begins to descend near Campbell Run, a small seasonal stream with cascades and a few campsites. This is a rocky 500-foot descent over almost .7 mile. At the bottom of this descent, the trail bears left and begins a gradual descent, passing and following old forest and logging roads. The MT stays about 200 to 300 feet above the Allegheny Reservoir. About 2.5 miles from Campbell Run, the trail reaches Morrison Campground, accessed by an unblazed side trail to the right. This is a popular place to camp in summer, as it is also used by boaters. It features a small beach, nice views of the reservoir, picnic tables, vault toilets, hand pump, and fire rings.

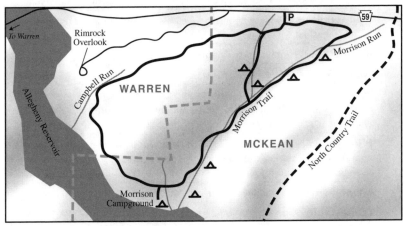

Hike 36: Morrison Trail

Cross a small seasonal stream and traverse the side of the plateau. The trail eventually joins scenic Morrison Run. A trail heading downstream to your right, with faded blue blazes, can be followed to several great campsites near the reservoir. Follow the run upstream; here is great scenery, including deep hemlocks, boulders, and rock outcrops. Pass the connector trail, where it and the West Branch join from the left, and continue upstream along Morrison Run, at times following the remnants of an old railroad grade. The scenery gets even better, with massive boulders and rock outcrops, cascades, and meadows. The MT bears left and climbs away from Morrison Run. Cross over the ridge and descend mildly to complete the loop.

A worthwhile side trip is to Rimrock Overlook, accessed by FR 454. This area features picnic tables, excellent views of the reservoir, and massive rock outcrops and boulders, some with deep fractures that emit cold air in summer.

🥾 37. Tracy Ridge Hiking Trail System

Length: 33.69-mile interconnecting trail system.

Duration: 1.5 to 3 days, depending on route taken.

Difficulty: Easy to moderate.

Terrain: Often level or rolling, but several ascents and descents range from 100 to 500 vertical feet and can be steep. Trails often follow narrow sidehills on steep embankments along streams and the Allegheny Reservoir.

Trail conditions: Trails generally are well blazed, but some are brushy and unestablished.

Blazes: Off-white/gray; North Country Trail, blue.

Water: Generally plentiful.

Vegetation: Open northern hardwoods predominate, with an understory of ferns, lowbush blueberries, grass, and mountain laurel; occasional pines and hemlocks, usually near water.

Highlights: Allegheny Reservoir, rock outcrops and boulders, scenic streams and woodlands, nice camping, North Country Trail, views, Allegheny National Recreation Area.

Maintained by: Allegheny National Forest, volunteers.

Contact info: Allegheny National Forest, P.O. Box 847, Warren, PA 16365; phone: 814-723-5150; websites: www.fs.fed.us/r9/forests/allegheny, www.allegheny-online.com/hikingtrails.html.

Maps and guides: Maps and pamphlet guide free from Allegheny
   National Forest.

Trailhead directions:

Tracy Ridge Campground (main trailhead): From Smethport, proceed west on
   PA 59 for 19.4 miles to PA 321. Turn right onto PA 321 north and proceed
   10.8 miles to Tracy Ridge Campground. Turn left and follow road for .5 mile
   to parking on left. From Warren, follow PA 59 east for 20 miles to PA 321
   north and turn left. From Bradford, follow PA 346 west for 18 miles. Turn
   left onto PA 321 south and proceed 3 miles. Turn right into the Tracy Ridge
   Campground.

Nelse Run: Follow directions above to PA 321 north. This trailhead is
   located 7.2 miles from PA 59 on the left. Small lot has parking for
   about four cars.

The Tracy Ridge Hiking Trail System (TRT) was originally a 4-mile-long linear trail that connected the Tracy Ridge Campground to the North Country Trail (NCT) along the Allegheny Reservoir. Together with the NCT and Johnnycake Trail, the TRT created a 10-mile-loop. In 1998, the trails here were greatly extended, with various loops, connector trails, and spur trails creating a complex 33.68-mile system. This new network was named the Tracy Ridge Hiking Trail System and connects with the NCT at various points. The Johnnycake Trail continues to exist but is now considered a part of the larger trail system. Numbers appear at trail junctures and are shown on the free map from the Allegheny National Forest, which also gives the distances between these numbered junctures. There are numerous route options on this network of trails. The description here will focus on what you should not miss. Backpacking this system will invariably require you to hike the NCT at some point.

From the trailhead, cross the gravel campground road and pass a side trail to the right that winds through rock outcrops and boulders. The trail is level and begins a slight descent as it passes more rock outcrops and curves behind the campground. Reach juncture No. 2 and bear right. The trail is level as it passes through open hardwoods. Reach No. 15; to the left, the trail descends to No. 16, which leads to the Johnnycake Trail at No. 17 or to a new trail following the contour of the plateau to No. 13 and No. 12. The trail is very curvy, and when I hiked here last, it featured no open vistas as indicated on the map. From No. 15, continue on to No. 14 and No. 12 along level terrain. Once you pass No. 12, the trail begins a 400-foot descent to the NCT

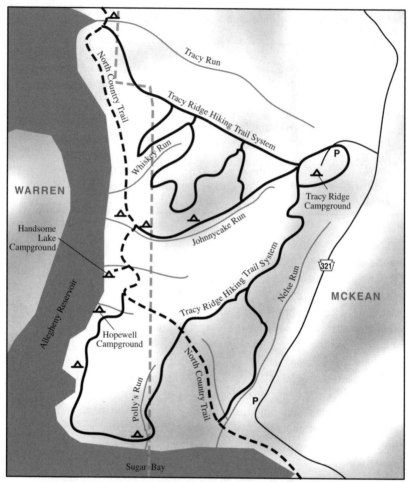

Hike 37: Tracy Ridge Hiking Trail System

over .7 mile. The trail steepens at the bottom and passes under hemlocks. The NCT joins from the right; if you turn right, there are nice views of the reservoir and beautiful camping where Tracy Run meets the reservoir.

Otherwise, bear left onto the NCT. For the next 2.4 miles, the trail traverses the steep bank of the reservoir, often along narrow sidehills. The NCT gradually moves farther from the reservoir and crosses seasonal streams, including Whiskey Run. Descend gradually through a pine plantation and reach No. 10, where the Johnnycake Trail joins from the left. This trail gradually follows its namesake run upstream, crossing it several times, and offers some nice campsites. It terminates at No. 3, along the Interpretive Trail.

Cross scenic Johnnycake Run. This area around the reservoir contains several nice campsites. Continue to follow the contour of the plateau and gradually climb above the reservoir. Enter a scenic hemlock-shaded glen, where a side trail to the left descends to Handsome Lake Campground, a hike-in- or boat-in-only campground featuring grassy campsites with picnic tables and fire rings, vault toilets, water, and nice views of the reservoir. Use of this facility requires self-registration and an $8 daily fee.

The NCT continues up this scenic glen, crosses the small stream, and climbs 200 feet over .3 mile to the crest of the plateau. At the top, the NCT turns left and follows the level top of the plateau, while the TRT descends 400 feet over a mile to scenic Hopewell Campground, which offers the same amenities and registration requirements as Handsome Lake. The segment of the TRT between No. 8 and No. 6 is isolated and scenic. The trail stays fairly close to the side of the reservoir and has many potential campsites. The forest is more diverse, with occasional pines and hemlocks. The reservoir is typically only a short distance from the trail. The terrain is level or rolling as the trail follows the contour of the plateau and passes through scenic side hollows and glens. Particularly nice views are where the trail bears left at the juncture of Sugar Bay and the reservoir. The TRT continues to be level and rolling as it enters the scenic glen of Polly's Run. Here you'll find hemlocks and nice campsites. Cross the run and begin to ascend the side of the glen, steeply at times, to a grassy grade. Turn left onto the grade and continue a mild ascent. The trail bears right off the grade and climbs steeply, passing through a side glen, then levels off along the side of the plateau. Descend to another grassy grade (possibly the same one) and bear right, following the grade gradually uphill. Sections of this trail are not well blazed; just follow the grade. At the top, the grade disappears and the trail is level as it meets the NCT at No. 6.

Bear right onto the NCT as it crosses over the top of the plateau and begins a 500-foot descent over 1.3 miles into a scenic glen of hemlocks and pines. The descent is gradual as you follow an old forest road, and the trail is generally high above the stream. There appear to be several potential campsites along the beautiful stream. The NCT levels off as it reaches No. 7 and continues on to cross beautiful Nelse Run, where a side trail leads to a trailhead and parking along PA 321.

At No. 7, turn left onto the TRT, which is initially level but soon begins its ascent. Watch carefully for the blazes through this section, as there are many turns. This is a scenic segment of trail as it climbs through hemlocks and crosses side glens and small streams. At times the ascent is steep. As you continue to climb, the hemlocks diminish and open hardwoods dominate. The climb continues until it reaches the top of the plateau, a total climb of 500 feet over .8 mile. The trail levels off but continues a moderate incline until it reaches No. 5. Turn left and continue to No. 4. This 2.3-mile-long segment is level or rolling through an open hardwood forest. Upon reaching No. 4, you can turn right onto the Interpretive Trail, which loops around the southern side of the Tracy Ridge Campground, or continue on to No. 3 and No. 2 and retrace your steps to the trailhead.